Africa Now

Africa Now is published by Zed Bo(respected Nordic Africa Institute. Featu...... .....-quality, cutting-edge research from leading academics, the series addresses the big issues confronting Africa today. Accessible but in-depth, and wide-ranging in its scope, Africa Now engages with the critical political, economic, sociological and development debates affecting the continent, shedding new light on pressing concerns.

Nordic Africa Institute

The Nordic Africa Institute (Nordiska Afrikainstitutet) is a centre for research, documentation and information on modern Africa. Based in Uppsala, Sweden, the Institute is dedicated to providing timely, critical and alternative research and analysis of Africa and to cooperation with African researchers. As a hub and a meeting place for a growing field of research and analysis, the Institute strives to put knowledge of African issues within reach for scholars, policy-makers, politicians, media, students and the general public. The Institute is financed jointly by the Nordic countries (Denmark, Finland, Iceland, Norway and Sweden).
www.nai.uu.se

Forthcoming titles

Henning Melber (ed.), *The Rise of Africa's Middle Class*
Anders Themnér (ed.), *Warlord Democrats in Africa*
Paul Higate (ed.), *Private Security in Africa*

Titles already published

Fantu Cheru and Cyril Obi (eds), *The Rise of China and India in Africa*
Ilda Lindell (ed.), *Africa's Informal Workers*
Iman Hashim and Dorte Thorsen, *Child Migration in Africa*
Prosper B. Matondi, Kjell Havnevik and Atakilte Beyene (eds), *Biofuels, Land Grabbing and Food Security in Africa*
Cyril Obi and Siri Aas Rustad (eds), *Oil and Insurgency in the Niger Delta*
Mats Utas (ed.), *African Conflicts and Informal Power*
Prosper B. Matondi, *Zimbabwe's Fast Track Land Reform*
Maria Eriksson Baaz and Maria Stern, *Sexual Violence as a Weapon of War?*
Fantu Cheru and Renu Modi (eds), *Agricultural Development and Food Security in Africa*
Amanda Hammar (ed.), *Displacement Economies in Africa*
Mary Njeri Kinyanjui, *Women and the Informal Economy in Urban Africa*
Liisa Laakso and Petri Hautaniemi (eds), *Diasporas, Development and Peacemaking in the Horn of Africa*
Margaret Lee, *Africa's World Trade*
Godwin R. Murunga, Duncan Okello and Anders Sjögren (eds), *Kenya: The Struggle for a New Constitutional Order*
Lisa Åkesson and Maria Eriksson Baaz (eds), *Africa's Return Migrants*
Thiven Reddy, *South Africa, Settler Colonialism and the Failures of Liberal Democracy*
Cedric de Coning, Linnéa Gelot and John Karlsrud (eds), *The Future of African Peace Operations*

About the editors

Tobias Hagmann is associate professor of international development at Roskilde University, a research associate with the Political Geography Chair at the University of Zurich and a fellow with the Rift Valley Institute in Nairobi and London.

Filip Reyntjens is professor of African law and politics at the Institute of Development Policy and Management, University of Antwerp. He is a full member of the Belgian Royal Academy of Overseas Sciences and a board member of several scientific organizations.

Aid and authoritarianism in Africa

Development without democracy

edited by Tobias Hagmann and Filip Reyntjens

Nordiska Afrikainstitutet
The Nordic Africa Institute

Zed Books
LONDON

Aid and Authoritarianism in Africa: Development without Democracy was first published in association with the Nordic Africa Institute, PO Box 1703, SE-751 47 Uppsala, Sweden, in 2016 by Zed Books Ltd, The Foundry, 17 Oval Way, London SE11 5RR, UK.

www.zedbooks.co.uk
www.nai.uu.se

Typeset in Minion Pro by seagulls.net
Index: Rohan Bolton
Cover design: www.alice-marwick.co.uk
Printed and bound by CPI Group (UK) Ltd, Croydon, CR0 4YY

A catalogue record for this book is available from the British Library.

ISBN 978-1-78360-629-0 hb
ISBN 978-1-78360-628-3 pb
ISBN 978-1-78360-630-6 pdf
ISBN 978-1-78360-631-3 epub
ISBN 978-1-78360-632-0 mobi

Contents

Introduction: aid and authoritarianism in sub-Saharan Africa after 1990

Tobias Hagmann
and Filip Reyntjens

Introduction

This book explores the motives, dynamics and consequences of international aid given to authoritarian African governments.[1] The relationship between foreign aid and autocratic rule in sub-Saharan Africa has a long-standing historical precedent (see for example McVety, 2012), but it is of renewed interest and salience. In the past decade, important donors have gradually traded their earlier commitment to political reform in Africa for the achievement of increasingly technocratic development successes such as the Millennium Development Goals (MDGs) and, more recently, the 'development effectiveness paradigm' with its focus on growth and productivity (Eyben, 2013). In 2013, four of the ten most important aid recipients in Africa – Ethiopia, Mozambique, Uganda and Rwanda – were ruled by one-party regimes that do not allow for democratic participation and criminalize political dissent. While bilateral and multilateral donors constantly claim to be promoting democracy, good governance and human rights in Africa, many are effectively complicit in fostering development without democracy. The recent revival of the complicity between foreign aid and authoritarianism in the name of 'development' is not only problematic, but also went largely unnoticed by both academics and the broader public. This book is thus a first – and certainly incomplete – attempt to draw attention to some of the illiberal effects of aid channelled to authoritarian political regimes in sub-Saharan Africa.

A significant body of scholarly work exists on why and how donors disburse aid, explaining both positive and negative impacts of development assistance with regards to economic growth, poverty, development and domestic governance. Yet much of this literature suffers from one of two shortcomings: it either conceives of aid in technocratic, managerial and ultimately apolitical terms or, alternatively, it seeks to explain the relationship between foreign aid – typically modelled as the independent variable – and democracy or democratization or the lack thereof – often represented as the dependent variable. In other words, while economists and political scientists have scrutinized how and whether foreign aid contributes to democracy in recipient countries, the more

I

sinister hypothesis that foreign aid strengthens autocracies has rarely been explored in the literature. Consequently, published research on the relationship between foreign aid and authoritarian governance in sub-Saharan Africa after 1990 – namely in countries that benefit from substantial aid flows – is close to non-existent.

The collusion between donors and one-party regimes or dictatorships in sub-Saharan Africa raises numerous questions. A main empirical puzzle, which has motivated the editors of this volume, is the following: why do donors not only support, but also align their policy agendas with authoritarian rulers who reject the very liberal democratic values that Western donors endorse? Where does this creeping 'African democracy fatigue', as Nicolas van de Walle puts it in his concluding chapter, emanate from and what is its significance for previous, current and future development paradigms? But donor assistance to undemocratic regimes also raises many moral questions, in particular concerning the manner in which prominent donor agencies such as the United States Agency for International Development (USAID), the UK Department for International Development (DFID) or the European Commission's (EC) various country development programmes have recently revised their earlier stances on democratization in favour of more narrow 'developmental' objectives that are easily quantifiable, but come without freedom (Sen, 1999). This shift is also due to competition from so-called emerging donors. More problematically, donors' rhetoric about the supposed trade-off between political rights and economic development is neither approved nor shared by taxpayers living in donor countries nor by 'beneficiaries' in Africa. Rather, the decision to continue or increase funding to authoritarian regimes is essentially the outcome of an elite bargain between donor and recipient governments.

Two main themes are at the centre of this book. They pertain to *i)* donors' motives for giving substantial amounts of aid to undemocratic recipient countries in sub-Saharan Africa (the 'why' question) and *ii)* the political and economic consequences that these aid flows generate (the 'what' question). While some of the chapters in this volume focus more on the 'why' question of donor motives to fund autocracies (Chapters 1, 3, 5 and the conclusion), others pay more attention to the 'what' question of aid impact in authoritarian contexts (Chapters 2 and 6) or do both (Chapter 4). The inquiry into the nexus between foreign aid and authoritarian rule in sub-Saharan Africa sparks many more vital questions, which this book does not or only partly addresses. These questions concern the various processes by which 'aid' contributes to oppression, but also the perceptions of those involved, both target groups and development agents. This includes issues such as the impact of aid on the daily workings of authoritarian regimes and how it affects those living under their rule, the reaction of local societies to donor-funded authoritarian regimes' policies and practices, the types of aid that are more prone to enhancing repressive mechanisms, and the reconciliation by donors – including their staff based in recipient countries – of their official rhetoric of promoting liberal goals with their support for authoritarian governments. Finally, we do not address the agency of domestic actors, and how aid can or should relate to local demands for democracy and human rights.[2]

Before we dwell on the issues raised in this book, three clarifications are in order. First, 'aid' can be conceived of in starkly different terms. While its vernacular use associates aid with altruism, solidarity or even an obligation of helping the poor, economists predominantly view international aid as a rent that accrues to recipient countries, often with negative effects (see Bräutigam & Knack, 2004: 265). From a policy perspective, aid represents a 'particular form of external influence' that limits recipient countries' policy autonomy (Brown, 2013). In this book, we use a generic definition of aid as consisting of material flows between donors and recipient countries, i.e. official development assistance (ODA) as defined by the Organisation for Economic Co-operation and Development's (OECD) Development Assistance Committee (DAC).[3] Evidently, close aid and diplomatic relations between donor and recipient countries also generate symbolic capital and recognition, but we are less concerned with these more immaterial dimensions of foreign aid. Foreign aid thus takes place in variegated forms, ranging from direct budget support to funding for particular policies, programmes and projects in a broad range of sectors and involving a multitude of intermediaries and implementers such as local and international NGOs and state, para-statal or community organizations.

Second, the analysis offered in this book is confined to interactions between selected sub-Saharan African countries and Western, meaning European and North American, donors. Even though very pertinent, apart from Chapter 5 and the conclusion, this book does not consider non-Western, namely Chinese and other non-DAC, donors and their interactions with African autocracies (see Bräutigam, 2009; Kragelund, 2008). This is both an omission and a plea for future research as a comparison between DAC and non-DAC donors' interactions with authoritarian African states potentially provides important and surprising new insights, debunking commonly held assumptions about the liberal or illiberal character of particular donors. For instance, Dreher, Nunnenkamp and Thiele (2011) find that, while new donors care less for recipient need than old donors, both behave similarly in several respects, and that new donors do not generally exhibit a stronger bias against better governed countries. On the whole, 'new donors resemble the old bunch in one important respect, namely that both categories disguise considerable variation within these groups with regard to need, merit, and self-interest as motives underlying aid activities' (Dreher, Nunnenkamp & Thiele, 2011: 1961). Similarly, although Northern Africa has been the home of several long-standing autocracies with long histories of external support, both civilian and military, we do not look at Algeria, Egypt, Libya, Mali, Morocco, Sudan and Tunisia.

Finally, aside from occasional references to the Cold War period, this book concentrates on donor–recipient relations in the post-1990 period. While this periodization is partly a matter of convention and while more historic research into long-term development practices is necessary (see Chapter 4), the choice of the post-Cold War era is motivated by the emergence and triumph of the (neo-)liberal donor agendas – namely democratization and liberalization – that are currently being redefined in Africa's development landscape. In keeping with the two main foci of this book, i.e. donors' motives for giving aid to undemocratic regimes and the consequences of their aid, the next two sections review the scholarly works on these subjects. Subsequently, we propose a number of more conceptual suggestions that aim to reframe the nexus between aid and authoritarianism and that have so far been overlooked by the existing literature. We then introduce the various chapters and case studies that make up the bulk of this book.

Donor motives for funding autocracies

How can we account for Western donors' support for authoritarian governments in Africa in the name of 'development'? The comparative literature provides numerous clues as to why donors may decide to give or withhold foreign aid. In-depth case-study research unearths the particular mix of motivations and considerations of an individual donor, a particular aid relation, or a particular time period (see Schraeder et al., 1998). Scholars are essentially in agreement that 'donor aid levels are not critically linked to needs in Africa' (Riddell, 1999). In other words, even though donors routinely profess to aiding the 'poorest of the poor', aid flows do not primarily reflect recipient countries' development needs, but rather donor priorities (Schraeder et al., 1998: 302). National security interests, cultural similarity, colonial past, economic potential for domestic economies, ideological proximity, the maintenance of aid budgets, and a host of other domestic and international factors explain donor calculations with regards to aid allocation (Olsen, 1998; Schraeder et al., 1998; Alesina & Dollar, 2000; Goldsmith, 2001; Fuchs et al., 2014).

Yet donor motives must not be seen in isolation from recipient governments' behaviour and assets. On the basis of eight case studies, Whitfield (2009: 329) argues that the ability of a recipient government to project non-negotiability and the confidence that its actions will not lead to donors pulling out (or that it can manage on its own if they do) distinguishes more from less successful recipient negotiating strategies. Contemporary Ethiopia and Rwanda are prime examples of the 'negotiating capital' identified by Whitfield. The volume of aid relative to the recipients' economies – and therefore their aid dependency – does not necessarily impact that capital: Rwanda, Ethiopia and Uganda, in that order, are major recipients of aid in sub-Saharan Africa in the time period, but their aid dependency has not affected their policy independence. The similarities between the two authoritarian one-party states and 'donor darlings' Ethiopia and Rwanda are striking in a number of regards. Both managed to convince donors that governance was 'technocratic' and 'developmental' and thus unrelated to politics and rights, both silenced their internal and external critics, and both obtained more aid as they became more dictatorial over time (for Rwanda see Reyntjens, 2013; for Ethiopia see Borchgrevink, 2008; Feyissa, 2011; Abbink & Hagmann, 2012). Ideologically, they both have a clearly articulated vision of state-led development. Geopolitically, they are key allies of the United States and the United Kingdom, though Ethiopia more so than Rwanda. Institutionally, 'a culture of discipline and performance pervades government and the civil service' in Ethiopia (Furtado & Smith, 2009: 132). In addition, the Rwandan Patriotic Front (RPF)-dominated regime has been able to claim moral authority over donors as a result of the genocide, using 'the legacy of the genocide to de-legitimize external interference in the country's domestic affairs' (Whitfield, 2009: 340). Uganda shares the geopolitical asset of Ethiopia and Rwanda, but its ideological asset has weaned off, and the institutional confidence that Museveni's National Resistance Movement (NRM)-led regime once inspired has eroded. This may explain in part why aid to Uganda has decreased over the last five years, suggesting that there may be a 'tipping point' at which the divergence grows too large for some donors to maintain the illusion of consistency.

Self-interest, as opposed to rhetorical support of democracy, is an obvious donor rationale that explains assistance to authoritarian regimes. Emmanuel (2012) shows how one critical donor, France, was able to shield its client and former colony, Cameroon, from pressure to pursue liberalization. While other donors applied negative conditionality to Cameroon in the early 1990s, the massive influx of French aid during that period helped the Biya regime to thwart the efforts by Cameroon's domestic political opposition and the wider donor community to encourage genuine democratic reform. France's interest here was not economic but political, namely to maintain a Francophone client whose most popular opponent was the Anglophone politician John Fru Ndi (Emmanuel, 2012; Pommerolle in this book). While this case echoes long-standing paternalistic foreign-policy practices of France vis-à-vis its former colonies, commonly referred to as the *Françafrique* (Schlichte, 1998), the close alliance with ruling autocratic governments is not specific to former colonial powers as the US and British support to Rwanda, Ethiopia and Uganda demonstrates.

Among the diverse and often incoherent reasons for the mismatch between donors' rhetoric and the actual aid flows to African autocracies identified in the literature are donors' security concerns (counter-terrorism and intelligence sharing), commercial interests, expectations about the effectiveness of sanctions (an issue linked to donor coordination), regional stability, the level of recipient aid dependency, the recipient country's linkage to the international community or political ties to donors (including voting behaviour at the UN), regimes' claims to domestic legitimacy or congruence of donor action with demands by national opinion, the regime's 'presentability', and a sense of fatigue with representative democracy, seen to engender conflict and chaos (Lynch & Crawford, 2011: 294–296; del Biondo, 2012; Grauvogel & von Soest, 2013; Nielsen, 2013; Resnick & van de Walle, 2013b). Studying US and European Union aid to Africa in the 1990s, Brown (2005: 188) concludes that 'donor motivations did not seem any less self-interested in the 1990s than they were during the Cold War, and recent years have further confirmed this'. More recently, Nielsen (2013: 11) found 'little evidence to support constructivist accounts that identify human rights norms as the foremost driver of rights-friendly foreign policies and principled ideals as the primary motivation for Western aid programs'.

Another major factor that intervenes in donor calculations and aid relations is the trade-off between technocratic and political governance, between the short to medium and the long term. This has recently been highlighted by the research conducted by the Africa Power and Politics Programme (APPP), funded by DFID, which asserts that 'developmental patrimonialism' can generate dynamic growth (Kelsall & Booth, 2010). However, others have claimed that 'the assumptions underpinning the grand visions of the illiberal state-builders are deeply flawed' and that counting on their ability to deliver 'may be a costly miscalculation' (Jones et al., 2013: 21). Donors' ambiguity is enhanced by lack of clarity on whether they believe that other values (such as business-friendly policies or security) are more important than democracy and respect for human rights, although they would prefer recipients to adhere to these, or if they actually think that authoritarianism can better promote development outcomes.

Beyond the aid nexus, there appears to be a more general trend towards the restoration and acceptance of authoritarianism. Cooley (2015) recently pointed at the resurgence of the primacy of state sovereignty and security, renewed challenges to liberal democracy's universalism and growing acceptance of 'civilizational diversity', and the defence of 'traditional values' by powers like Russia. Cooley argues that this evolution is also facilitated by new 'authoritarian regionalism' across Eurasia, the Middle East, Africa and Latin America, and by the advent of new providers of international public goods as a consequence of the rise of emerging powers, in our case alternative donors.[4]

Managerial issues too play an important role in the everyday life of ODA programmes. Despite what appears as paying lip service to democracy, aid agencies tend to insulate aid from politics, as 'developmental states' and 'authoritarian enclaves' are more comfortable to cope with and seen as delivering effective results, at least in the short and perhaps medium term. Developers' tendency of reframing political issues in host countries into technical development challenges has of course been a staple feature of international aid's 'anti-politics machine' (Ferguson, 1990). Brown (2005: 187) notes the technical bias of assistance when 'donors forget about politics'. Hout (2010) demonstrated how the World Bank's governance-related publications contain more frequent use of depoliticized notions such as 'management', 'public sector' or 'decentralization', whereas academic publications tend to associate governance with political issues and institutions as witnessed by notions like 'interests', 'conflict' or 'democracy'. Likewise, Uvin (2010: 176) notes 'a tendency towards the "technicalisation" of all political issues by the development community'. Consequently, some donors are content with procedural compliance and tolerate evading tactics by authoritarian regimes. As Young observed, already at the end of the 1990s (1999: 39), 'semi-democracy is probably sufficient to deflect international system pressures for more complete political opening, particularly if macroeconomic management earns external approbation'.

Another explanation for this is that decision-making by donors in Western capitals is often informed by their officials in the host countries who, not unlike diplomats, are immersed in close working relations with their counterparts whose viewpoints they begin to appreciate or even replicate. Brown (2011) found that locally based development agents frequently claim that their host country is more democratic than it actually is, or that it could not be any more democratic for the time being. His interviews show three recurrent methods to deflect criticism of the democratic credentials of recipients: *i)* focusing on election day, rather than the electoral campaigns and broader political conditions; *ii)* setting the standard very low ('don't expect too much'); and *iii)* setting a long time-horizon ('don't expect it too soon'). Because embassies and aid missions have short institutional memories as a result of permanent staff rotation and short postings, because it is easier to tolerate abuse than to prevent it, because career-wise it is better not to rock the boat and to follow the path of least resistance, because there is a strong need to 'feel good', and because of the 'Stockholm syndrome' that makes over-identification with host governments difficult to escape, Brown observes that these officials 'often express sympathy for autocratic behaviour – and when they do so, they use a remarkably limited set of faulty arguments and clichés' (Brown, 2011: 513). Brown's findings square with our own observations about the defensive reactions of foreign aid officials in both Ethiopia and Rwanda when confronted with criticism about their host countries' political record.

A final professional factor that shapes donors' attitudes towards authoritarian recipient governments is what Uvin describes as 'a lack of fine knowledge of (recipient) countries: donors largely see what they want to see, and largely interact with people who have a vested interest in making sure this continues' (Uvin,

2010: 176). Finally, for all sorts of reasons, donors sometimes differ radically in their assessment of the dynamics at play in recipient countries, thus preventing coordination and allowing recipients to play one donor against another.[5]

Foreign aid's impact on domestic governance

Since the end of the 1990s a growing body of large-N scholarship building on statistical datasets has examined the impacts of foreign aid on democracy and democratization in recipient countries. Most of this literature considers bilateral aid, using the OECD-DAC's official development assistance indicator as well as Freedom House, Polity and other indicators as proxies of regime type. Given that African countries figure prominently among aid recipients, much of this literature has focused on sub-Saharan Africa. The literature shows indecisive results, some studies suggesting a positive relationship between aid and democracy, others showing disparate impacts, and others still finding none, or a negative relationship (Resnick & van de Walle, 2013a: 3–5). Few authors conclude that foreign aid has contributed to democracy promotion on the continent. Among them is Goldsmith, who finds development assistance to be 'associated with slightly higher levels of political and civil liberty in Africa' (2001: 141) and with economic liberalism (144). Alesina and Dollar (2000: 34) find that countries that have improved their democratic record have benefited from a subsequent surge in foreign aid. This finding is supported by Hariri (2013), who shows that, while democracy is not generally associated with higher rates of economic growth, democratization is followed by growth that is accounted for by a substantial influx of aid into young democracies.

However, most studies challenge donor claims that aid furthers democratic governance. In his study on the impact of aid on democratization between 1975 and 2000, Knack (2004: 251) concludes that 'no evidence is found that aid promotes democracy'. To the contrary, Bräutigam and Knack (2004: 276) report a 'robust statistical relationship between high aid levels in Africa and deteriorations in governance'. The causal reason for this, the authors add, remains unclear. Similar conclusions have been drawn by scholars who study political conditionality in aid disbursements. In his study of democracy promotion in post-1991 Africa, Brown (2005: 182) notes that 'the relationship between political conditionality and democratization is unclear'. More significantly, he observes that donor enthusiasm for political conditionality quickly waned after the mid-1990s (Brown, 2005: 168) while security interests again started to override other concerns. Indeed, Fisher and Anderson (2015) show that the politics of Western aid and international development have become increasingly 'securitized', and that African governments have eagerly embraced that agenda. As a consequence of Western enthusiasm for supporting, training and arming the military and security services, 'illiberal states are emerging and growing stronger' (Fisher & Anderson, 2015: 131).

If foreign aid cannot be associated with democracy promotion, can it be correlated with the promotion of autocracies? In their paper aptly titled 'Does Foreign Aid Support Autocrats, Democrats, or Both?', Kono and Montinola (2009) argue that this is not the case either. Although long-term aid helps dictators more than democrats, large amounts of aid given to dictatorships reduce the marginal impact of current aid flows, and the latter are more beneficial for democracies. Dutta et al. (2013) provide maybe the most interesting explanation for the causal relation between foreign aid and domestic political institutions. They argue that foreign aid neither improves nor deteriorates governance in recipient countries, but that it essentially amplifies recipients' existing political–institutional orientations (Dutta et al., 2013: 209).[6] In their own words, 'Aid makes dictatorships more dictatorial and democracies more democratic.' The political implications of their statistical analysis, if correct, are far reaching for donors: whoever provides large amounts of aid to authoritarian governments in Africa and elsewhere is likely to enhance the regime's oppressive capacities rather than further democratization.[7]

Have authoritarian countries received more aid recently? In terms of aggregate patterns of increasing foreign aid, the answer appears to be a qualified yes. Table 1.1 offers an overview of the distribution of average ODA per capita to sub-Saharan African countries between 1990 and 2013.[8] Countries are categorized according to the Freedom House political rights score, with 1 representing the most free and 7 representing the least free.

The overall trend of ODA per capita to sub-Saharan African states is one of decline from the end of the Cold War to today (1990–2013), but that decline has been sharpest in countries in the lower score categories than those higher scores, and overall, more authoritarian states have seen a per capita increase. For example, in the years 1990–1994, countries with a score of 7 in political rights received an average of 36.28 USD ODA per capita, compared to 45.07 in the years 2010–2013. By contrast, countries with a score of 1, 2 and 3 all

Political rights score	Average ODA per capita (in constant 2012 USD)				
	1990–1994	1995–1999	2000–2004	2005–2009	2010–2013
1	165.59	22.58	21.06	53.68	77.17
2	69.21	58.80	58.43	45.70	43.07
3	101.33	72.07	62.63	70.38	68.62
4	85.77	29.15	24.33	54.92	28.86
5	21.33	44.95	35.63	36.03	54.97
6	61.69	37.42	43.91	43.02	46.95
7	36.28	16.51	28.97	52.28	45.07

Table 1.1 Political rights score (Freedom House) and average ODA per capita in sub-Saharan Africa (1990–2013)

witnessed a reduction of over 30 per cent in per capita aid in the same time period. While the data indicate that a general stagnation or decline in average ODA per capita across all categories of political rights occurred between 1990 and 2004, more importantly, the existing data reveal an overall increase in the levels of aid given to higher-scoring – or, more repressive – countries in particular. For example, average ODA per capita to countries in the most authoritarian categories (5–7) in 2010–2013 represents on average 150 per cent of levels in 1990–1994, compared to just under 60 per cent to countries in the least authoritarian categories (1–3).

Future inquiries into the aid and authoritarianism nexus

Existing scholarship on the politics of aid has been limited by its predominant use of highly aggregated data, its unilateral focus on the increase or decrease of democratic governance in recipient countries, and its overly technocratic and narrow institutionalist view of aid relations. There is a need to pursue a series of complementary research inquiries into the aid and authoritarianism nexus in Africa and beyond.[9] A more interdisciplinary approach that draws on qualitative research traditions such as the burgeoning anthropology of aid literature (Li, 2007; Mosse, 2005; Olivier de Sardan, 2006), diplomatic history or more ethnographic studies of international organizations and global policy regimes (Neumann, 2012; Stepputat & Larsen, 2015) appears very much relevant for a more fine-grained analysis of the micropolitics inherent in the nexus between aid and authoritarianism. In this section, we suggest four future strategies of inquiry, some of them taking on the form of propositions, for future empirical research.

Beyond donor speak Donor positions towards recipient countries are often gauged in function of their official intentions as manifest in policy documents, speeches or media statements. The exclusive focus on visible and audible donor speak misleads us into considering donor governments or agencies as homogeneous entities and to discount unofficial donor narratives and views. Within governments there is often competition and disagreement between and among line ministries, headquarters and country offices, different levels of hierarchy as well as personalities. Moreover, bureaucrats in development agencies might be – in their personal capacity – rather critical of their own government's policies and programmes. Although critics often accuse donors of naivety, there is every reason to assume that foreign ministries and development agencies are populated by self-reflective actors/individuals. The fact that several donors have instituted economy analysis and country risk assessments that aim to critically evaluate the potential impact of their aid in a particular country evidences a certain degree of organizational reflexivity (see Hout, 2012).[10] Increased attention to donor bureaucrats' perceptions of their work in and for authoritarian regimes will add more nuance and provide a fuller picture of the often very complex and contentious relations between donors and recipient authoritarian countries. What might appear to outsiders as smooth cooperation and alignment between development partners might in reality be a very rocky aid relation prone to escalation into open confrontation despite substantial aid allocation.[11] A close examination of development officials' worldviews and experiences, but also their personal aspirations and concerns, will contribute to unpacking the everyday making of foreign aid in authoritarian polities.

The accountability gap A second, very different research angle consists in paying more attention to the 'accountability gap' that emerges in the aid and authoritarianism nexus. Development programmes financed by foreign donors and implemented in or by undemocratic administrations are characterized by an almost complete lack of accountability. As Martens (2005) argued, aid agencies exist primarily because they mediate the absence of direct accountability between donor-taxpayers and beneficiaries in recipient countries. As the two live in separate worlds, there is no 'feedback loop' between aid recipients and taxpayers in predominantly Western countries. Put simply, although foreign aid decisions are subject to scrutiny by national parliaments and although aid agencies – both governmental and NGOs – use a plethora of methods to demonstrate the ownership, sustainability and effectiveness of their activities, foreign aid is essentially not accountable to recipients (see de Renzio, 2006; Wenar, 2006). This absence of accountability is further compounded by the fact that Western publics have little interest in and knowledge about political dynamics in the countries supported by their governments. Consequently, domestic debates about development assistance are mostly informed by partisan positions about whether or not aid is effective and how much should be spent. An even greater lack of accountability exists in autocratic recipient countries; undemocratic regimes are not responsive to their citizens and operate with a near complete lack of accountability. 'Development' in these countries may well mean material progress for some, but policies are framed and implemented without consulting the citizenry. Foreign aid to authoritarian countries thus often operates with minimal accountability as domestic and foreign politicians, diplomats and development workers govern development programmes that affect the lives of millions of people who are only nominally involved in decision-making. This is not surprising as technical expertise and democratic accountability are contradictory organizing principles of modern governance, namely in the realm of global governance (Barnett, 2015). Barnett (2015) suggests that the balance between expertise and accountability is likely to more heavily favour the former in global governance, including international aid, as opposed to domestic governance.

Historical trajectories A third research strategy into the aid and authoritarianism nexus consists in historicizing the 'strategies of extraversion' (Bayart, 2000) that have figured so prominently in aid-dependent postcolonial Africa. Our proposition is that foreign aid – in particular bilateral aid – is path dependent and informed by historical relations between donor and recipient countries. A case in point are aid flows between former colonial powers and their ex-colonies, for example in West Africa's *Françafrique*. But there are also long-standing bilateral and aid connections between countries without common colonial history, for example between the US and Ethiopia and Egypt. The important point here is that foreign aid needs to be seen in the *longue durée*, allowing the changing justifications given by donors for supporting authoritarian clients-cum-partners in the global South to be traced. Some of these aid relations span several decades and survive government and even regime changes in both donor and recipient countries. A good example is, again, Ethiopia, which has a long history of aid-supported authoritarianism. In her book on the history of US foreign aid to Ethiopia, McVety (2012) identifies numerous historical continuities of US assistance towards Ethiopia from the imperial to the current period (also see Fantini and Puddu, this volume). Among them are the imperial Ethiopian government's ability to make use of 'development' discourse to obtain funds, the alignment of US and Ethiopian interests towards the Middle East and the realization, on behalf of American aid officials, that US aid contributed to helping an unpopular autocrat in power, fuelling popular unrest, which eventually led to the demise of Emperor Haile Selassie. An historical approach to 'development aid' (Cullater, 2000) thus unearths the trajectories, continuities and ruptures between past and present aid flows to African autocrats.

Autocratic modernities Finally, aid allocated to authoritarian governments in the name of liberal internationalism is part and parcel of a modernity that is concomitantly liberal and illiberal. Rather than conceiving of international aid and its (neo-)liberal rhetoric of good governance, democracy and human rights as being fundamentally at odds with autocratic politics in recipient countries, what we see is the emergence of illiberal autocratic modernities in recipient countries whose political elites effectively amalgamate authoritarian politics with (neo-)liberal discourses emphasizing efficiency, effectiveness and performance (see for example Jones, 2015). Illiberal democracies are thus not pre-modern, outdated or on the road to perdition (Kagan, 2008). Rather, they persist as an increasing number of 'competitive authoritarian' (Levitsky & Way, 2010) regimes that have institutionalized selected elements of multi-party democracy – namely elections – which are won by the ruling party. Foreign aid may thus play a support role in generating, maintaining and legitimizing contemporary illiberal African regimes that combine autocratic rule with trappings of liberal democracy.

Case studies and contributions

The chapters in this book scrutinize donor motives for supporting authoritarian regimes in sub-Saharan Africa and the various, often negative, impacts created by foreign aid. Five of the seven chapters consist of country case studies that offer in-depth analyses of donor motives and development dynamics in authoritarian Rwanda, Uganda, Ethiopia, Cameroon, Angola and Mozambique. As is evident from this country list, with the exception of Angola these cases are all selected on the dependent variable, i.e. they all examine prominent recipient countries marked by the concomitance of important levels of foreign aid and domestic autocratic rule. This selection is deliberate and in line with the exploratory ambition of this book. We hope that future research into the aid and authoritarianism nexus will make use of more stringent cross-country comparisons that factor in variation of both aid levels and political regime type in recipient countries. While relatively few Africanists study foreign aid, considered as being 'non-African', many scholars who research foreign aid lack the kind of country-specific knowledge that results from long-term immersion. Although the contributors to this book employ different methodological and theoretical approaches, they are all country experts as well as long-time students of international development.

In Chapter 1, Rita Abrahamsen argues that the manner in which democracy is conceptualized in development discourse and democracy promotion has implications for the very practice of democracy. Among the consequences of development discourse's shifting conceptualization of democracy can be the support and maintenance of authoritarian practices, and in some cases even authoritarian regimes. Abrahamsen concludes that donor discourse that defines democracy as a means to another end, be it economic growth or security, inevitably risks undermining democracy as a value in itself. The diverse and often conflicting liaisons between aid and political regimes by both donors and recipients highlighted by Abrahamsen are very well illustrated and complicated by the six cases studies presented here. They all underscore a major thread of this book, namely that aid relations are influenced both by donor interests and priorities, and by recipients' agency and autonomy.

In Chapter 2, which focuses on Rwanda, Zoë Marriage challenges a core tenet of contemporary aid, namely that development, democracy and security reinforce each other. Conventional analysis assumes progressions towards liberal economy, democracy and peace, but Rwanda's recent history counters these assumptions. While economic and social indicators have shown impressive improvements, political opposition has been muted, and Rwanda's involvement in the neighbouring Democratic Republic of Congo (DRC) has aggravated regional insecurity. Marriage addresses paradoxes of the ongoing aid relationship between donors and Rwanda. Hopes of donors that they could influence political governance through 'constructive engagement' have not materialized.

On the contrary, President Paul Kagame has been defiant in the face of donor demands, but this paradox is resolved by donors' acceptance of the Rwandan government's autocratic and violent behaviour as a central mechanism of the development indicators that donors demand.

Chapter 3 looks at Uganda, another (former) donor darling. David M. Anderson and Jonathan Fisher argue that Western donors not only offered muted or insignificant criticism of abuses by the Museveni regime, but also enhanced its capacity to do so by funding large parts of its budget, and by training and equipping its military and strengthening its security forces at home and abroad. The Ugandan government itself has played a pivotal role in fostering and maintaining this dispensation by capitalizing on major shifts in the international and regional contexts in order to 'securitize' its relations with donors and increasing international support for its military and security forces. The authors argue that by consenting to the gradual securitization of their relationship with the Museveni regime, donors have assisted in the creation of an increasingly militarized, illiberal state.

Chapter 4 focuses on Ethiopia, which has managed to attract an impressive amount of foreign aid, and has become one of the largest beneficiaries of ODA in sub-Saharan Africa in the past decade. While several explanations have been offered for this apparent paradox (e.g. the Ethiopian government's ability to manipulate international development discourse, donors' ignorance of local political dynamics, Western geopolitical priorities, the need of a showcase for the international aid industry), Emanuele Fantini and Luca Puddu highlight the historical continuities between foreign aid and authoritarian politics in Ethiopia, from the imperial to the current federal government. Using two case studies, one in the 1960s, the other in the 2000s, they demonstrate how high-modernist schemes carried out in the name of 'development' ordinarily work according to logics of exceptionality, circumventing the rule of law and thereby contributing to the authoritarian exercise of power. The two cases also show the internal plurality and contradictions among donors: rather than a homogeneous 'community', international donors operate in a competitive arena shaped by a multiplicity of actors, agendas and conflicting interests. This chapter also draws attention to the involvement of private contractors in implementing authoritarian development schemes.

Chapter 5 considers Cameroon, which, unlike some other countries discussed in this book, has not been a donor darling, as it was not seen as a model of political or economic reform. Apart from a brief period in the early 1990s, Cameroon has, however, benefited from constant financial and political support. When the USA and Germany reduced aid flows over concerns about the 1992 presidential elections, France increased its support. As Marie-Emmanuelle Pommerolle demonstrates, during the next two decades donors reached consensus on the 'acceptability of elections', endorsing the electoral victories of Paul Biya, in power for over thirty years, and his Cameroon People's Democratic Movement (CPDM). The Biya regime has considerable political and economic leverage as Cameroon is not really dependent on donor funding. Pommerolle shows that, in an 'internationalized political field', donors interact with domestic political parties, state institutions and civil society actors. With regard to the running of elections in Cameroon, she finds that the latter are the results of political negotiations in which national actors and international donors need to safeguard 'credible' institutions to ensure the country's stability while abiding, even in contested ways, to international criteria of democratic credibility.

The comparison between Angola and Mozambique offered by Helena Pérez Niño and Philippe Le Billon in Chapter 6 is revealing for the way in which donors and recipients interact. Both countries have competitive authoritarian regimes, but there are important differences between the two long-standing regimes in terms of their economic and political power. Angola was never a significant aid recipient, and international actors have had very little leverage over the ruling People's Movement for the Liberation of Angola (MPLA). Mozambique for its part was already a darling of some Western donors during its wartime socialist period, and it remains one of the most aid-dependent countries on the continent. While the Angolan regime survived on the basis of patronage, co-option and disciplining mechanisms funded on natural-resource revenues, Pérez Niño and Le Billon argue that ODA has functionally sustained the ruling Mozambique Liberation Front's (Frelimo) undemocratic policies. Western donors' willingness to pick up a substantial share of social expenditure has provided a buffer that extended the dominance of Frelimo, protecting it from a popular backlash of its regressive fiscal, monetary, investment and natural-resource policies. They conclude that, if Angola exemplifies the advantages and pitfalls of restricted engagement with promoters of liberal peace-building, Mozambique represents the ambiguous effects of foreign aid on the 'political settlement' as the regime becomes more authoritarian.

In the conclusion, Nicolas van de Walle challenges the current academic and policy literature that promotes the idea of an authoritarian development advantage in Africa. He dissects donors' current 'democratic fatigue' in Africa by drawing attention to parallels with modernization theory of the mid-twentieth century, which provided an intellectual justification for authoritarian state-led development interventions. Van de Walle expounds the reasons for donors' endorsement of authoritarian African regimes, which reflect their disappointment with failed democratization on the continent as much as the aid industry's recent return to top-down expertise and centralized planning. He then confronts four sets of key claims made by the scholarly literature that advocates aiding authoritarian regimes in Africa, namely that multi-party elections are anathema to sound policy-making, that the relation between states and capital is more important than political regime type, that the East Asian Developmental State model can be exported to Africa, and that good governance may delay economic growth driven by domestic rent seeking.

Taken together, our book highlights how donors increasingly abandoned their earlier commitment to democratic governance in recipient countries over the past decade in favour of a, once again, more technocratic approach to development that sits well with the authoritarian policies of a number of sub-Saharan African regimes. While withholding aid remains, at least in theory, a policy option for donors, the multiple agendas, interests and entanglements that link Western donors with a select number of African autocracies prove once more stronger, furthering development without democracy.

Notes

1 We are indebted to Lars Buur, Martin Doornbos, Rachel Hayman, Peter Kragelund and an anonymous reviewer for valuable comments on earlier versions of this chapter as well as to Caitriona Dowd and Lara Cockx for their help in statistical analysis. The idea for this book was sparked when the editors compared notes on how Rwanda and Ethiopia had both managed to attract mounting levels of donor support despite their shortcomings in terms of political governance and human rights. We explored the relation between foreign aid and authoritarian governments in Africa at a panel convened at the 5th European Conference on African Studies (ECAS) in Lisbon in June 2013. This introduction and three chapters of this book are revised versions of papers presented at this panel.

2 For instance, Afrobarometer (2015) found that African publics strongly support presidential term limits and resist leaders' attempts to extend their tenure.

3 http://www.oecd.org/dac/stats/officialdevelopmentassistancedefinitionandcoverage.htm

4 On the global spread of authoritarianism and the current 'authoritarian resurgence', see the recent issues published by the *Journal of Democracy* (vol. 26, no. 2, 3).

5 A telling example with regard to Rwanda can be found in Uvin (2001).

More concretely on how the need for democratization in Rwanda was differently judged, see Silva-Leander (2008).

6 Their paper also explains why much of the previous large-N literature, which tended to focus on democratic governance, produced inconclusive results.

7 How aid impacts on domestic political governance also depends on its modalities of delivery. For instance, Gibson *et al.* (2015) argue that technical aid to African governments can be associated with increasing democratization.

8 The table excludes any country for which no political rights score was assigned, affecting all years pre-2011 in South Sudan, and two years (1990 and 1992) in Eritrea. At the time of writing, no ODA data for 2014 was available, meaning the final year group (2010–2013) is one year shorter than its comparison groups. For this reason, any observed decline in this final year group should be considered in light of the fact that the actual years are fewer, meaning we might expect a proportionate drop in aid corresponding to this. By contrast, an observed increase in this time period, in spite of the fact that this group contains fewer years, could be seen to indicate a greater increase.

9 A point shared by Bader and Faust, whose recent review paper concludes

that 'recipient behavior in authoritarian and semi-authoritarian settings still lacks sufficient academic attention' (Bader & Faust, 2014: 589).

10 We thank Lars Buur for this observation.

11 For example, when the US and other donors in 2013 cut military and other aid to Rwanda over a combination of Rwandan complicity in the violence in the eastern Democratic Republic of Congo (DRC) and its assassinations of political opponents. Or when the British government decided to discontinue its support to the Ethiopian government's controversial Promotion of Basic Services (PBS) programme in the run-up to the May 2015 elections. We thank one of the reviewers for bringing this point to our attention.

References

Abbink, J & Hagmann, T (eds) (2012), *Reconfiguring Ethiopia. The politics of authoritarian reform*, Routledge, Abingdon.

Afrobarometer (2015), *African publics strongly support term limits, resist leaders' efforts to extend their tenure*, Afrobarometer, Dispatch No. 30, 25 May 2015.

Alesina, A & Dollar, D (2000), 'Who gives foreign aid to whom and why?', *Journal of Economic Growth*, vol. 5, no. 1, pp. 33–63.

Bader, J & Faust, J (2014), 'Foreign aid, democratization, and autocratic survival', *International Studies Review*, vol. 16, no. 4, pp. 575–95.

Barnett, M (2015), 'Accountability and global governance: the view from paternalism', *Regulation & Governance*, forthcoming, doi: 10.1111/rego.12083.

Bayart, JF (2000), 'Africa in the world: a history of extraversion', *African Affairs*, vol. 99, no. 395, pp. 217–67.

Borchgrevink, A (2008), 'Limits to donor influence: Ethiopia, aid and conditionality', *Forum for Development Studies*, vol. 35, no. 2, pp. 195–220.

Bräutigam, DA (2009). *The dragon's gift: the real story of China in Africa*, Oxford University Press, Oxford.

Bräutigam, DA & Knack, S (2004), 'Foreign aid, institutions and governance in sub-Saharan Africa', *Economic Development and Cultural Change*, vol. 52, no. 2, pp. 255–85.

Brown, S (2011), '"Well, what can you expect?": donor officials' apologetics for hybrid regimes in Africa', *Democratization*, vol. 18, no. 2, pp. 512–34.

Brown, S (2005), 'Foreign aid and democracy promotion: lessons from Africa', *European Journal of Development Research*, vol. 17, no. 2, pp. 179–98.

Brown, W (2013), 'Sovereignty matters: Africa, donors, and the aid relationship', *African Affairs*, vol. 112, no. 447, pp. 262–82.

Cooley, A (2015), 'Countering democratic norms', *Journal of Democracy*, vol. 26, no. 3, pp. 49–63.

Cullater, N (2000), 'Development? Its History', *Diplomatic History*, vol. 24, no. 4, pp. 641–53.

Del Biondo, K (2012), 'Norms, self-interest and effectiveness: explaining double standards in EU reactions to violations of democratic principles in sub-Saharan Africa', *Afrika-Focus*, vol. 25, no. 2, pp. 109–20.

Dreher, A, Nunnenkamp, P & Thiele, R (2011), 'Are "new" donors different? Comparing the allocation of bilateral aid between non DAC and DAC donor countries', *World Development*, vol. 39, no. 11, pp. 1950–68.

Dutta, N, Leeson, PT & Williamson, CR (2013), 'The amplification effect: foreign aid's impact on political institutions', *Kyklos*, vol. 66, no. 2, pp. 208–28.

Emmanuel, NG (2012), '"With a friend like this …": shielding Cameroon from democratization', *Journal of Asian and African Studies*, vol. 48, no. 2, pp. 145–60.

Eyben, R (2013), 'Struggles in Paris: the

DAC and the purposes of development aid', *European Journal of Development Research*, vol. 25, no. 1, pp. 78–91.

Ferguson, J (1990), *The anti-politics machine: 'development', depoliticization, and bureaucratic power in Lesotho*, University of Minnesota Press, Minneapolis.

Feyissa, D (2011), 'Aid negotiation: the uneasy "partnership" between EPRDF and the donors', *Journal of Eastern African Studies*, vol. 5, no. 4, pp. 788–817.

Fisher, J & Anderson, DM (2015), 'Authoritarianism and the securitization of development in Africa', *International Affairs*, vol. 91, no. 1, pp. 131–51.

Fuchs, A, Dreher, A & Nunnenkamp, P (2014), 'Determinants of donor generosity: a survey of the aid budget literature', *World Development*, vol. 56, no. 4, pp. 172–99.

Furtado, X & Smith, WJ (2009), 'Ethiopia: retaining sovereignty in aid relations', in L Whitfield (ed.), *The politics of aid. African strategies for dealing with donors*. Oxford University Press, Oxford, pp. 131–55.

Gibson, CC, Hoffman, BD & Jablonski, RS (2015), 'Did aid promote democracy in Africa? The role of technical assistance in Africa's transitions', *World Development*, vol. 68, no. 4, pp. 323–35.

Goldsmith, AA (2001), 'Foreign aid and statehood in Africa', *International Organization*, vol. 55, no. 1, pp. 123–48.

Grauvogel, J & von Soest, C (2013), *Claims to legitimacy matter: why sanctions fail to instigate democratization in authoritarian regimes*, GIGA, Hamburg, Working Paper No. 235.

Hariri, JG (2013), 'Foreign aided: why democratization brings growth when democracy does not', *British Journal of Political Science*, vol. 45, no. 1, pp. 53–71.

Hout, W (2012), 'The anti-politics of development: donor agencies and the political economy of governance', *Third World Quarterly*, vol. 33, no. 3, pp. 405–22.

Hout, W (2010), 'Governance and the rhetoric of international development', Inaugural Address, Institute of Social Studies, Erasmus University Rotterdam, 27 May 2010.

Jones, CW (2015), 'Seeing like an autocrat: liberal social engineering in an illiberal state', *Perspectives on Politics*, vol. 13, no. 1, pp. 24–41.

Jones, W, Soares de Oliveira, R & Verhoeven, H (2013), *Africa's illiberal state-builders*, University of Oxford, Refugee Studies Centre, Oxford, Working Paper Series No. 89.

Kagan, R (2008), 'The end of the end of history', *New Republic*, April 23.

Kelsall, T & Booth, D (2010), *Developmental patrimonialism? Questioning the orthodoxy on political governance and economic progress in Africa*, Africa Power and Politics Programme, London, APPP Working Paper No. 9.

Knack, S (2004), 'Does foreign aid promote democracy?', *International Studies Quarterly*, vol. 48, no. 1, pp. 251–66.

Kono, DY & Montinola, GR (2009), 'Does foreign aid support autocrats, democrats, or both?', *Journal of Politics*, vol. 71, no. 2, pp. 704–18.

Kragelund, P (2008), 'The return of non-DAC donors to Africa: new prospects for African development?', *Development Policy Review*, vol. 26, no. 5, pp. 555–84.

Levitsky, S & Way LA (2010), *Competitive authoritarianism: hybrid regimes after the Cold War*, Cambridge University Press, Cambridge.

Li, TM (2007), *The will to improve: governmentality, development and the practice of politics*, Duke University Press, Durham and London.

Lynch, G & Crawford, G (2011), 'Democratization in Africa 1990-2010: an assessment', *Democratization*, vol. 18, no. 2, pp. 275–310.

Martens, B (2005), 'Why do aid agencies exist?', *Development Policy Review*, vol. 23, no. 6, pp. 643–63.

McVety, AK (2012), *Enlightened aid: U.S. development as foreign policy in Ethiopia*, Oxford University Press, Oxford.

Mosse, D (2005), *Cultivating development: an ethnography of aid policy and practice*, Pluto Press, London.

Neumann, IB (2012), *At home with the diplomats: inside a European foreign ministry*, Cornell University Press, New York.

Nielsen, RA (2013), 'Rewarding human rights? Selective aid sanctions against repressive states', *International Studies Quarterly*, vol. 57, no. 4, pp. 791–803.

Olivier de Sardan, JP (2006), *Anthropology and development: understanding contemporary social change*, Zed Books, London.

Olsen, GR (1998), 'Europe and the promotion of democracy in post Cold War Africa: how serious is Europe and for what reason?', *African Affairs*, vol. 97, no. 388, pp. 343–67.

de Renzio, P (2006), 'Aid, budgets and accountability: a survey article', *Development Policy Review*, vol. 24, no. 6, pp. 627–45.

Resnick, D & van de Walle, N (2013a), 'Introduction: why aid and democracy? Why Africa?', in D Resnick & N van de Walle (eds), *Democratic trajectories in Africa. Unravelling the impact of foreign aid*, Oxford University Press, Oxford, pp. 1–27.

Resnick, D & van de Walle, N (2013b), 'Democratization in Africa: what role for external actors?', in D Resnick & N van de Walle (eds), *Democratic trajectories in Africa. Unravelling the impact of foreign aid*. Oxford University Press, Oxford, pp. 28–55.

Reyntjens, F (2013), *Political governance in post-genocide Rwanda*, Cambridge University Press, New York.

Riddell, RC (1999), 'The end of foreign aid to Africa? Concerns about donor policies', *African Affairs*, vol. 98, no. 392, pp. 309–35.

Schlichte, K (1998), 'La Françafrique – Postkolonialer Habitus und Klientelismus in der französischen Afrikapolitik', *Zeitschrift für Internationale Beziehungen*, vol. 5, no. 2, pp. 309–43.

Schraeder, PJ, Hook, SW & Taylor, B (1998), 'Clarifying the foreign aid puzzle: a comparison of American, Japanese, French and Swedish aid flows', *World Politics*, vol. 50, no. 2, pp. 294–323.

Sen, A (1999), *Development as freedom*, Oxford University Press, New York.

Silva-Leander, S (2008), 'On the danger and necessity of democratisation: trade-offs between short-term stability and long-term peace in post-genocide Rwanda', *Third World Quarterly*, vol. 29, no. 8, pp. 1601–620.

Stepputat, F & Larsen, J (2015), *Global political ethnography: a methodological approach to studying global policy regimes*, Danish Institute for International Studies, Copenhagen, DIIS Working Paper 2015:1.

Uvin, P (2010), 'Structural causes, development co-operation and conflict prevention in Burundi and Rwanda', *Conflict, Security & Development*, vol. 10, no. 1, pp. 161–79.

Uvin, P (2001), 'Difficult choices in the new post-conflict agenda: the international community in Rwanda after the genocide', *Third World Quarterly*, vol. 22, no. 2, pp. 177–89.

Wenar, L (2006), 'Accountability in international development aid', *Ethics and International Affairs*, vol. 20, no. 1, pp. 1–23.

Whitfield, L (2009), 'Aid and power: a comparative analysis of the country studies', in L Whitfield (ed.), *The politics of aid. African strategies for dealing with Donors*. Oxford University Press, Oxford, pp. 329–60.

Young, C (1999), 'The third wave of democratization in Africa: ambiguities and contradictions', in R Joseph (ed.), *State, conflict and democracy in Africa*, Lynne Rienner, Boulder, CO, pp. 15–38.

1 | Discourses of democracy, practices of autocracy: shifting meanings of democracy in the aid–authoritarianism nexus

Rita Abrahamsen

Introduction

Since the early 1990s, democracy and good governance have been core tenets of development discourse and policy, with donors proclaiming the importance of freedom, rights and accountability for development and prosperity. Yet, not only does the process of democratization appear to have stalled in many African countries, foreign aid also seems to be flowing freely to some of the continent's more autocratic and repressive states. As this volume shows, countries like Ethiopia, Rwanda and Uganda have continued to attract substantial donor support, despite their dwindling democratic credentials and decreasing respect for human rights and political freedoms. In other countries, democracy has fared better and multi-party elections are now a routine event across the continent. Nevertheless, when describing the results of two decades of democracy promotion, observers conjure unlikely terms like 'electoral dictatorships', 'competitive authoritarianism' and 'hybrid regimes', or point to continued presidentialism and the need to qualify democracy 'with adjectives' (Collier & Levitsky, 1997; Carothers, 2002; Diamond, 2002; Levitsky & Way, 2002; van de Walle, 2003; Lynch & Crawford, 2011; Peiffer & Englebert, 2012).

This chapter analyses the trajectory of African democracies in the context of the changing meanings ascribed to democracy in donor discourses. Put simply, I argue that the manner in which democracy is conceptualized in development discourse and democracy promotion has implications for the practice of democracy. Approaching democracy as an essentially contested concept, the chapter charts democracy's shifting status and the meaning ascribed to it in development discourse and thus reveals its contingent and constructed character. Combining a theoretical and textual analysis with an empirical discussion of processes of democratization on the continent, it shows how the practical and political consequences of development discourse's narrations of democracy can be the support and maintenance of authoritarian practices, and in some cases even authoritarian regimes. Emerging at the end of the

Cold War, donors' support for democracy has followed a path from an initial focus on economic liberalization, to poverty reduction, to increasing securitization. Thus, in the 1990s, the close association of democracy with economic liberalization had the paradoxical effect of contributing both to the creation and maintenance of (an imperfect) democracy and the persistence of social and political unrest, which in turn posed a continuing threat to the survival of pluralism. Despite the abandonment of structural adjustment programmes and the attention to poverty reduction in the 2000s, these tensions continue to haunt many African democracies. More recently as part of the merger of development and security, democracy has been subtly reconceptualized and incorporated into a broader security strategy, where democracy is valued for its perceived contribution to a more peaceful and stable international environment. The result is frequently a development policy that ends up privileging security and stability over democracy, despite donors' insistence that the two are always and everywhere perfectly coterminous. Democracy, in other words, is not a definitional constant, but has its own history and is given meaning in interaction with the broader conditions of possibility of donor discourses and policies.

There are of course multiple complex reasons for democracy's fate in Africa, and the relationship between foreign aid, democracy and authoritarianism cannot be captured in a singular narrative or explanatory frame. In arguing that the shifting conceptualization of democracy matters in explaining how foreign aid can end up supporting authoritarianism, this chapter rejects characterizations of the good governance agenda and democracy promotion as mere rhetoric, empty words or quite simply 'spin', but it does not suggest that development discourse is the only explanation. While democracy as a foreign policy objective is frequently trumped by national interests such as security and trade, the manner in which democracy is defined and related to other objectives and values influences how political rights and freedoms are promoted and put into practice. Particular interpretations of democracy legitimize particular political practices, while delegitimizing and marginalizing other models and possibilities. While the effects will play out differently in different settings, depending on the history and politics of specific countries, this means that engaging in debate about the meaning of democracy in development is not merely an abstract conceptual exercise, but an intrinsic part of broader global struggles over social and political power. In short, recovering the essential contestability of democracy is a political task alongside practical struggles for the widening of democratic space in Africa.

The absence and rise of democracy in donors' development discourse

Historically, democracy has not figured prominently on donors' development and foreign policy agendas. On the contrary, a neglect or even an outright dislike of democracy appears as one of the few invariants of development discourse and donors have traditionally interacted closely, if not always comfortably, with autocrats of variable brutality. Early political development theories and models of the 1950s and 1960s regarded democracy as the almost inevitable outcome of the relatively unproblematic transition from 'traditional' society to 'modernity'. As Gabriel Almond put it, 'in the new and modernizing nations of Asia, Africa and Latin America, the process of enlightenment and democratization will have their inevitable way' (1970: 232). Such optimism, underpinned by a prevailing structural functionalism and determinism, soon gave way to a Cold War perspective that feared political freedom as a potential harbinger of Communism and upheld political order and stability as its main values (Pye, 1966; Zolberg, 1966; Pool, 1967; Huntington, 1968). In a classic statement: 'in the Congo, in Vietnam, in the Dominican Republic, it is clear that order depends on somehow compelling newly mobilized strata to return to a measure of passivity and defeatism from which they have been aroused by the process of modernization. At least temporarily, the maintenance of order requires a lowering of newly acquired expectations and levels of political activity' (Pool, 1967: 26).

Even as superpower rivalries faded, foreign aid retained a preference for political order and strong government, with democracy and freedom frequently seen as a luxury to be deferred until other, more pressing development problems had been solved. During the heyday of structural adjustment in the 1980s, for example, unpopular economic reforms had to be protected from the demands of an active citizenry, leaving little room for democratic participation and debate. As Depak Lal, an influential figure in the Research Department of the World Bank, put it at the time, 'a courageous, ruthless and perhaps undemocratic government is required to ride roughshod over newly created interest groups' (1983: 33). Foreign aid kept many reform-minded African governments in power during this period by providing them with sufficient resources to overcome (and suppress) domestic protest against adjustment, and thus simultaneously ensured the survival of authoritarianism (see Bangura, 1986; Beckman, 1992; Toye, 1992).

It took the end of the Cold War for democracy to emerge as the 'new global zeitgeist' (Diamond et al., 1988) and, almost overnight, democracy rose from obscurity to become the panacea for Africa's development ills. There is thus a clear geopolitical dimension to the inclusion of democracy as a development objective. Freed from the restraints of bipolarity and intoxicated by the perceived victory of democracy and capitalism over Communism, donors were 'free at last' (Clough, 1992) to insist on democracy without fearing a loss of allies or the rise of the political left. The World Bank's 1989 report 'Sub-Saharan Africa: From Crisis to Sustainable Growth' marks a key turning point in this regard, although it presents the need for democracy in terms of 'lessons learnt' rather than geopolitics. By proclaiming that a 'crisis of govern-ance' underlies the 'litany of Africa's development problems', the report placed the concept of good governance at the heart of the development agenda for Africa. Defining governance in rather general terms as the 'exercise of political power to manage a nation's affairs', the World Bank stressed the need not only for less, but for better government. 'History suggests', the Bank argued, 'that political legitimacy and consensus are a precondition for sustainable develop-ment (World Bank, 1989: 60). Hence, the solution to Africa's predicament was presented as greater openness and accountability, the rule of law, freedom of the press, increased grassroots participation, and legitimate, pluralistic political structures. The message of the report was unequivocal: liberal democracy was not only a human right, but also conducive to and necessary for economic growth (World Bank, 1989: 60, 192).

Where the World Bank leads, others follow. One by one, bilateral donors lined up to announce that henceforth development assistance would only be granted to countries committed to democratization. Already in February 1990, the United States announced that foreign assistance would be used to promote democracy and would favour countries pursuing 'the interlinked and mutu-ally reinforcing goals of political liberalization and market-oriented economic reforms' (Clough, 1992: 57, 59). The British position was spelt out in no uncertain terms by Foreign Secretary Douglas Hurd in June 1990, when he announced that countries that 'tend toward pluralism, public accountability, respect for the rule of law, human rights, market principles, should be encouraged'. Governments that 'persist with repressive policies', on the other hand, 'should not expect us to support them in their folly with scarce aid resources' (ODI, 1992: 1). A couple of weeks later in France, President Mitterrand announced to the Conference of Heads of States of Francophone Africa that he expected 'true democracies with multi-partyism, free elections and respect for human rights' to be established (*IDS Bulletin*, 1993: 7). The OECD and the European Council issued similar statements, linking continued support to democratic transition (*ibid.*: 8). The outcome of this newfound veneration for democracy was the birth of political aid conditionality, whereby foreign assistance was made conditional on specific reforms towards multi-party democracy.

In political theory, the meaning of democracy has been vigorously debated for more than 2,000 years. It is often classified as an essentially contested concept (Gallie, 1955–56) in the sense that any neutral definition is impossible as rival interpretations embody different and indeterminate social and political allegiances, operating within particular moral and political perspectives. Put differently, democracy is one of those concepts that 'inevitably involves endless disputes about their proper uses on the part of their users' (*ibid.*: 169). It is political, contested and open to multiple definitions. It is part of social and economic struggles for power and influence, and thus beyond consensus. Not so in development! Since its inclusion in official development documents and speeches in the early 1990s, democracy has been presented as an uncontested concept, an unquestionable 'good' about which there is little or no difference of opinion. In common with most mainstream literature on democratization at the time, lengthy theoretical discussions of the meaning and value of democracy are almost entirely absent from development discourse and the notion of contestability is expelled in favour of a convergence towards procedural and minimalist definitions of liberal democracy and an exclusion of more participatory models (see Abrahamsen, 2000; Kurki, 2010). More recently, the limits of focusing too much on elections have been acknowledged, giving rise to an emphasis on the quality of democracy and the extent to which citizens can participate in elections, influence decision-making and hold those in power accountable (see e.g. Klugman, 2002; Diamond, 2008; Levine and Molina, 2011). Nevertheless, as Milja Kurki observes, after more than twenty years 'nothing fundamental has changed ... in democracy promotion' (2010: 363) and donor promoted democracy is primarily about certain key procedures, including elections, the institutionalization of the rule of law, and freedom of expression and association.

Liberal democracy in the form of elections, the rule of law and individual rights is undoubtedly valuable and worth fighting for, and it is not my intention to dismiss electoral democracy as unimportant. Nevertheless, it is crucial to recognize how particular understandings and definitions of democracy, despite protestations to the contrary, can end up supporting authoritarian practices. Liberal democracy, like all models of democracy, is linked to social and political contexts and represents specific social and political positions and power relations (Held, 1987; Arblaster, 1999). The formation of development policy, as all forms of knowledge production, occurs within these social relations of power and is embedded within specific historical and political conditions and change in complex interaction with this wider socio-political environment. Thus, in order to understand how a development discourse that insists on the importance of democratization can end up supporting authoritarian practices, it is necessary to investigate in greater detail exactly how democracy is defined and how it relates to other development objectives, and to existing socio-political orders and power relations. Below, I do this by focusing first on how donor discourses conceive of the relationship between democracy and economic liberalization, and second, the relationship between democracy and international security.

Democracy and economic liberalization

When democracy emerged from the cold to become the centrepiece of development discourse in the early 1990s, it was touted as an unquestionable 'good' about which there could be little or no difference of opinion. The image in development documents and speeches was of a worldwide democracy move- ment with shared goals and aspirations, where donors and creditors joined forces with the 'people' of the South against oppressive and authoritarian leaders. The kind of democracy that Africans should strive for, according to the good governance agenda, was minimalist and procedural – an institutional arrangement or political method centred on the competitive struggle between political parties for people's votes. Democracy, in other words, was primarily about political and civil rights, not about concrete socio-economic rights. Here donors discourses were in accordance with mainstream literature on democratization, which dismissed more participatory models focusing on welfare and inclusion as outdated and unrealistic (O'Donnell & Schmitter, 1986; Huntington, 1991). Huntington, for example, celebrated the fact that US political scientists had made democracy 'less of a hurrah word and more of a common sense word' (1991: 7), whereas Di Palma argued that democracy's 'disengagement from the idea of social progress is a silver lining ... which gives democracy more realistic, more sturdily conscious grounds for claiming superiority in the eyes of public opinion and political practitioners (1990: 23). In this way, definitions of democracy were gleaned from already-existing political systems rather than from democratic ideals (see Held, 1987).

Correspondingly, democracy was linked to continued economic liber- alization and structural adjustment programmes. By this time, the failure of structural adjustment to generate economic growth on the African continent had become an almost inescapable fact, as more than a decade of adjustment policies had failed to produce a single definite success story (Mosley, Harrigan & Toye, 1991; Corbo, Fischer & Webb, 1992). Yet, economic liberalism could hardly be abandoned at the moment of capitalism's victory over Communism and there was therefore an urgent need for a new development paradigm. In many ways, this is precisely what the World Bank's 1989 report provided. By arguing that political factors had prevented the implementation of the right economic policies and identifying the 'root cause of weak economic performance in the past' as 'the failure of public institutions' (World Bank, 1989: xii), the report not only rehabilitated structural adjustment but also brought it into line with post-Cold War ideology. The reason for the failure of structural adjustment was not the programmes themselves, nor imbalances in the global political economy, unfair markets, or adverse domestic conditions, but African governments and their autocratic behaviours. Drawing attention to the lack of accountability, transparency, and predictability, the Bank concluded that 'poor governance' had made it almost impossible for the right economic policies to work.

The 1989 World Bank report constructed a binary opposition between state intervention, which it associated with past development failures, and economic liberalism, which represented the basis for future development success. According to the Bank, Africa's 'postindependence development effort failed because the strategy was misconceived' and 'pinned too much hope on rapid state-led industrialization' (1989: 3, 83). It drove 'entrepreneurs into the informal sector' and 'crowded local firms out of access to markets and financial resources' (*ibid.*: 136–7). While there is no denying the dismal performance of many African states as entrepreneurs and providers of public goods, the effect of this order of discourse was to bestow legitimacy on further contraction of the state and its services in accordance with structural adjustment programmes (see Abrahamsen, 2000: 47–52). Because state intervention was associated with development failure, authoritarianism, predation and oppression, the curtailment of state activities came to appear as a people-friendly, democratic venture, so much so that in the post-Cold War climate democratization became almost synonymous with state contraction or de-statization. A positive synergy was thus constructed between democracy and economic growth, and economic reform was said to be 'wasted if the political context is not favourable' (World Bank, 1989: 192). This interpretation echoed across the development community, with the UK Foreign Secretary Robin Cook, for example, stating that 'the past two decades have repeatedly demonstrated that political freedom and economic development are mutually reinforcing' (1998). In brief, democracy and economic liberalization were regarded as two sides of the same coin, inseparable and mutually reinforcing in the sense that democracy was perceived as the necessary political framework for economic liberalization and growth. The context in which African countries embarked on the process of democratization was accordingly one where donors and creditors insisted that economic liberalization was to continue unabated, and African countries were expected to achieve development by implementing political and economic reforms simultaneously.

The pursuit of simultaneous economic and political reform presented newly elected governments in the 1990s with complex and intractable dilemmas, where economic and political logic often appeared contradictory and conflicting: on the one hand, the demand for further economic adjustment by donors and creditors, and, on the other, domestic expectations of social improvements in the wake of democracy; on one side, instructions to privatize state-owned enterprises and, on the other, hopes for gainful employment. Many newly elected governments thus had two irreconcilable constituencies: external donors and creditors and their poor domestic majorities (Abrahamsen, 2000). While governments were crucially dependent on both, for their financial survival and re-election respectively, they could not satisfy the two at the same time. External sponsors demanded continued economic liberalization, which was sure to create domestic dissatisfaction and unpopularity at the polls. Conversely, responding to popular demands for social improvements was likely to result in loss of vital financial assistance from donors.

In many countries, the first casualty of this dilemma was the democratic process itself, as governments reverted to the tried and tested methods of the authoritarian past in order to contain civil disorder and silence critics. We can see this clearly in several countries where the second and third elections were considerably less 'free and fair' than the first transitional elections. Zambia is a particularly good illustration. As the 1990s' austerity measures bit deeper and deeper and life under democracy proved to be just as bad or worse as under authoritarianism, protests, demonstrations and unrest escalated. So too did support for the opposition. Faced with this new uncertain environment of political competition and popular unrest, the government of President Chiluba reacted by closing down democratic space, harassing the opposition, and rigging elections (Abrahamsen, 2000; Simon, 2005). The 1996 elections were the most blatantly authoritarian, as constitutional reforms disqualified former President Kenneth Kaunda, the 'Father of the Nation', from running and a boycott by the opposition ensured Chiluba and the incumbent party a landslide victory. Even as elections have become routinized, and despite a promising change of governing party in 2011, undemocratic practices have continued. President Michael Sata and his Patriotic Front have failed to deliver on their populist promises, and instead opposition parties have fallen afoul of the notorious Public Order Act and an overzealous police force. In the last year alone, the leaders of at least four prominent parties have been harassed and arrested, simply for criticizing the government, whereas NGOs are under attack from a new law that requires civil-society organizations to be registered by a government-controlled board. The media has also been subdued, and journalists have been physically attacked and online news sites shut down in a further attempt to silence critics (Gilbert & Mureriwa, 2014).

Zambia thus conforms to Caryn Peiffer and Pierre Englebert's recent observation that the consolidation of democracy in Africa has stalled at the level individual countries had reached by 1995, and the overall distribution of regimes classified as 'free', 'partly free' and 'not free' has remained steady for almost two decades (Peiffer & Englebert, 2012). In other words, the 'partly free' or hybrid regimes have become a permanent feature of the African political landscape, neither transitioning to more democracy, nor reverting to fully fledged authoritarianism. These countries hold elections as a matter of routine, and although these are often far from free and fair, they are supported, encouraged and also often endorsed by donors. Between elections, significant breaches of democratic practice will lead to the suspension of assistance, or assistance is withheld in the lead-up to elections in protest against unconstitutional or undemocratic practices. Almost without fail, however, foreign aid is reinstated in an almost ritual performance.

Malawi, a highly aid-dependent country where about 40 per cent of the national budget comes from donors, provides a good example. When President

Bingu wa Mutharika and his Democratic Progressive Party (DPP) won a landslide second term in 2009, it was generally interpreted as a reward for their sound economic policies, which had produced a 7 per cent growth in the period from their first election in 2004 (Wroe, 2012). Shortly afterwards, the UK withheld a small portion of its annual aid package after development funds had been diverted to buy a jet for the personal use of the president (*ibid.*). Then again in 2011, donors, including the EU and DFID, suspended aid in protest of the government's failure to devalue the currency and its increasingly unconstitutional behaviour. Just as the reinstatement of assistance was considered, the government used the police and the army to suppress popular protests. Nineteen civilians were killed in the clashes, and donors, this time including the US, suspended aid indefinitely (*ibid.*). This on-and-off approach to Malawi continued under the presidency of Joyce Banda, when a high-level corruption scandal known as Cashgate led to the suspension of aid worth US$150 million. Banda lost the elections in 2014, and aid is expected to resume as new budget controls are implemented. In Kenya, too, donor support has been turned on and off in response to democratic malpractice, but has done little to enhance and deepen democratization (see Brown, 2001; 2005).

Countries that perform well in terms of economic reforms seem to have an even easier time in terms of getting away with undemocratic behaviour without losing access to development assistance. Uganda, for example, has periodically encountered the wrath of donors in response to its authoritarian practices and persecution of the opposition, but aid has inevitably been restored to a country that has become a 'donor darling' due to its economic liberalization, its successful HIV/AIDS campaign and more recently its support for counter-terrorism (Lindemann, 2011; Fisher, 2012). Never mind that Uganda is a de facto one-party system, which according to the Afrobarometer's surveys has one of the continent's biggest gaps between citizens' demand for democracy and its perceived supply (Bratton & Houessou, 2014: 20). It remains to be seen if recent international outrage at the country's anti-gay legislation will lead to a more permanent suspension of assistance, but in most cases it takes large-scale political violence and military coups to trigger more serious and enduring sanctions. In Mauritania and Niger, for example, aid was suspended following a military coup and unconstitutional changes to the presidential term limits respectively, but in both countries assistance was restored following elections in 2009 and 2011.

As in Mauritania and Niger, elections or the promise of elections often function as the trigger for the restoration of foreign aid. Elections, in this sense, are treated as a proxy for democracy; they are easy to monitor, they have a defined beginning and end, and they create a presumption of relative democracy. In this way, donors appear satisfied with hybrid democracy and content to support the holding of periodic elections as opposed to a deepening of democracy, especially as long as recipient countries are good economic reformers. In this way, development discourse and practice allow for a form of electoralism that is compatible with a high degree of authoritarianism.

Seen in this light, the enduring instability and fragility of many African democracies is in part a reflection of the very design and conceptualization of democracy in development discourse. This is not to say that other factors, interests and actors are irrelevant or less important, but in analysing the outcome of democratization it is disingenuous to ignore the manner in which the definition of democracy has conditioned the outcome of democratic struggles since the initial transitions in the early 1990s. Born as exclusionary democracies that allow some political competition but that cannot incorporate or respond to the demands of the majority in any meaningful way, African democracies and the choices available to elected governments have remained constrained by the definition of democracy and economic liberalism as two sides of the same coin. Although structural adjustment was formally abandoned in 1999, following strong critiques and a growing recognition that the programmes had not been effective in changing economic polices, the underlying, defining features of democracy as promoted in development have not changed and remain primarily procedural and electoral and allied to continued economic liberalization (Kurki, 2010). Despite the new emphasis on partnerships, ownership and poverty reduction, the hopes and expectations of the democratic transitions have not been fulfilled and the quality of life has still to improve for the vast majority of people. Reviews of Africa's democratic experience thus often conclude that Africans are disappointed with democracy's ability to reduce poverty, inequality and suffering (Lumumba-Kasongo, 2005; Whitfield & Mustapha, 2009; Lynch & Crawford, 2011). As Peter Lewis observes, 'growth has not been accompanied by rising incomes or popular welfare', giving rise to the paradox of 'growth without prosperity' (2008: 97). In several countries like Ghana, Kenya, Nigeria, South African and Tanzania, 'indicators of public welfare lag behind strong overall economic performance [and] officials and average citizens alike often note the "disconnect" between macroeconomic indicators and microeconomic performance' (ibid.: 97). To date, there are few signs that the spectacular double-digit growth experienced by many countries since the mid-2000s (The Economist, 2011) has significantly improved the socio-economic conditions, and recent surveys conducted by the Afrobarometer in thirty-four countries suggest that the 'Africa rising' narrative is not shared by ordinary Africans (Hofmeyr, 2013). Instead, 53 per cent of respondents rated the state of their national economy as 'fairly bad' or 'very bad', and 48 per cent described their personal living conditions as 'fairly bad' or 'very bad' (ibid.). This massive gap between the glowing reports of Africa's rapid GDP growth and Africans' personal accounts of everyday hardships means that the contradictions and tensions of exclusionary democracies are likely to remain. And, as the Afrobarometer concludes, if 'growth exacerbates social inequalities, the outcome may be increasing political instability' (*ibid.*: 12). In this way, the effects of simultaneous economic and political liberalization can be seen as paradoxical; they contribute both to the maintenance of (an imperfect) democracy and the persistence of social and political unrest, which in turn pose a continual threat to the survival of pluralism.

Democracy and international security

Following the attacks of 11 September 2001 and the ensuing global fight against terrorism, the status of democracy in development discourse has changed in subtle, but important ways. While in the 1990s, the concern with democracy reflected the perceived victory over Communism and was seen as a route to economic liberalism and growth, today democracy, freedom and accountability are arguably valued first and foremost as potential contributors to international security and stability. Donors, of course, stress the mutually reinforcing nature of democracy, development and security, as exemplified by President George W. Bush's declaration in 2007 that there are 'no hard lines between our security interests, our development interests and our democratic goals' (in Epstein, 2010: 2). The so-called 'war on terror', as launched by President Bush, was in part based on the conviction that promoting democracy would bring an end to international terrorism, or at the very least significantly reduce the prevalence of attacks. According to this view, people who can freely express their opinions in the public domain and through the ballot box are less likely to find the bomb and the gun a tempting political strategy. Attractive as this interpretation may appear, the relationship between democracy and terrorism is unfortunately much more complicated. Democracy and security are always and everywhere awkward bedfellows: in the aftermath of 9/11, many established democracies have curtailed civil liberties and citizens' rights in the face of heightened attention to homeland security (Huysmans, 2004; Wilkinson, 2006; Webb, 2007) and there is little evidence to support the idea that democracy prevents terrorism, at least not in any straightforward way (Gause III, 2005; Weinberg, 2013). By contrast, many recent terrorist attacks have been planned and executed from within established democracies, whereas the policy of linking democracy to the 'war on terror' tarnished democracy promotion by associating it too much with 'regime change', as for example in Iraq (see Carothers, 2006).

Democracy and good governance remain key tropes in post-9/11 development discourse, but they now stand in a new, and frequently subservient, relationship to the relatively recent discovery of security by development policy.[1] The immediate aftermath of 9/11 saw an increase in official development assistance (ODA) and a noticeable redirection of the aid effort towards countries considered of strategic importance and/or affected by conflict. While growth in development spending has subsequently levelled off, the direction of assistance towards security issues and strategic countries has persisted (Woods, 2005). Accordingly, strategic but often undemocratic countries like Afghanistan, Pakistan and Yemen, as well as Ethiopia, Uganda, and Rwanda, have emerged as major recipients of foreign assistance in return for their support for global counter-terrorism and security policies. While development discourse has never valued liberal democracy primarily for its intrinsic properties such as participation, inclusion and equality, the current manner of narrating democracy increases the risks that it will be further sacrificed on the altar of international security.

One of the characteristics of contemporary development assistance is an unashamed acknowledgement that it must serve the national security interest of donors. Whereas in the past such geopolitical motivations were dressed up in humanitarian language, today the straightforward assumption is that 'development and security goals can be pursued in a mutually reinforcing way' (DFID, 2005: 13). Or as President Obama proudly announced to the UN, 'My national security strategy recognizes development not only as a moral imperative, but as a strategic and economic imperative' (The White House, 2010a). In strikingly similar terms, the UK Conservative Party's 'One World Conservatism' stated that 'tackling global conflict is not only a moral imperative but a clear national security concern' and advocated a 'hard-headed but not hard-hearted' approach to development (UK Conservative Party, 2009: 5). Echoes of these policy shifts can be heard in the statements of most bilateral donors, even those often associated with a softer, more progressive development agenda. Denmark, for example, made combating and preventing terrorism a priority for the disbursement of development assistance already in 2004 (DANIDA, 2004), stating that a 'modern and effective foreign policy requires that many facets of foreign policy, such as development, security, defence and trade policies, are integrated in a mutually reinforcing manner' (Royal Danish Ministry of Foreign Affairs, 2003). Canada, another traditionally humanitarian-oriented donor, declared unambiguously that 'Development has to be the first line of defence for a collective security system that takes prevention seriously ... Development makes everyone more secure' (Government of Canada, 2005). Japan too has fallen into line with this dominant discourse on development and terrorism, and in 2003 devised its ODA charter so as to allow development assistance to be used in the national interest and as part of counter-terrorism efforts (Kiyokazu, 2006). The EU, the largest provider of development aid to Africa, has also explicitly assigned greater importance to security in its development agenda, and its 'Declaration on Combating Terrorism' announced that 'the commitment of countries to combat terrorism on an ongoing basis would be an influencing factor in EU relations with countries' (Gavas, 2006).

In the US, this new discourse has coalesced around the three 'Ds' of develop-ment, diplomacy and defence – notably missing a fourth 'D' for democracy. The three 'Ds' are considered mutually reinforcing tools of foreign policy that are in turn integrated into an overall security strategy. Development policy, in other words, is also security policy. This is clearly evident from President Obama's Presidential Directive on Global Development, the first of its kind by a US administration, which seeks to forge a new bipartisan consensus on development policy 'within the broader context of our National Security Strategy' (The White House, 2010b: 2). The Directive recognizes development as 'a central pillar of our national security policy, equal to diplomacy and defense' (*ibid.*: 5). As part of this integration, the Administrator of USAID is now included in meetings of the National Security Council, and a new Interagency Policy Committee on Global Development is led by the National Security staff, not development experts (*ibid.*: 6).

The UK has followed a similar path of synchronizing development and defence spending, and has adopted an 'integrated approach' that again combines the three 'Ds' of development, diplomacy and defence as well as intelligence resources to ensure effective coordination in fragile and conflicted states (DFID, FCO & MOD, 2011). Analogous to the institutional collaboration between USAID and the National Security Council, DFID is now one of the permanent members of a new British National Security Council. The 2010 Strategic Defence and Security Review, entitled 'Securing Britain in an Age of Uncertainty', emphasized the link between national security and fragile states. The Review assigned a central role to DFID, and, while acknowledging that development aid is primarily about poverty reduction, the goal is to ensure that develop-ment assistance makes the 'optimal contribution to national security within its overall objective of poverty reduction' (HM Government, 2010: 11). A full 30 per cent of British ODA is now directed towards fragile and conflict-affected states, an increase from £1.9 billion to £3.8 billion in 2014 (*ibid.*: 44). The aim of UK development assistance is to 'focus on those fragile and conflict-affected countries or regions where the risks are high, our interests are most at stake and where we know we can have an impact' (DFID, FCO & MOD, 2011: 19). This, Development Secretary Andrew Mitchell said, is not only 'cost-effective and beneficial for the security of the UK, it will also help to improve the lives of some of the poorest and most vulnerable people on the planet' (DFID, 2011).

The three 'Ds' of development, diplomacy and defence come together in a concern for the national security of donors, and there is little doubt that security today figures more prominently on the development agenda than at any other time since the end of the Cold War. This discourse constructs the development needs of the poor as coterminous with the security priori-ties of donors, and there is little or no room for conceiving of conflict or contradictions between them. It is of course possible that these interests do align, and thus that the two birds of underdevelopment and insecurity can be killed with the one stone of foreign assistance: some of the world's poorest and most vulnerable people do, as the UK development secretary suggests, live in fragile and conflict-affected states. A well-functioning security sector with security personnel that respect human rights is vital to democracy, and may have beneficial effects on development. Ensuring that African people are protected against acts of violence and terror is of central importance, and using development aid to enhance security is not in and of itself wrong or detrimental to the objective of poverty reduction or democracy.

The question is: what happens if and when the needs and priorities of donors and recipients do not align, or when the national security interests of donors clash with democratic principles or the objectives of democracy and good governance? Consider the Trans-Saharan Counter-Terrorism Partnership, which has five objectives. Three refer to security: strengthening regional counterterrorism capabilities; enhancing and institutionalizing cooperation among the region's security forces; and reinforcing bilateral military ties with the US. The two others refer to 'promoting democratic governance' and 'discrediting terrorist ideology' (AFRICOM, 2010).

The inherent danger in this order of priorities is that foreign assistance ends up being driven by donors' security interests rather than the development needs of recipient countries. While many projects carried out in the name of security are focused on seemingly traditional development concerns, such as education, employment and health, there is nevertheless a shift away from poverty and poor countries in general towards what is sometimes referred to as 'populations at risk', 'at-risk' geographic locations, or 'vulnerable groups'. 'At risk' and 'vulnerable' here refers to radicalization, not poverty, and the target populations are Muslims, and Muslim youth in particular, in fragile and conflict-affected countries rather than simply the poorest and most vulnerable people in the poorest countries (see Howell and Lind, 2009). The securitization of poverty and underdevelopment, in other words, may facilitate policy responses informed by a desire to safeguard the 'here' against the 'elsewhere', with detrimental effects for both development and democracy. The absence of a fourth 'D' in contemporary development discourse has to be understood in the context of the value placed on security and stability; democracy heralds potential uncertainty and change in a world where order and predictability is of prime importance. That said, the values of democracy and good governance have not been entirely abandoned, but their meaning has been reinterpreted in subtle, yet important ways, especially when it comes to the issue of democracy in so-called fragile environments or in conflict-affected states. Here, democracy is valued to the extent that it contributes to a more peaceful, stable and predictable environment, but is simultaneously feared for the potential uncertainty that follows from political competition.

The World Bank's 2011 World Development Report 'Conflict, Security and Development' is instructive in this regard. The report not only confirms the centrality of security within contemporary development discourse, but, as Gareth Jones and Dennis Rodgers (2011: 993) suggest, also sets out a pragmatic agenda that privileges security before development and democracy. The report identifies 'capable, accountable and legitimate institutions' as 'the common "missing factor" explaining why some societies are more prone to violence than others' (World Bank, 2011: 46). The central message is accordingly that 'strengthening legitimate institutions and governance to provide citizen security, justice and jobs is crucial to breaking the cycle of violence' (*ibid.*: 2). Democracy – in the form of legitimate institutions and governance – is thus emphasized, but in a highly functionalist view where democracy appears primarily as a tool for producing security and stability. In line with this approach, one of the central concepts of the report is 'inclusive-enough coalitions'. Such coalitions, the report suggests, include the parties necessary for implementing the initial stages of confidence building and institutional transformation and need not be 'all-inclusive' (*ibid.*: 12). Instead of calling for broad-based participation and inclusion, the report stresses the need for a 'national leader … to lay out clear priorities' (*ibid.*: 20) and warns that democracy is frequently associated with a short-term upsurge in violence, and that it might therefore make sense to postpone elections until a more secure, less coercive environment is established (*ibid.*: 164). 'Elections', the report notes, 'are a means of institutional transformation not its end' (*ibid.*).[2]

There is much to commend these observations, and it is certainly the case that elections are not ends in themselves and that perfect, inclusive elections are unlikely in the immediate aftermath of large-scale violence or civil war. Nevertheless, care is needed lest the desire to achieve security overrules the value and aspiration of democracy. As Jones and Rodgers point out in their review of the report, for all its emphasis on legitimate institutions, the World Bank actually pays shockingly scant attention to democracy. The first full mention of democracy is on page 101, and then simply to note that transitions from authoritarianism to democracy can increase violence (Jones & Rodgers, 2011: 986). Overall, there are fewer than a dozen mentions of democracy (*ibid.*), and instead the report seems to be preoccupied with the 'legitimacy of institutions'. The concept of 'inclusive-enough coalitions' indicates a highly restrictive vision of democracy, participation and representativeness, in that legitimacy is anchored in the ability of institutions to produce results and impose order and security rather than arising from the active endorsement and support of the people. 'Inclusive enough' by definition also means 'exclusion', and the question is, accordingly, exclusion of which groups and interests and for how long. 'Inclusive-enough coalitions' risk becoming deeply sedimented inequalities, embedded in the very structures of governance and reproduced through the procedures and formal channels of elections. In the World Development Report, however, the representativeness and inclusiveness of institutions appear less important than the production of security and stability.

The results of this reinterpretation of democracy in development discourse are by no means uniform across the continent, and therefore merit close attention when assessing democracy's fate in recent years. Whereas some countries are largely unaffected, others have experienced significant changes in their interactions with donors and foreign assistance due to securitization. This is particularly the case for conflict-affected countries and countries considered strategic allies, where the emphasis on security and stability has often furnished African states and their leaders with greater capacities to avoid further democratization. Ethiopia is a case in point; as a key contributor to the counter-terrorism efforts in Somalia and East Africa, the country receives an estimated US$3 billion annually in foreign aid (Jones, Soares de Oliveira & Verhoeven, 2013: 18). Similarly, Rwanda has positioned itself as central to African peace and security, and through its high troop contributions to various peacekeeping missions has succeeded in securing substantial foreign assistance for military capacity building and training (Beswick, 2014). In Uganda, President Museveni has also successfully played the 'war on terror' to his advantage, bargaining strategic support for increased assistance and political negotiating space (Fisher, 2012). Meanwhile, progress on democracy has stalled in all three countries, with human rights organizations frequently expressing concerns about freedom of expression, persecution of civil society and harassment of the opposition (Human Rights Watch, 2010; Lindemann, 2011; Reyntjens 2011; chapters in this volume). In North Africa, Algeria has become pivotal in the fight against violent extremism in the Sahel, and has benefited from considerable foreign assistance despite its poor record on democracy and human rights. The manner in which donors perceive the relationship between democracy and security makes these incongruities both easier to explain and to tolerate.

The reinterpretation of democracy and security has not only led to a re-allocation of aid towards countries considered strategically important, it has also led to increased support for various security and military efforts on the continent. After the OECD's influential Development Assistance Committee broadened the definition of what counts as official development assistance (ODA) to include contributions to security sectors, reported spending on security sector reform (SSR) increased threefold from 2004 and 2007 (Muggah & Downes, 2010: 144). In addition, there are now a plethora of more direct military assistance initiatives, designed to enhance Africa's military capacity and ability to deter and defeat perceived transnational threats. AFRICOM, the US Africa Command authorized by President Bush in December 2006, is the most well known and controversial of these. In addition, there is the Pan-Sahel

Initiative, which expanded into the Trans-Saharan Counter-Terrorism Partnership (TSCTP) in 2005, the Partnership for Regional East African Counter-Terrorism (PREACT) and the Combined Joint Task Force-Horn of Africa (CJTF-HOA), to mention but a few of the acronyms that make up the continent's by now complex network of foreign-funded military, security and intelligence apparatuses.

There is nothing inherently undemocratic about training and funding police and militaries, but the substantial allocation of resources and development assistance to security efforts raises numerous questions and challenges. Given the frequency of military coups and the tendency of African militaries and police to be focused on regime security rather than citizen security, strengthening a state's security apparatus is potentially hazardous both for the survival of democracy and the protection of human rights (see Krogstad, 2012; Beswick, 2014). From the perspective of African states, the current emphasis on security can be seen as a resource and the language of anti-terrorism can be appropriated to strengthen their military capacities, repress perceived political opponents and silence civil society critics. According to William Miles (2012: 41), Burkina Faso's inclusion in the Trans-Saharan Counter-Terrorism Partnership reflects a 'reward' for hosting AFRICOM training exercises and contributing to conflict mediation rather than any real risk from violent extremism, and the US State Department actively downplayed 'the less-than-democratic nature of Blaise Compaoré's decades-long rulership' (*ibid.*). Rwanda, Uganda and Ethiopia have all been major recipients of military assistance and training programmes. Yet, Rwandan society is becoming increasingly militarized (Reyntjens, 2011; Beswick, 2014), Ethiopia has suppressed opposition parties and journalists by branding them 'terrorists' (Human Rights Watch, 2010), while Museveni has linked the Lord's Resistance Army to the war on terror and al-Qaeda in order to attract foreign assistance (Fisher, 2012). Other countries, like Mauritania and Guinea, have arrested alleged 'Islamists', 'warlords', and other transnational 'subversive threats' in an effort to frame their domestic and foreign policies in ways that resonate with international discourses and thereby obtain either more support from Western states or lower their democratization pressure (or both) (Jourde, 2007: 481).

In Kenya, the Anti-Terrorism Police Unit, established with US assistance in 2003, has been accused of targeting Muslims, especially ethnic Somalis, and for using extreme tactics (Howell & Lind, 2009; Patinkin, 2014). Operation Usalama Watch, launched in April 2014 as part of Kenya's counter-terrorism strategy, has been found to target Somalis in the name of national security, and widespread police abuse, arbitrary arrests, forced encampment, as well as the deportation of nearly 400 people to Somalia have been documented (Amnesty International, 2010). Yet, given Kenya's strategic position, its undoubted security challenges and its support for global anti-terrorism efforts, the country and its leaders continue to receive the support of Western donors – despite concerns about democracy and human rights and despite early protestations about the impossibility of diplomatic relations with a president and vice president that are both charged by the International Criminal Court (see Republic of Kenya, 2014).

In short, the current discourse on development, security and stability constitutes a resource that African leaders can employ to their own advantage, frequently enhancing their own security apparatus while weakening the opposition and civil society critics. It is in this sense a new take on the classic game of 'extraversion' (Bayart, 2000) whereby internationally available resources are skilfully adapted to the benefit of domestic elites. While it would be insincere to suggest that donors are not aware of these tensions between security and democracy, it remains the case that development discourse glosses over the considerable challenges involved in seeking security and democracy at the same time.

Conclusion

In assessing the progress of democracy in Africa and the relationship between foreign aid and authoritarianism, the different, historically specific interpretations of democracy are rarely considered a relevant factor. However, as this chapter shows, the manner in which democracy is defined matters in at least three important ways. First, the conceptualization of democracy has practical consequences and influences how and what kind of democracy is promoted and supported. The definition of democracy in development discourse has not been static, but has changed in interaction with broader historical and political conditions. Thus, the linking of democracy to economic liberalization and to security has had concrete effects in terms of policy formulation and implementation and in terms of politics in recipient countries. These outcomes are by no means uniform, nor dictated by discourse in the sense of there being no political agency or other causal factors, but they are influenced and conditioned by the manner in which democracy is defined and promoted. This in turn helps to explain why, after more than two decades of democracy promotion, foreign aid can still flow freely to countries that by most assessments are far from democratic.

Second, a focus on the conceptualization of democracy in development discourse broadens our analysis away from a reading centred only on *real*politik and interests in foreign assistance. By approaching development as a discursive formation – that is a historically contingent form of knowledge intimately connected to prevailing structures and relations of power at the time of its formation – we can better appreciate its sometimes contradictory outcomes and internal tensions. It is also a form of analysis that makes visible the political consequences of particular representation of social reality, leading directly to my third and final point. A focus on definitions of democracy is part of a critical project, and recovering the essentially contested character of democracy matters for critical and political engagement. Particular conceptualizations of democracy legitimize particular practices, while delegitimizing and marginalizing other possibilities and democratic models. In this way, debates about the meaning of democracy are not purely conceptual or theoretical, but deeply practical and political. Challenging the aid–authoritarianism nexus in Africa therefore also involves recovering the essential contestability of democracy. This entails a constant interrogation of donor discourses and policies. The label 'democracy' has the effect of making almost any policy appear more palatable, but a discourse that defines democracy as a means to another end, be it economic growth or security, inevitably risks undermining democracy as a value in itself.

Notes

1 Security has arguably always been part of development discourse, but there is no doubt that its prominence increased after the Cold War and then again after 9/11. On the merger of development and security, see Duffield (2000); on the securitization of Africa, see Abrahamsen (2005).

2 This statement is indicative of the extent to which academic critiques of earlier models of democracy promotion have been taken into account by development donors, and echoes recent academic debates about the quality of democracy and the dangers of focusing on elections alone. Just as in the 1990s, when democracy was reinterpreted by for example Huntington as 'less of a hurrah word', there is thus an interaction between academic approaches to democracy and donor discourses and policies. This relationship is multifaceted, and far from straightforward.

References

Abrahamsen, R (2005), 'Blair's Africa: the politics of securitization and fear', *Alternatives*, vol. 30, no. 1, pp. 55–80.

Abrahamsen, R (2000), *Disciplining democracy: development discourse and good governance in Africa*, Zed Books, London.

AFRICOM (2010), 'Trans-Saharan Counter Terrorism Partnership', United States Africa Command, viewed 22 September 2015, www.africom.mil/Doc/7432

Almond, GA (1970), *Political development. Essays in heuristic theory*, Little, Brown & Company, Boston, MA.

Amnesty International (2014), *Somalis are scapegoats in Kenya's counter-terrorism crackdown*, Amnesty International, London.

Arblaster, A (1999), 'Democratic society and its enemies', *Democratization*, vol. 6, no. 1, pp. 33–49.

Bangura, Y (1986), 'Structural adjustment and the political question', *Review of African Political Economy*, vol. 14, no. 37, pp. 24–37.

Bayart, JF (2000), 'Africa in the world: a history of extraversion', *African Affairs*, vol. 99, no. 395, pp. 217–67.

Beckman, B (1992), 'Empowerment or repression? The World Bank and the politics of adjustment', in P Gibbon, Y Bangura & A Ofstad (eds), *Authoritarianism, democracy and adjustment. The politics of economic reform in Africa*, Nordiska Afrikainstitutet, Uppsala, pp. 127–68.

Beswick, D (2014), 'The risks of African military capacity building: lessons from Rwanda', *African Affairs*, vol. 113, no. 451, pp. 212–31.

Bratton, M & Houessou, R (2014), *Demand for democracy is rising in Africa, but most political leaders fail to deliver*, Afrobarometer, Policy Paper No. 11.

Brown, S (2001), 'Authoritarian leaders and multiparty elections in Africa: how foreign donors help to keep Kenya's Daniel Arap Moi in power', *Third World Quarterly*, vol. 22, no. 5, pp. 725–39.

Brown, S (2005), 'Foreign aid and democracy promotion: lessons from Africa', *European Journal of Development Research*, vol. 17, no. 2, pp. 179–98.

Carothers, T (2006), 'The backlash against democracy promotion', *Foreign Affairs*, vol. 85, no. 2, pp. 55–68.

Carothers, T (2002), 'The end of the transition paradigm', *Journal of Democracy*, vol. 13, no. 1, pp. 5–21.

Clough, M (1992), *Free at last? US policy toward Africa and the end of the Cold War*, Council of Foreign Relations, New York.

Collier, D. and S. Levitsky (1997), 'Democracy with adjectives: conceptual innovation in comparative research, *World Politics*, vol. 49, no. 3, pp. 430–51.

Cook, R (1998), 'Human rights: making a difference', Speech to the Amnesty International Human Rights Festival, London, 16 October 1998.

Corbo, V, Fischer, S & Webb, SB (eds) (1992), *Adjustment lending revisited: policies to restore growth*, World Bank, Washington, DC.

DANIDA (2004), 'Security, growth – development: priorities of the Danish government for Danish development assistance, 2005–2009', Ministry of Foreign Affairs, Copenhagen.

DFID (2011), 'New strategy to help build stability overseas', 19 July 2011, viewed 24 September 2015, http://www.dfid.gov.uk/news/latest-news/2011/new-strategy-to-build-stability-overseas/

DFID (2005), *Fighting poverty to build a safer world: a strategy for security and development*, Department for International Development, London.

DFID, FCO & MOD (2011), *Building stability overseas strategy*, Department for International Development, Foreign and Commonwealth Office and Ministry of Defence, London.

Diamond, L, Linz JJ & Lipset, SM (eds) (1988), *Democracy in developing countries. Volume 2: Africa*, Adamantine Press, London.

Diamond, L (2008), 'The democratic roll-back: the resurgence of the predatory state', *Foreign Affairs*, vol. 87, no. 2, pp. 36–48.

Diamond, L (2002), 'Thinking about hybrid regimes', *Journal of Democracy*, vol. 13, no. 2, pp. 21–35.

Di Palma, G (1990), *To craft democracies: an essay on democratic transitions*, University of California Press, Berkeley, CA.

Duffield, M (2000), *Global governance and the new wars*, Zed Books, London.

Epstein, SB (2010), *Foreign aid reform, national strategy, and the quadrennial review*, CRS Report for Congress, Congressional Research Service, Washington, DC.

Fisher, J (2012), 'Managing donor perceptions: contextualizing Uganda's 2007 intervention in Somalia', *African Affairs*, vol. 111, no. 444, pp. 404–23.

Gallie, W B (1955-56), 'Essentially contested concepts', *Proceedings of the Aristotelian Society*, vol. 56, pp. 167–98.

Gause III, FG (2005), 'Can democracy stop terrorism?', *Foreign Affairs*, vol. 84, no. 5, p. 62–76.

Gavas, M (2006), 'EC aid: at the forefront of poverty reduction or global security?', in Aid Management Committee (ed.), *The reality of aid 2006*, Zed Books, London, pp. 268–73.

Gilbert, C & Mureriwa, J (2014), 'Zambia's president threatens both democracy and his own party's survival', *Freedom at Issue Blog*, Freedom House, 7 March 2014, viewed 24 September

2015, http://www.freedomhouse.org/blog/zambia-president-threatens-both-democracy-and-his-own-partys-survival#.U9qnO_1gPwJ

Government of Canada (2005), *Canada's international policy statement: a role of pride and influence in the world*, Queen's Printer, Ottawa.

Held, D (1987), *Models of democracy*, Polity Press, Cambridge.

HM Government (2010), *Securing Britain in an age of uncertainty: the strategic defence and security review*, HM Government, London.

Hofmeyr, J (2013), 'Africa rising? Popular dissatisfaction with economic management despite a decade of growth', Afrobarometer, Policy Brief No. 2.

Howell, J & Lind, J (2009), *Counter-terrorism, aid and civil society: before and after the war on terror*, Palgrave-Macmillan, Basingstoke, UK.

Huysmans, J (2004), 'Minding exceptions: the politics of insecurity and liberal democracy', *Contemporary Political Theory*, vol. 3, no. 3, pp. 321–41.

Human Rights Watch (2010), *Development without freedom. How aid underwrites repression in Ethiopia*, Human Rights Watch, New York.

Huntington, SP (1991), *The third wave: democratization in the late twentieth century*, University of Oklahoma Press, Norman & London.

Huntington, SP (1968), *Political order in changing societies*, Yale University Press, New Haven, CT.

Jones, W, Soares de Oliveira, R & Verhoeven, H (2013), *Africa's illiberal state-builders*, University of Oxford, Refugee Studies Centre, Oxford, Working Paper Series No. 89.

Jones, GA & Rodgers, D (2011), 'The World Bank's World Development Report 2011 on Conflict, Security and Development: a critique through five vignettes', *Journal of International Development*, vol. 23, no. 7, pp. 980–95.

Jourde, C (2007), 'The international relations of small neoauthoritarian states: islamism, warlordism, and the framing of stability', *International Studies Quarterly*, vol. 51, no. 2, pp. 481–503.

IDS Bulletin (1993), 'The emergence of the "good government" agenda: some milestones', *IDS Bulletin*, vol. 24, no. 1, pp. 1–8.

Kiyokazu, K (2006), 'Japan's ODA at a crossroad: counter-terrorism or poverty eradication', in Aid Management Committee (ed.), *The reality of aid 2006*, Zed Books, London, pp. 190–94.

Klugman, J (ed.) (2002), *A sourcebook for poverty reduction strategies*, World Bank, Washington, DC.

Krogstad, EG (2012), 'Security, development, and force: revisiting police reform in Sierra Leone', *African Affairs*, vol. 111, no. 443, pp. 261–80.

Kurki, M. (2010), 'Democracy and conceptual contestability: reconsidering conceptions of democracy in democracy promotion', *International Studies Review*, vol. 12, no. 3, 362–86.

Lal, D (1983), *The poverty of 'development economics'*, Institute of Economic Affairs, London.

Levine, D & Molina, J (eds) (2011), *The quality of democracy in Latin America*, Lynne Rienner, Boulder.

Levitsky, S & Way, L (2002), 'The rise of competitive authoritarianism', *Journal of Democracy*, vol. 13, no. 2, pp. 51–65.

Lewis, P (2008), 'Growth without prosperity in Africa', *Journal of Democracy*, vol. 19, no. 4, pp. 95–109.

Lindemann, S (2011), 'Just another change of guard? Broad-based politics and civil war in Museveni's Uganda', *African Affairs*, vol. 110, no. 440, pp. 387–416.

Lumumba-Kasongo, T (ed.) (2005), *Liberal democracy and its critics in Africa. Political dysfunction and the struggle for social progress*, Zed Books, London.

Lynch, G & Crawford, G (2011), 'Democratization in Africa 1990–2010:

41

an assessment', *Democratization*, vol. 18, no. 2, pp. 275–310.

Miles, WFS (2012), 'Deploying development to counter terrorism: post-9/11 transformation of US foreign aid to Africa', *African Studies Review*, vol. 55, no. 3, pp. 27–60.

Mosley, P, Harrigan, J & Toye, J (1991), *Aid and power: the World Bank and policy based lending. Volume 1*, Routledge, London.

Muggah, R & Downes, M (2010), 'Breathing room: interim stabilization and security sector reform in the post-war period', in Sedra, M. (ed.), *The future of security sector reform*, The Centre for International Governance Innovation, Waterloo, pp. 136–53.

O'Donnell, G & Schmitter, P (1986), *Transitions from authoritarian rule. Volume 4: Tentative conclusions about uncertain democracies*, Johns Hopkins University Press, Baltimore.

Overseas Development Institute (ODI) (1992), *Aid and political reform*, Overseas Development Institute, London, Briefing Paper.

Patinkin, J (2014), 'Will Kenya mosque assault radicalize Muslim youths?', *Christian Science Monitor*, 18 February, viewed 25 September 2015, http://www.csmonitor.com/World/Africa/2014/0219/Will-Kenya-mosque-assault-radicalize-Muslim-youths

Peiffer, C & Englebert, P (2012), 'Extraversion, vulnerability to donors, and political liberalization in Africa', *African Affairs*, vol. 111, no. 444, pp. 355–78.

Pool, I de Sola (ed.) (1967), *Contemporary political science: towards empirical theory*, McGraw-Hill, New York.

Pye, L (1966), *Aspects of political development*, Little, Brown & Company, Boston, MA.

Republic of Kenya (2014), 'President Uhuru Kenyatta meets UK, US, Canadian and Australian envoys at State House', Ministry of Foreign Affairs and International Trade, Nairobi, 5 April 2014.

Reyntjens, F (2011), 'Constructing the truth, dealing with dissent, domesticating the world: governance in post-genocide Rwanda', *African Affairs*, vol. 110, no. 483, pp. 1–34.

Royal Danish Ministry of Foreign Affairs (2003), 'A changing world – the government's vision for new priorities in Denmark's foreign policy 2003', Royal Danish Ministry of Foreign Affairs, Copenhagen.

Simon, D (2005), 'Democracy unrealized: Zambia's third republic under Fredrick Chiluba', in L Villalón & P von Doepp (eds), *The fate of Africa's democratic experiments*, Indiana University Press, Bloomington, IN, pp. 199–220.

The Economist (2011), 'The hopeful continent: Africa rising', 3 December, pp. 2–3.

The White House (2010a), 'Remarks by the president at the Millennium Development Goals summit in New York', New York, 22 September, viewed 25 September 2015, http://www.whitehouse.gov/the-press-office/2010/09/22/remarks-president-millennium-development-goals-summit-new-york-new-york

The White House (2010b), 'Fact sheet: US global development policy', The White House, Washington, DC, 22 September 2010, viewed 25 September 2015, https://www.whitehouse.gov/the-press-office/2010/09/22/fact-sheet-us-global-development-policy

Toye, J (1992), 'Interest group politics and the implementation of adjustment policies in sub-Saharan Africa', in P Gibbon, Y Bangura & A Ofstad (eds), *Authoritarianism, democracy and adjustment. The politics of economic reform in Africa*, Nordiska Afrika Institutet, Uppsala, pp. 106–26.

UK Conservative Party (2009), 'One world conservativism: a conservative agenda for international development'. Conservative Party, London, Policy Green Paper No. 11.

van de Walle, N (2003), 'Presidentialism and clientelism in Africa's emerging party systems', *Journal of Modern African Studies*, vol. 41, no. 2, pp. 297–321.

Webb, M (2007), *Illusions of security: global surveillance and democracy in the post-9/11 world*, City Light Books, San Francisco.

Weinberg, L (2013), *Democracy and terrorism: friend or foe?*, Routledge, Abingdon.

Whitfield, L & Mustapha, AR (2009), 'Conclusion: the politics of African states in the era of democratization', in AR Mustapha & L Whitfield (eds) *Turning Points in African Democracy*, James Currey, Woodbridge, pp. 202–27.

Wilkinson, P (2006), *Terrorism versus democracy. The liberal state response*, Routledge, Abingdon.

Woods, N (2005), 'The shifting politics of foreign aid', *International Affairs*, vol. 81, no. 2, pp. 393–409.

World Bank (2011), *World development report: conflict, security and development*, World Bank, Washington, DC.

World Bank (1989), *Sub-Saharan Africa: from crisis to sustainable growth*, World Bank, Washington, DC.

Wroe, D (2012), 'Donors, dependency and political crisis in Malawi', *African Affairs*, vol. 111, no. 442, pp. 135–44.

Zolberg, A (1966), *Creating political order: the party states of West Africa,* Rand McNally, Chicago.

2 | Aid to Rwanda: unstoppable rock, immovable post

Zoë Marriage

Introduction

A core tenet of contemporary aid is that development, democracy and security reinforce each other. This tenet is often explicit in policy designed for countries that have experienced violent conflict and in which there is widespread destitution and devastated political and physical infrastructure (DAC, 1998; DFID, 2000; DFID, 2005). Correspondingly, mainstream Northern analysis of African states and their trajectories following war rests on the assumption of linear progressions from distorted to liberal economies, dictatorship to democracy, and war to peace.

Rwanda's recent history provides evidence that counters this assumption. Since the genocide that took place in the country in 1994, and under the political leadership of President Paul Kagame, Rwanda's economic and social development indicators have been impressive, political opposition has been muted, and these outcomes have been shored up by the violence inflicted in the Democratic Republic of Congo, where Rwanda has operated through military or militia forces, aggravating regional insecurity (Longman, 2002; Stearns, 2011).

Kagame also challenges many of the critics of aid as he is not preying on the Rwandan population's economic resources or nurturing a sycophantic relationship of accountability towards his donors. Corruption by officials is punished, and Rwanda is lauded for its financial probity in aid administration and more widely (Purcell *et al.*, 2006: 103; Booth & Golooba-Mutebi, 2011: 14). The military is disciplined, is sustained by salaries, and is not deployed to subdue or impoverish the population. The economic situation for most Rwandans has improved steadily if not dramatically over the last twenty years. Further, there are negligible economic or strategic returns on donor involvement, so charges that donors provide aid as a cover for access to mineral wealth do not obviously have traction in the Rwandan case.

This chapter investigates how budget support to the government of Rwanda influences the mechanisms of domestic governance and international relations.

Budget support, which channels ODA directly to partner governments, has been the centrepiece of the aid given to Rwanda since 2000. It signals a close and innovative relationship between donors, particularly the UK's Department for International Development (DFID), which often makes the largest bilateral contributions (currently projected at £54 million),[1] and the Rwandan government. Other large donors have been multilateral: the EC, the World Bank and the African Development Bank (Swedlund, 2013: 363).

The provision of aid to Rwanda resembles the irresistible force paradox, which focuses on what happens when an unstoppable rock (aid, driven by naive liberalism) strikes an immovable post (the Rwandan president's convictions). The paradox's assumption that both are indestructible is reflected by the ongoing aid relationship between donors and Rwanda, despite elements of incompatibility. This paradox is presented to philosophy students to test their logical faculties, but, when applied to politics, the questions swivel to an enquiry of why the rock is unstoppable, why the post is immovable and what the political perspectives are on their interaction at the moment of collision.

The post and the rock The characterization of Kagame's political convictions as an immoveable post derives from his uncompromising political stance in domestic affairs and international relations. The ruling party, the RPF, established its power and credentials in its decisive action against the former Rwandan government, army and allied militias by taking the capital, Kigali, and ending the genocide in July 1994. Paul Kagame rose through posts as defence minister and vice president, and to president in 2000. His crucial role in the armed struggle granted him political leverage domestically, and has also strengthened his hand in negotiations with donors (Kagame, 2012).

Aid driven by a 'naive conception of liberal form' (Dillon & Reid, 2001: 45) is characterized as an unstoppable rock not because it is impossible to withdraw funding: withdrawing funds is a sanction that has been threatened or used many times in Rwanda (Hayman, 2011: 677–8). It is characterized as unstoppable because it is embedded in the patterns of the dominant neoliberal agenda. This agenda is presented as accountable and representative, espousing 'universally acclaimed values' (Dillon & Reid, 2001: 45), and therefore there are no means of questioning the processes of providing aid or the legitimacy of the approach.

In the immediate aftermath of the genocide in Rwanda, the USA and many European donors were impressed by Kagame's order and dynamism, as well as his modest personal style; he was part of an 'African Renaissance' perceived by then-US President Clinton among others (Liebenberg, 1998: 42). Those who became acquainted with Kagame during the Second Congo War, which started in 1998 when Rwanda invaded eastern Congo, tend to look much less favourably on the president. As opinions crystallized around Kagame's merits and misdemeanours, camps of 'believers' and 'non-believers' formed. Some distinction has been maintained between these perspectives in academic circles, but the falseness of the dichotomy that it implies is captured by the *New York Times* article that described Kagame as 'The Global Elites' favourite Strongman' (Gettleman, 2013): at differing levels of acknowledgement, many agree that he is both favoured and a strongman.

Definitions of 'autocracy' identify the rule by a single person and the unlimited and uncompetitive nature of the power wielded (van de Walle, 2002; Marshall, 2013). In Rwanda, the combination of militaristic political infrastructure and strong individual political skills concentrates power in Kagame's hands. Booth and Golooba-Mutebi observe, 'promoters and critics of the regime seem to agree on one thing [...]: that Kagame has personally transformed much of what happens in Rwanda and that he is both visionary and determined to the point of ruthlessness' (Booth & Golooba-Mutebi, 2011: 15). Kagame has not altered his political persuasion in the light of the reprimand he has received from his donors. The practically unlimited nature of his power is reflected in the extremely low level of resistance or challenge that he faces from the Rwandan population.

Budget support: partnership and innovation The development trajectory of Rwanda since the genocide in 1994 owes its direction and intensity to the domestic leadership of the president and his ability to attract donor funding and devise and implement domestic policy. The government elaborated its development priorities through Vision 2020, which was laid out between 1998 and 2000 (Government of Rwanda, 2000). The Poverty Reduction Strategy Paper in 2002 embraced Northern donors' predilection for the poverty agenda (Government of Rwanda, 2002), and further policies were established in the Economic Development and Poverty Reduction Strategy 2008–12, written by the Ministry of Finance and Economic Planning (Government of Rwanda, 2007).

International aid, particularly that given to Africa, had come under criticism through the 1990s for being ineffective and self-serving, and for stymieing domestic political development (Duffield, 1994; de Waal, 1997; Keen, 1998). Kagame's leadership provided something of a riposte to these charges. He explicitly rejected the moral superiority of aid providers and by setting his own agenda he gave aid the edginess needed for its credibility. Rwanda has received relatively high aid spends per capita and is the world's fifth most aid-dependent country, receiving around a billion US dollars of aid per year. The three largest donors are the UN, USA and UK, with Germany, Japan and the Netherlands also providing significant support (Action Aid, 2012: 28).

The UK is the only country to have committed to long-term funding in Rwanda. New Labour came to power in the UK in 1997 and embarked on an episode of policy innovation. Tony Blair, then prime minister, formed a close and lasting relationship with Rwanda, extending his advisory role even after he had left office. The fact that the UK, unlike Belgium and France, had no colonial or neo-colonial history in Rwanda allowed the notion to float that there was a discontinuity with the aid-giving of the past, which had been vilified for contributing to the genocide by supporting the military structure and ignoring ethnic tensions (Uvin, 1998). Other 'new' donors after the genocide were Norway, the Netherlands and Sweden.

Clare Short, secretary of state for international development in Blair's cabinet, established strong ties with Kagame, defending – rather than denying – Rwanda's operations in Congo at the turn of the century with reference to the insecurity posed by the ousted regime. Two years after the insurgency in the north of Rwanda had been defeated, Short asserted, 'Rwanda has what I might call the best case for being involved in the DRC. Fighters there wish to return to Rwanda to complete the genocide. For Rwanda, to fight back means that the north of the country has been pacified [...] Rwanda needs peace in the DRC and security'.[2]

The preferential relationship between Rwanda and the UK was maintained under the coalition government of Conservatives and Liberal Democrats, which came to power in 2010 and increased aid to Rwanda. Andrew Mitchell, who later became secretary of state for international development, had established 'Project Umubano' ('friendship', in Kinyarwanda) in 2007, facilitating British volunteers to travel to Rwanda for two weeks to participate in development-related activities. This provided David Cameron with a launch pad for his development policy, and Cameron claimed that 'Project Umubano has had a profound impact on our party' (Conservatives, 2010: 1). For its critics, Umubano was an attempt to 'detoxify' the Conservative Party, which was in opposition when the project was set up (Hale, 2012).

Budget support was designed at a time when donors were exploring new development paradigms: the MDGs and the holistic approach of the Poverty Reductions Strategy Papers opened discussions on how expectations arising from these initiatives could be fulfilled (Lawson *et al.*, 2002; Koeberle & Stavreski, 2006). At the same time, the need to respond to 'failed states' brought a new urgency to development discourse, intertwining it with security policy and processes aimed at state-building. Rwanda provided an environment for policy innovation and experimentation as it had a low base line and a weak but ambitious bureaucracy (Purcell *et al.*, 2006: 17).

Budget support to Rwanda is potentially progressive in incorporating a mechanism for priorities to be shaped and pursued at national level. In theory, it provides a high level of predictability, allowing the government to plan in the short and medium terms (Action Aid, 2012: 31). It was initiated at a time when 'partnership' was gaining currency in aid discourse, particularly in the UK's Department for International Development. The UK initiated the

Partnership Global Budget Support (PGBS) in 2000 and Sweden followed suit the next year; these contributions replaced debt-relief support. The EC started providing budget support in 2003, and the World Bank and African Development Bank in 2004 (Purcell *et al.*, 2006: S7).

The UK, EC and government of Rwanda signed a Partnership Framework for Harmonisation and Alignment of Budget Support in 2003, and this was endorsed by the World Bank, the African Development Bank and Sweden (Purcell *et al.*, 2006: 19). PGBS rose steeply from $13.7 million in 2000 to $32.5 million in 2002, to $34.2 million in 2003 and to $129.7 million in 2004 (Purcell *et al.*, 2006: 35). This took place alongside the HIPC initiative from 2000–2004, which gave $20 million interim debt relief from IMF and 56.5 million from the International Development Agency (Purcell *et al.*, 2006: 8). In 2008, Rwanda signed a Memorandum of Understanding, with its budget support donors outlining their 'mutual commitment.' Contributions levelled at a total of just under $200 million general budget support in 2009 and around a further $20 million in other forms of budget support (Chiche, 2008: 20). PGBS suggests a closeness that not all donors were comfortable with: major non-PGBS donors are the USA, France and Belgium.

A Joint Evaluation of General Budget Support was published in 2006, this being the most comprehensive assessment of the aid modality. It was commissioned by a consortium of donors and the partner government and its purpose was to assess budget support with relation to poverty reduction and growth. It conveys some oscillation in its findings. On the one hand, there are details of the budget support and the assumption that the Agreement can be taken at face value (i.e. that the Rwandan government and donors have priorities in common and the challenge is to operationalize them). On the other hand, there are references to the possibility that the whole process is stoking unsavoury political and military activity (referred to in the evaluation as the problems nationally and in the region and with conditionality and the disruption that it causes). The report finds that the 'combination of Rwanda's heavy reliance on aid and its vulnerability to "political aid" in an uncertain regional and national context makes the necessity of a long-term commitment all the more important and at the same time more difficult' (Purcell *et al.*, 2006: 23).

The evaluation mechanism is based around a 'causality' map that charts the path from government and donor readiness to the 'impacts' of income poverty reduction, non-income poverty reduction and empowerment and social inclusion of poor people. This projected form of causality highlights the assumption of shared processes and outcomes between donor and recipient, and the technical inclination of budget support (Molenaers, 2012: 792). The donors are assumed to be neutral and to take their decisions on provision and withdrawal of budget support with reference to events in Rwanda, rather than according to their own interests.

High aid spends and returns: a halting and disjointed dialogue Rwanda has generated some key success stories for aid. In mid-2012, it was largely on target to attain the majority of the MDGs, an achievement that puts it ahead of many other countries on the continent as far as conventional measures are concerned (Action Aid, 2012: 6). In September 2013, DFID produced a summary of its work in Rwanda and, under the title 'Why we work in Rwanda', it wrote:

> Rwanda has achieved tremendous progress since the devastating genocide of 1994. By 2020, the Government of Rwanda aims to complete the country's transformation from a poor, post-conflict nation to a thriving, middle income, regional trade and investment hub. Rwanda uses aid very well, both in terms of the results it achieves and accounting for its use. (DFID, 2013)

Emerging from violent conflict in the mid-1990s, Rwanda's recovery took place in an era of aid intervention formulated with respect to liberal assumptions. These held there to be linear progressions from distorted to liberal economies, from dictatorship to democracy, and from war to peace, and maintained that these economic, political and military transitions were mutually reinforcing. Fifteen years on, there were remarkable economic indicators, elections had been hosted and there had been no large-scale return to violence in Rwanda.

Alongside Rwanda's economic success and its progress towards the MDGs, though, the two purportedly complementary elements of transition – towards democracy and security – are less convincing. The democratization, signalled by presidential elections in 2003 and 2010 and parliamentary elections in 2008 and 2013, has involved the suppression of opposition and near-total victory for the incumbent president and party. As far as security was concerned, despite the withdrawal of Rwandan troops from eastern Congo and the pervasive rule of law in Rwanda, regional security has remained extremely poor, freedom of expression in Rwanda is limited, and a series of credible reports have linked Kagame's administration to the ongoing violence over the border. 'Fighting back', as Clare Short would have it, has not brought peace.

Development

Economic growth and reduction in poverty provide a set of quantifiable indicators around which donors and the Rwandan government can rally. From both perspectives, economic recovery is positively linked to security: for donors informed by neoliberal policy, underdevelopment and poverty are key threats to security (DFID, 2005). For Kagame, the eradication of poverty – through pro-poor policies and through economic growth – is the backbone of reconciliation through development (Golooba-Mutebi & Booth, 2013). The UK's MOU (Memorandum of Understanding) with Rwanda states,

[Government of Rwanda] recognises the linkages between conflict and poverty and will work with others towards the aim of peaceful resolution of disputes and the restoration of regional stability. GOR will work towards a negotiated settlement of the conflict in the DRC which will respect the sovereignty and territorial integrity of all countries in the region, protect the interests of their people and which will take account of the legitimate security concerns of all these countries. (Purcell *et al.*, 2006: 184)

Budget support has been successful in channelling a large budget for reconstruction through the government and moving towards longer-term capacity (Purcell *et al.*, 2006: S50). Macroeconomic stability has been good, and poverty rates have reduced consistently since the genocide. The majority of Rwandans have seen their incomes and service provision improving over time, although there have been increases in inequality. Within the context of the technical aims of the modality, it has recorded significant successes.

The government's stated aim in its aid policy was to 'assert genuine ownership and leadership in development activities' (Government of Rwanda, 2006) and the development taking place in Rwanda is not merely a technical project. Strides have been made in education, health insurance, employment, reducing infant mortality and increasing computer literacy. The country has a higher percentage of women in parliament than anywhere else in the world. Micromanagement has also been prominent: the 'one-cow-per-family' policy (designed to ensure all families had a source of milk) and the outlawing of grass-roofed houses have been accompanied by directives regarding personal hygiene and self-respect – including strictures for wearing shoes in public to not sharing drinking straws (French, 2013).

From the beginning, though, Kagame's vision for development was controversial and there was a strong element of re-education: of prisoners, soldiers and rough sleepers (Gettleman, 2013). Observers criticized the villagization project, which oversaw the obligatory re-housing of tens of thousands of people, including many who had returned to Rwanda following the genocide, to areas in which they could be provided for and monitored (HRW, 2001). The *gacaca* system of local courts established to try genocide suspects was decried for failing to uphold international standards of justice (HRW, 2011: 27–82). Despite the lack of favour garnered among donors by these policies and the fragility of the economic situation, the government has been forthright in pushing ahead with its agenda (Hayman, 2008: 169).

Democracy

Post-genocide Rwanda was characterized by a divided society headed by a government that had come to power through insurgent force. Kagame moved quickly towards the establishment of civilian rule and elections were held at cell (sub-village) level in 1999 and at district level in 2001. A constitution was agreed with no dissenting opinions in a referendum – quietly deplored by the EU observer mission – in 2003 (EU, 2003). The RPF won forty out of fifty-three seats in the parliamentary elections of 2003, and forty-two in 2008.

Presidential elections, the gold-standard for post-conflict countries at the turn of the century, were first held in 2003, when Kagame gained 95 per cent of the vote. As the population was invited to enter post-genocide political space, the prime minister was sacked and the main opposition party was banned; the Netherlands briefly froze part of its aid. Reflecting on the elections in 2003, Uvin warned,

> What Rwanda is currently going through is not a process of democratization as much as a formal election painted on top of an increasingly totalitarian state. The closing off of all political space, the maintenance of a climate of fear, the intimidations and disappearances of potentially critical voices, the banning of the sole opposition party with some possible popular grounding, the attacks on key civil society organizations and the further muzzling of the press – all point to the undeniable fact that there is, in 2003, no free choice in Rwanda. (Uvin, 2003: 1)

Political space became further restricted and increasingly associated with intimidation and violence (HRW, 2003; Hayman, 2008: 172). The presidential elections of 2010 returned Kagame with 93 per cent of the vote. The two opposition parties were effectively banned from standing, meaning that all candidates were aligned with the RPF, and the arrests and deaths of people with opposition voices, including journalists, marred the political victory (McConnell, 2010). Freedom House ranked Rwanda as 'not free'.[3] Meanwhile, Rwanda was awarded a grade 'A' from OECD in 2010 for its implementation of the Paris Agenda on aid effectiveness, which had introduced targets and a commitment to mutual accountability between donors and recipients.

The prospect of opening political space is viewed with suspicion in Rwanda, not least because pressure towards inclusivity in the early 1990s contributed to the civil war and the genocide. Space is tightly demarcated even within the institutions of government as 'parliament has a relatively subdued role in policy-making [...] [which] is marked by continuous, strong leadership from the president and a small number of persons around him' (Purcell *et al.*, 2006: 52). Golooba-Mutebi and Booth make the case that there is widespread agreement across the government that the international donors are pushing to open political space that would allow a return to sectarian politics (Golooba-Mutebi & Booth, 2013: 17). The law banning 'genocide ideology', promulgated in 2008, was vague and harsh in its implementation and effectively muted opposition voices (ARB, 2010; Polity IV, 2010).

The Rwandan political system has been assessed by some observers as a de facto one-party state (Reyntjens, 2004; Front Line, 2005). Despite other interpretations of it as 'multi-party power-sharing' based on consensus rather than contestation (Golooba-Mutebi & Booth, 2013), its processes are not reconcilable with DFID's aspirations for inclusive political structures. According to Beswick, 'DFID regards inclusive political settlements as characterised by continuous negotiation between state and society on the form and content of politics' (Beswick, 2011: 1924), referring to a higher degree of contestation than occurs in Rwanda.

The issue of ethnicity, which was central to the organization of the genocide and preceding episodes of violent history, has been dealt with through political and legal mechanisms that ban parties from mobilizing along ethnic lines. This supports Kagame's 'One Rwanda' policy, which supersedes references to ethnic identities according to the Divisionist Law of 2002 (Law 47/2001). While this policy has aspects that are reconciliatory, there is also political expediency in distracting attention from the perspective that reveals that the group that dominates politics comprises only 15 per cent of the population (Gettleman, 2013). The 'One Rwanda' policy allows for the normalization of the under-privilege experienced by sections of the population previously identified as Hutu and charges of divisionism have been used to control politics and public life.

In addition, there has been more cynical deployment of the legislation and the lack of definition in terms of what constitutes infringement of the law on divisionism has raised concerns that it is used to stifle freedom of expression (HRW, 2003: 15). High-profile cases of individuals being prosecuted and imprisoned for falling foul of the law sent ripples of intimidation across society (Reyntjens, 2004). This form of intimidation undermines the development of contested forms of democracy, but allows political actors to maintain a situation with a veneer of calm, and does not impact negatively on the indicators of economic development.

Security

Rwanda has been stable since the insurgency was put down in the north of the country in 1998, but continuing violence in the Kivu region in eastern Congo has kept security high on the political agenda. The Democratic Forces for the Liberation of Rwanda (FDLR), the armed group that is associated with the Interahamwe militias who participated in the 1994 genocide, has maintained a varying presence in the Kivus (ICG, 2009; Marriage, 2012). The existence of this group has been cited by the Rwandan government as a persistent menace to national security.

Rwanda's military operations in Congo, either described as defensive action against the FDLR or denied outright, have iteratively prompted donor threats to withdraw aid funding. The donor position was problematic from the outset as budget support started in 2000, when Rwanda was leading the occupation of Congo during the Second Congo War. The Panel of Experts report on the mining and export of resources detailed 'mass-scale looting' and 'systematic and systemic exploitation' by Rwandan-backed forces (UNSC, 2001; 2002), and a review of the decade of violence from 1993 to 2003 in Congo recorded,

The apparently systematic and widespread nature of the attacks [by the Rwandan army], which targeted very large numbers of Rwandan Hutu refugees and members of the Hutu civilian population, resulting in their death, reveal a number of damning elements which, if proven before a competent court, could be classified as crimes of genocide. (UNSC, 2010)

After the signing of the Global and All-Inclusive Agreement on the Transition of the Democratic Republic of Congo in 2002 (finalized in 2003), which brought a formal end to the Second Congo War, there was further evidence of a widespread understanding among donors that Rwanda's operations in Congo were aggressive, rather than defensive. The Evaluation of General Budget Support noted the 'unilateral decisions' by the UK and Sweden to cut funding when Kagame threatened to reinvade Congo in 2004. These moves, though, did not restore credibility and the report documents that there was 'no dialogue, even though provisions for such dialogue are foreseen in the bilateral MOUs between the UK and Rwanda and between Sweden and Rwanda' (Purcell *et al.*, 2006: 190). Late in the year, the World Bank and the EU disbursed funds to cover the money withheld by DFID and Swedish SIDA (Purcell *et al.*, 2006: 40). At the time, Richard Sezibera, Rwanda's special envoy to the Great Lakes accepted that the 8,000–15,000 strong FDLR 'no longer constitute[d] an immediate threat to the Government' (Front Line, 2005: 1).

In 2006, the UK signed a MOU with the Rwandan government, committing £46 million to general or sector budget support over the next ten years (DFID, 2006). The militia group the National Congress for the Defence of the People (known by its French acronym of CNDP) formed in Congo at the end of the year and took control of much of North Kivu, engaging the Congolese army and FDLR, and inflicting high costs on the civilian population (HRW, 2007). Its leader, Laurent Nkunda, had fought for the Rwandan-backed Congolese Rally for Democracy (RCD) during the war, had been integrated into the Congolese army when the peace was signed and had defected to lead the insurgents. His service in each armed group embodied the continuity of the perpetration of the violence (Marriage, 2013: 115).

The Netherlands and Sweden cut aid in 2008. Nkunda was arrested in January 2009 but many of the former-CNDP fighters re-grouped as the M23 two months later following the breakdown of the 23 March 2009 peace agreement between the government of Congo and the CNDP. Espousing the same set of objectives and means of operation as the CNDP, the M23 was a force of around 1,500 fighters, headed by Bosco Ntaganda, formerly of the RPF, who had been wanted by the International Criminal Court since 2006 (and has since surrendered to their custody) (Stearns, 2013). By 2011, the UK was becoming 'internationally isolated in its support for the RPF' (Beswick, 2011: 1911).

A further UN report was released in June 2012, accompanied by a forty-eight-page addendum a week later (UNSC, 2012a). It detailed the Rwandan support for the M23 and six other armed groups in Congo, naming individual high-profile Rwandans' involvement. The same month, DFID's 'Country Plan' announced,

> DFID is: Scaling up UK support in Rwanda in recognition of Rwanda's
> excellent development performance. DFID will continue to provide
> a significant proportion of the UK's support through budget support
> (an average of 65% over the four years) because this is spent well and
> accountably; delivers measurable results; and maintains the UK's influence
> over development expenditure and results and ability to engage in debate on
> governance/political issues. (DFID, 2012a: 3)

The change in government in the UK renewed British interest in Rwanda as a country that avowed neoliberal development, but did not signal any fundamental change in the power relations of aid-giving. HRW published an article entitled 'Rwanda should stop aiding war crimes suspect', referring to the accusations against Bosco Ntaganda and the support Rwanda was accused of providing to him (HRW, 2012b). DFID committed to maintaining its yearly £37 million budget support, acknowledging,

> Strong performance in these areas co-exists with constraints on political
> rights and freedom of expression. And the long term stability of the Great
> Lakes region remains in question – with the continued risk that Rwanda
> will again be drawn into the conflict in Eastern Congo. (DFID, 2012: 2)

The terminology of being 'drawn into the conflict' was obscure, given the weight of evidence of Rwandan aggression and the lack of any empirical work to support alternative interpretations (HRW, 2012a). A month after scaling up support, the UK cut its budget support to Rwanda on the basis of the UN report and under pressure from the USA and Germany, which had already withdrawn theirs. The EU, the Netherlands and Sweden also suspended aid, suggesting that consensus was being reached among the major donors on the violence in Congo and donor complicity with it if they continued to assist Rwanda. The UK's contribution was reinstated fifty-three days later by Secretary of State for International Development Andrew Mitchell. On his last day in office Mitchell signed off £16 million, asserting that Rwandan support to the M23 had ended (Hale, 2012). Britain was the largest bilateral donor at the time.

The aid cuts brought no capitulation from the Rwandan government, which instead salvaged political gain from the situation by portraying donors as overbearing and thus galvanizing domestic opinion against them. The government protected itself in the short term with the 26.4 billion Rwandan francs accrued in the Agaciro Development Fund, established to offset the aid cuts (Behuria, forthcoming). The violence in Congo continued unabated and, in September 2012, a Human Rights Watch report charged that 'several hundred […] possibly more' Rwandan troops had given direct support to M23 fighters in Congo between June and August (HRW, 2012a). In mid-November, a UN report followed up on the June findings by naming General Jacques Nziza, Rwandan permanent secretary of the Ministry of Defence, and James Kabarebe, Rwandan minister of defence, at the head of M23. Both men were accused of recruiting Rwandan children, and the report detailed the procedures by which Rwanda supplied weapons and ammunition to the M23 (UNSC, 2012b: 3).The M23 took Goma, the provincial town of North Kivu, on 20 November 2012, while the UN troops stationed in the town looked on.

On 30 November, the UK announced that it would suspend £21 million of its budget of £75 million (projected to rise to £90 million by 2015), and at the beginning of 2013, 40 per cent of Rwanda's budget was withheld (*The Economist*, 2013). In March, the UK announced that it would be restoring £16 million of aid, the majority now channelled through the Rwandan government as part of the Vision 2020 Umurenge Programme. This signalled a shift from general budget support to sector budget support, and implied that the aid would not be subject to the partnership principles (Roopanarine, 2013). Germany, the World Bank, the EU and the African Development Bank also restored aid while the Netherlands, Sweden and the USA did not.

Zone of perpetual non-collision: clarity and controversy The dissolution of the M23 in November 2013 was the ironic denouement of the halting and disjointed dialogue between donors and the Rwandan government. The funders could not claim policy victory as their differing approaches and priorities meant that there was no clear or common withdrawal, and many had already reinstated funding. Kagame could not appear or be presented as a cooperative negotiator as he had denied funding militias all along. More fundamentally, the surrender of the M23 did not imply the end of Rwandan involvement in Congo: its own mobilization had resulted from the dissolution of the previous movement, the CNDP.

While events such as the formation and surrender of particular groups move on, the relationship between donors and Kagame has remained more constant. It is characterized by a collusion around the high aid spends and positive indicators of development. The development indicators associated with budget support are the strongest indication of progress in the country and reflect well both on the donors and on Rwanda: there has been an inexorable rise in ODA since 1994 alongside a fall in Rwanda's reliance on aid: as a percentage of the budget, it has declined from 86 per cent in 2000 to 43 per cent in 2012 (Action Aid, 2012: 5).

Budget support has played a significant role in this, routinely accounting for over 20 per cent of ODA in the first five years and double that thereafter (Chiche, 2008: 23). A table in the Evaluation of General Budget Support recorded in note form:

> No specific political condition, rather reference to MOU, which lays down
> the expected broad political governance framework. Hence, PGBS as a
> form of 'political reward'. Appears to be little explicit analysis among donor
> community of impact/consequence of withholding PGBS and not project
> aid, bearing in mind issues of fungibility. (Purcell *et al.*, 2006: 184)

It is the achievements of high spends and returns to both parties that act as a buffer, precluding the unstoppable rock (naive liberalism of aid) from ever quite colliding with the unmoveable post (Kagame's political convictions). The agreement on the budget support and what it buys stands in stark contrast to the surrounding controversy over the violence in Congo and the constriction of political space in Rwanda, and this controversy in turn bolsters the buffer.

The controversy is functional for Kagame and his donors in splitting opinion and distracting attention, and it has three layers to it: whether Kagame is autocratic in domestic governance and supporting violence in Congo, whether he is justified in these activities given the divisionist voices at home and the threats he faces from insurgent forces across the border, and whether donors have any legitimacy to comment on Rwandan politics anyway.

The first layer of controversy is over the question of whether Kagame supports violence in Congo and oppresses opposition voices domestically. Despite the evidence amassed by human rights organizations and the UN on Rwanda's military activities in Congo and Kagame's political activities at home, the enthusiastic and intermittent provision of aid gives the impression that these are areas that are in dispute. The fact that nearly all donors have at some stage threatened to withdraw on account of the violence in Congo suggests that there are none who sincerely think that Rwanda is not involved. The reinstatement of aid, though, at different times and without clear reference to events in the region, suggests that they are unsure, do not know how to influence the situation, or are not concerned about the outcome.

Kagame is astute in stoking this controversy. Rather than accepting or ignoring the accusations, Kagame meets them with outrage and categorical responses. In a BBC interview, he claimed,

> We are not connected at all with the cause of the uprising of M23; we are
> not supporting it. We don't intend to because we don't know what they

are about or what they want. We are not involved at all [...]. There is no support for what is going on and there will be no support for what is going on. (Dowden, 2012)

This form of rebuttal reasserts Kagame's image as a politician who engages in rational negotiations and is concerned for his international reputation. By opening up a line of discussion in which he plays the aggrieved – apparently wrongly accused – party, Kagame draws attention away from his behaviour at home. For those who believe that he is supporting the violence in Congo, autocratic behaviour at home is not shocking, but by keeping the debate open on whether Rwanda is supporting insurgent activity in Congo, he provides the opportunity for his more sympathetic donors to speculate on whether he is simply badly misunderstood.

The procedural question of whether Kagame supports violence in Congo and oppression at home is surrounded by a layer of controversy on a more political level concerning his justification in terms of protecting himself from cross-border attacks or divisionism. The contradictions involved for donor decision-making were captured in the Evaluation of General Budget Support:

> In 2004, attacks by rebel groups (ex-genocide militia) from within the Democratic Republic of the Congo (DRC) prompted a reaction from the Rwandan president, who indicated that Rwanda might enter DRC to tackle this vital security issue. Reactions from the international community, including the PGBS International Partners in Rwanda, led to the temporary withholding of PGBS releases. (Purcell *et al.*, 2006: 18)

The compromise according to this version of events is that there is a credible threat posed by militias, but that Kagame is not justified in responding militarily to this threat. Positions taken with regard to the questions of whether the threat from the FDLR was a 'vital security issue' and the suitability of an armed response bind donors into a version of events and, as these can be controversial or untenable, justifying themselves becomes interlocked with justifying Kagame. The effect is to protect current and future aid spends on the strength of the fact that those made in the past have been claimed to have been justified.

The third layer of controversy surrounds the moral question on the legitimacy of Northern donors to attempt to influence Kagame's behaviour. Donors know that their history in Rwanda is inglorious and that they abandoned the country during the genocide (Melvern, 2000). Global budget support was established in 2000, demonstrating optimism in the government at a time when Rwanda was occupying a third of the territory of neighbouring Congo and exerting extraordinary violence there. The compromise that this entails is compounded by the fact that the UN is not credible as a neutral or authoritative voice on account of its incapacity to respond to the genocide and its lengthy and disastrous mission in eastern Congo (Autesserre, 2010).

This controversy, too, is fuelled by Kagame, who is assiduous in pointing out that donors have money but no high moral ground. Promoting his position further, Kagame has been proactive in forging a version of history that writes out RPF violence and foregrounds the hypocrisy of Northern powers. Under the title 'Masterclass in surreal diplomacy', Pottier analyses how, by the turn of the century, 'Kigali's new leaders had convinced the world that they – and they alone – had the right to know and determine what was going on in those parts of the Great Lakes region they now controlled' (Pottier, 2002: 151).

Reinforcing the post What is the significance of this non-collision and how has budget support interacted with Rwandan politics in ways that influence autocratic behaviour? DFID claims that, by restoring aid, it 'maintains the UK's influence over development expenditure and results and ability to engage in debate on governance/political issues', though it had withdrawn aid seemingly for the same reason (DFID, 2012: 3). The provision and withdrawal of budget support are part of the same approach and have both been used as an ineffective way of urging Kagame to adopt a more liberal and peaceful approach without endangering the returns on budget support.

Kagame's forthrightness discounts a proposition that budget support has been the single or seminal cause of autocracy in Rwanda but two key mechanisms are detectable by which budget support has encouraged autocratic behaviour. One is that it strengthens Kagame politically and economically, allowing him to consolidate his power, and the second is that it reiterates the use of illegitimate power in politics.

Consolidation of Kagame's strength

Crucial to the opportunities for autocracy has been the precision with which budget support buys its positive development indicators by strategically ring-fencing the terms of its evaluation, and the ways in which this enables Kagame to exploit the political space created for him both when it is given and when it is withdrawn. Budget support is favoured by donors because it is technocratic but Storey recorded in 2001 the 'strong sense of history repeating itself' as the World Bank threw its support behind state power without consideration of the interests of the population (Storey, 2001: 381). The contemporary situation implicates the providers of budget support in the domestic and regional violence committed by the Rwandan leadership.

According to the Evaluation of General Budget Support, 'PGBS is a powerful tool to show [donor] support to a government which they believe is on the whole on the right track' (Purcell *et al.*, 2006: 85). Budget support is credited with improving aid effectiveness, although it is critiqued both for enabling continued donor attempts to influence recipient countries and for failing to bring political reform (Hayman, 2011: 673; Swedlund, 2013: 357; Tavakoli & Smith, 2013: 59). The ability to support does not imply the ability to censure, a point made by Tony Blair, who, reflecting on the budget support cuts in 2012, assessed, 'Cutting aid does nothing to address the underlying issues driving conflict in the region; it only ensures that the Rwandan people will suffer – and risks further destabilizing an already troubled region' (Murphy, 2013). Any persuasive power that withholding aid was intended to wield was weakened by the fact that, for administrative or non-specified reasons, often donors simply do not disburse large tranches of aid (Action Aid, 2012).

From Kagame's side, the pressure is wasted: Rwandan 'officials clearly state that the "carrot and stick" approach will not work', particularly with regard to issues of national security, which are deemed non-negotiable and with which conditionality should not be used to interfere (Purcell *et al.*, 2006: 24 & 99). No donor is calling for Kagame to go: they are calling in various ways for him to act differently, but they have no way of forcing his hand and the withdrawal of budget support, like its provision, brings potentially high costs for donors. The possibility of slippage on the MDGs threatens one of the few aid and economic success stories of the continent. If support were to unravel, though, the possibility would not simply be that services were not funded but that the fragile structure would fall apart and Kagame lose his grip. The implication of this is that budget support is provided to stop Kagame losing his grip and that donors perceive his authoritarianism to be crucial to the form of development that they are promoting.

Donors are bound by the collusion around development activities that Kagame agrees to but this is not politically neutral activity as, by nurturing their development indicators, they strengthen his rule with economic and political resources. They become complicit in events over which they have no leverage, and experience has shown that when Kagame has promoted controversial policies he has pushed on through donor scepticism and they have tended to acquiesce or rally round later (Hayman, 2008: 173).

As far as operations in Congo and the oppressive domestic politics are concerned, Kagame also has no alternative plan and remains immoveable; but the resources that he has accrued through budget support have allowed him to build on successes and rupture the stalemate of aid politics by raising his international profile. On 30 November 2009, Rwanda joined the Common-wealth; despite being largely ceremonial, this was declaration of a preferential relationship with the UK and an openness towards the economic, political and cultural opportunities that the Commonwealth offered. Louise Mushiki-wabo, Rwandan foreign minister, was quoted by the government-aligned daily newspaper *The New Times* as saying, 'My government sees this accession as recognition of the tremendous progress this country has made in the last fifteen years' (Kagire, 2009).

Another step to strengthen Rwanda's international profile was made by providing 3,500 Rwandan peacekeeping troops for the UN mission in Darfur (UNAMID). This increases Rwanda leverage in discussions over its operations in Congo: in 2010 it threatened to withdraw the troops, following a leak of the UN report accusing Rwanda of genocide in Congo. The threat to withdraw from Darfur provides protection from Northern censure, and gives Rwanda a more prestigious voice than Congo in negotiations between them.

Further headway in international relations was made through Rwanda's election in October 2012 as a non-permanent member of the UN Security Council. This placed Rwanda in a collegial relationship with the countries that have been its key aid providers, and by improving his international political standing Kagame has decreased his economic dependence on aid and the political relationships that it implies. This shift in power has been funded by donors but has not involved Kagame in consultation with his constituency; instead it has propelled his individual political trajectory.

Reiteration of illegitimate power

The second mechanism by which budget support has encouraged autocracy is in the reiteration of illegitimate power: the exercise of coercive authority by donors undermines the espoused project of partnership by reasserting the unequal and differentiating relationship of donor and recipient. 'Partnership', with its inherent denial of power, is not a robust mechanism for negotiating and is undemocratic. However innovative the budget support and Vision 2020 were presented as being in policy, they have turned out to constitute another lesson in reinforcing political hierarchies.

The lesson is not lost on the Rwandan leadership. Following the suspension of aid by donors in 2012, Reuters quoted Louise Mushikiwabo, Rwandan foreign minister, as saying, 'This child-to-parent relationship has to end [...] there has to be a minimum respect [...]. As long as countries wave cheque books over our heads, we can never be equal' (Miriri, 2012). The comment turned the tables on the donors' moralizing and the reinstatement of aid was no more inspiring: Andrew Mitchell's assertion that Rwanda was no longer supporting the M23 was apparently made without advice from ministers and has since been questioned by his successor. The ability to change course with no reason and with no accountability confirms the patronizing and irresponsible approach of the UK government as a donor.

In 2010, Knox Chitiyo, head of the Africa programme at the Royal United Services Institute (RUSI) observed, 'The UK has an awful lot invested in Rwanda and Kagame – financially, emotionally, symbolically', continuing, 'The irony is that the UK needs Rwanda more than Rwanda needs the UK' (McConnell, 2010). This part is not ironic: great power involvement in Africa has conventionally been associated with forms of exploitation that privilege the powerful. It is, though, ironic that it is the scrambling to gain political credit from the investment made on budget support that underpins the failure of the operation, and that it is the constant rescuing of the story that perpetuates failure and binds donors into the aggravation of the situation that they apparently decry.

The budget support to Kagame has generated a situation that has profoundly affected the life chances of millions of people in the Great Lakes region: by providing budget support that deliberately blinds itself to the political situation in which it is operating, and compounding this through the reiteration of illegitimate power, donors have encouraged the Rwandan leadership to exert violent force over Congo and Rwanda's domestic opposition. Kagame's plans for the future, focusing largely on maintaining the high levels of economic growth, increase the stakes for Rwanda and its donors: the more ambitious his plans, the more aid he needs to maintain his project, the higher the stakes become for his donors too.

The problems that now confront donor decision-making are not caused by the FDLR in Congo or divisionism stemming from genocide denial in Kigali. They emanate from the insecurity that Kagame has stirred up to protect himself. According to Theogene Rudasingwa, the former Rwandan ambassador to Washington turned opponent,

> After the first Congo war, money began coming in through military channels and never entered the coffers of the Rwandan state [...]. It is RPF money, and Kagame is the only one who knows how much money it is – or how it is spent. In meetings it was often said, 'For Rwanda to be strong, Congo must be weak, and the Congolese must be divided'. (Murphy, 2013)

Kagame's economic survival depends on his development performance and 'whether the fiscal situation is sustainable depends [...] on whether aid inflows are sustainable' (Purcell *et al.*, 2006: 66). His physical and political survival is bound up with his status as both victim and victor, perpetually under threat from the continuing unrest in eastern Congo and thrown to the fore of contentious politics at home.

Conclusion

It is difficult to credit the budget support with specific positive impact. The technical outcome of aid has been impressive, but the dramatic rebound was underway before budget support was initiated. The accompanying political story is problematic: the Evaluation of General Budget Support noted that donors adopt PGBS 'because they think [...] that constructive engagement is providing them with better opportunities to influence government through dialogue and to reach greater convergence between their preferences and government's over political governance' (Purcell *et al.*, 2006: 103). This has not happened; on the contrary, Kagame has been defiant in the face of donor demands. Without having to modify his political ambitions, Kagame has produced good results that flatter the donors and allow for the naive liberalism of aid to keep tumbling on.

The provision of budget support to Rwanda has demonstrated that the assumption that development, democracy and security reinforce each other is misplaced. Kagame has shown himself to be simultaneously transparent and oppressive, financially astute and aggressive. The implication follows that there is no linearity in the economic, political and military transitions after war. In examining the ways in which development has taken place to the detriment of democracy, it has also become apparent that security is not shared. A secured eastern border to Congo would deprive Rwanda of an important source of revenue; it would also reorder the security patterns in the region, and would be likely to lead to catastrophic threats to Rwanda in retaliation for the violence that has been committed in Congo.

Although the unstoppable rock and the immovable post appear to be in contradiction to each other, they are mutually constitutive: the processes of aid generate the political space and strength for Kagame to remain tenacious in his political ambitions, and, as agreed progress can be made without modifying policy, liberalism persists, despite the contradictions it faces. The rock and the post are perpetually in near collision, buffered by the high aid spends and development indicators, and maintained in debate by the layers of controversy.

The paradox is resolved by the donor acceptance of autocratic and violent behaviour as a central mechanism of the form of development indicators that they demand, despite the claims they make. The implication of this is that the 'naivety' of the donor position is contrived: the compromises made in the interactions with Kagame are calculated to deflect or diminish costs to the donors without opening discussion on the legitimacy of the aid relationship or donor complicity in violence. Equally, while appearing to be a lone figure, Kagame is buttressed by a set of political relationships domestically and internationally that have enabled him to further his political ambitions.

That there is a relationship of denial on both sides to please domestic audiences (on the part of the donors) and pursue aggressive policies (on Kagame's part) is not exceptional. Aid has theatrical and political roles beyond the provision of material help and the pragmatics of its implementation (Marriage, 2006). Rwanda is particular because Kagame has presented donors with a new challenge, giving rise to an unconventional relationship that the donors have been unable to chart successfully: he has an independent and impressive development programme, he does not need advice and he does not have ungoverned regions. Unable to meet this challenge in a constructive way, donors provide support and accommodate differences until it becomes too politically embarrassing or other opportunities occur and then the vacillation starts again.

Notes

1 http://devtracker.dfid.gov.uk/
countries/RW/ viewed 22 April 2014.

2 *Hansard*, 7 June 2000: 272, http://
www.parliament.uk/business/publications/
hansard/

3 http://africanelections.tripod.com/
fh2012.html, viewed 30 December 2013.

References

Action Aid (2012), *Aid effectiveness in Rwanda: who benefits?* Action Aid, Kigali.

ARB (2010), 'Rwanda: opposition harassment', *Africa Research Bulletin*, vol. 47, no. 2, pp. 18294C–18295B.

Autesserre, S (2010), *The trouble with The Congo: local violence and the failure of international peacebuilding*, Cambridge University Press, Cambridge.

Behuria, P (forthcoming), Building Agaciro: self-reliance as a political and economic instrument in Rwanda.

Beswick, D (2011), 'Aiding state building and sacrificing peace building? The Rwanda–UK relationship 1994–2011', *Third World Quarterly*, vol. 32, no. 10, pp. 1911–30.

Booth, D & Golooba-Mutebi, F (2011), *Developmental patrimonialism? The case of Rwanda*, Africa Power and Politics Programme, London, APPP Working Paper No. 16.

Chiche, M (2008), *Putting aid on budget: a case study of Rwanda. A study for the Collaborative Africa Budget Reform Initiative (CABRI) and the Strategic Partnership with Africa (SPA)*, Mokoro Ltd., Oxford.

Conservatives (2010), 'The Conservative Party's social action project in Rwanda and Sierra Leone. Project Umubano', Conservatives, London, viewed 30 September 2015, http://projectumubano.com/

DAC (1998), *Conflict, peace and development co-operation on the threshold of the 21st century*, Organisation for Economic Co-operation Development, Paris.

de Waal, A (1997), *Famine crimes: politics and the disaster relief industry in Africa*, James Currey, Oxford.

DFID (2013), *Summary of DFID's work in Rwanda 2011–2015*, Department for International Development, London.

DFID (2012), *DFID Rwanda operational plan 2011–2015*, Department for International Development, London.

DFID (2006), *Memorandum of Understanding between the Government of the United Kingdom of Great Britain and Northern Ireland and the Government of the Republic of Rwanda*, Department for International Development, London.

DFID (2005), *Fighting poverty to build a safer world: a strategy for security and development*, Department for International Development, London.

DFID (2000), *Security sector reform and the management of military expenditure: high risks for donors, high returns for development. Report on an international symposium sponsored by the UK Department for International Development*, Department for International Development, London.

Dillon, M & Reid J (2001), 'Global liberal governance: biopolitics, security and war', *Millennium*, vol. 30, no. 1, pp. 41–66.

Dowden, R (2012), 'Kagame and Congo: how long can he deny Rwandan involvement in the East?', *African Arguments*, viewed 25 September 2015, http://africanarguments.org/2012/07/17/kagame-and-congo-how-long-can-he-deny-rwandan-involvement-in-the-east-by-richard-dowden/

Duffield, M (1994), 'The political economy of international war: asset transfer, complex emergencies and international aid', in J Macrae & A Zwi (eds), *War and hunger: rethinking international responses to complex emergencies*, Zed Books, London, pp. 50–69.

EU (2003), *Mission d'observation électorale de l'Union Européenne, référendum* constitutionnel, Rwanda 2003, European Union, Kigali.

French, H (2013), 'The case against Rwanda's President Paul Kagame', *Newsweek*, 14 January 2013, viewed 25 January 2013, http://www.newsweek.com/case-against-rwandas-president-paul-kagame-63167

Front Line (2005), *Front Line Rwanda. Disappearances, arrests, threats, intimidation and co-option of human rights defenders 2001–2004*, The International Foundation for the Protection of Human Rights Defenders, Dublin.

Gettleman, J (2013), 'The global elite's favorite strongman', *New York Times*, 4 September 2013, viewed 25 September 2015, http://www.nytimes.com/2013/09/08/magazine/paul-kagame-rwanda.html

Golooba-Mutebi, F & Booth, D (2013), *Bilateral cooperation and local power dynamics. The case of Rwanda*, Overseas Development Institute, London.

Government of Rwanda (2007), *Economic development and poverty reduction strategy 2008–12*, Government of Rwanda, Kigali.

Government of Rwanda (2006), *Rwanda aid policy*, Government of Rwanda, Kigali.

Government of Rwanda (2002), *The Government of Rwanda poverty reduction strategy paper (PRSP)*, Government of Rwanda, Ministry of Finance and Economic Planning, Kigali.

Government of Rwanda (2000), *Rwanda vision 2020*, Government of Rwanda, Kigali.

Hale, M (2012), 'Why did Andrew Mitchell reinstate aid to Rwanda on his last day at DFID?' *New Statesman*, 27 September 2012, viewed 27 September 2014, http://www.newstatesman.com/blogs/politics/2012/09/why-did-andrew-mitchell-reinstate-aid-rwanda-his-last-day-dfid

Hayman, R (2008), 'Rwanda: milking the cow. Creating policy space in spite of aid dependence', in L Whitfield (ed.), *The politics of aid. African strategies for dealing with donors*, Oxford University Press, Oxford, pp. 156–184.

Hayman, R. (2011), 'Budget support and democracy: a twist in the conditionality tale', *Third World Quarterly*, vol. 32, no. 4, pp. 673–88.

HRW (2012a), *DR Congo: M23 rebels committing war crimes*, Human Rights Watch, London.

HRW (2012b), *DR Congo: Rwanda should stop aiding war crimes suspect*, Human Rights Watch, London.

HRW (2011), *Rwanda. Justice compromised. The legacy of Rwanda's community-based gacaca courts*, Human Rights Watch, London.

HRW (2007), *Renewed crisis in North Kivu. Democratic Republic of Congo*, Human Rights Watch, London.

HRW (2003), *Preparing for elections: tightening control in the name of unity*, Human Rights Watch, London.

HRW (2001), *Uprooting the rural poor in Rwanda*, Human Rights Watch, London.

ICG (2009), *Congo: une stratégie globale pour désarmer les FDLR*, Rapport Afrique de Crisis Group No. 151, International Crisis Group, Brussels.

Kagame, P (2012), 'From massacres to miracles: a conversation with Paul Kagame, president of Rwanda', *World Policy Journal*, vol. 29, no. 4, pp. 18–26.

Kagire, R (2009), 'Rwanda joins Commonwealth', *The New Times*, 29 November 2009, viewed 30 September 2015, http://www.newtimes.co.rw/section/article/2009-11-29/80423/

Keen, D (1998), 'Aid and violence, with special reference to Sierra Leone', *Disasters*, vol. 22, no. 4, pp. 318–27.

Koeberle, S & Stavreski, Z (2006), 'Budget support: concepts and issues', in S Koeberle, Z Stavreski & J Walliser (eds), *Budget support as more effective aid? Recent experiences and emerging lessons*, World Bank, Washington, DC, pp. 3–26.

Lawson, A *et al.* (2002), *General budget support evaluability study, phase 1. Final synthesis report to DFID*, Oxford Policy, Oxford.

Liebenberg, I (1998), 'The African renaissance: myth, vital lie, or mobilising tool?', *African Security Review*, vol. 7, no. 3, pp. 42–50.

Longman, T (2002), 'The complex reasons for Rwanda's engagement in Congo', in J Clarke (ed.), *The African stakes in the Congo war*, Palgrave Macmillan, New York, pp. 129–44.

Marriage, Z (2013), *Formal peace and informal war. Security and development in Congo*, Routledge, London and New York.

Marriage, Z (2012), 'The case of the FDLR in DR Congo: a facade of collaboration?', in A Giustozzi (ed.), *Post-conflict disarmament, demobilization and reintegration: bringing state-building back*, Ashgate, London, pp. 87–98.

Marriage, Z (2006), *Not breaking the rules, not playing the game. International assistance to countries at war*, Hurst, London.

Marshall, MG (2013), 'Polity IV project: political regime characteristics and transitions, 1800–2012', Center for Systematic Peace, viewed 25 September 2015, http://www.systemicpeace.org/polity/polity4.htm

McConnell, T (2010), 'An uncivil partnership', *The New Statesman*, 18 November 2010, viewed 18 November 2010, http://www.newstatesman.com/africa/2010/11/rwanda-british-kagame-genocide

Melvern, L (2000), *A people betrayed: the role of the West in Rwanda's genocide*, Zed Books, London and New York.

Miriri, D (2012), Rwanda demands respect from the West after aid cuts, *Reuters*, 28 July 2012, viewed 25 September 2015, http://uk.reuters.com/article/2012/07/28/uk-congo-democratic-rwanda-idUKBRE86R11920120728

Molenaers, N (2012), 'The great divide?

Donor perceptions of budget support, eligibility and policy dialogue', *Third World Quarterly*, vol. 33, vol. 5, pp. 791–806.

Murphy, T (2013), 'Why Blair and Buffett are wrong about giving international aid to Rwanda', *The Guardian*, 12 April 2013, viewed 25 September 2015, http://www.theguardian.com/world/2013/apr/12/rwanda-kagame-blair-aid

Polity IV (2010), *Polity IV country report 2010: Rwanda*, Center for Systematic Peace, Vienna.

Pottier, J (2002), *Re-imagining Rwanda: conflict, survival and disinformation in the late 20th century*, Cambridge University Press, Cambridge.

Purcell, R *et al.* (2006), *Evaluation of general budget support – Rwanda country report. A joint evaluation of general budget support 1994–2004*, International Development Department, School of Public Policy, University of Birmingham, Birmingham.

Reyntjens, F (2004), 'Rwanda, ten years on: from genocide to dictatorship', *African Affairs*, vol. 103, no. 411, pp. 177–210.

Roopanarine, L (2013), 'UK to channel £9m in aid through Rwanda government programme', *The Guardian*, 13 March 2013, viewed 25 September 2015, http://www.theguardian.com/global-development/2013/mar/13/uk-aid-rwandan-government-programme

Stearns, J (2013), *Strongman of the eastern DRC: A profile of General Bosco Ntaganda*, Rift Valley Institute, London.

Stearns, J (2011), *Dancing in the glory of monsters. The collapse of the Congo and the Great War of Africa*, Public Affairs, New York.

Storey, A (2001), 'Structural adjustment, state power and genocide: the World Bank and Rwanda', *Review of African Political Economy*, vol. 28, no. 89, pp. 365–85.

Swedlund, H (2013), 'From donorship to

ownership? Budget support and donor influence in Rwanda and Tanzania', *Public Administration*, vol. 33, no. 5, pp. 357–70.

Tavakoli, H & Smith, G (2013), 'Back under the microscope: insights from evidence on budget support', *Development Policy Review*, vol. 31, no. 1, pp. 59–74.

The Economist (2013), 'Aid to Rwanda. The pain of suspension. Will Rwanda's widely praised development plans now be stymied?', *The Economist*, 12 January 2013, viewed 25 September 2015, http://www.economist.com/news/middle-east-and-africa/21569438-will-rwandas-widely-praised-development-plans-now-be-stymied-pain

UNSC (2012a), *Letter dated 26 June 2012 from the Chair of the Security Council Committee established pursuant to resolution 1533 (2004) concerning the Democratic Republic of the Congo addressed to the President of the Security Council*, United Nations Security Council, New York.

UNSC (2012b), *Letter dated 12 November 2012 from the Chair of the Security Council Committee established pursuant to resolution 1533 (2004)* concerning the Democratic Republic of the Congo addressed to the President of the Security Council, United Nations Security Council, New York.

UNSC (2010), *Final report of the Group of Experts on the Democratic Republic of the Congo*, United Nations Security Council, New York.

UNSC (2002), *Final Report of the Panel of Experts on the illegal exploitation of natural resources and other forms of wealth of the Democratic Republic of the Congo*, United Nations Security Council, New York.

UNSC (2001), *Report of the Panel of Experts on the illegal exploitation of natural resources and other forms of wealth of the Democratic Republic of the Congo*. United Nations Security Council, New York.

Uvin, P (2003), *Wake up! Some policy proposals for the international community in Rwanda*, mimeo.

Uvin, P (1998), *Aiding violence: the development enterprise in Rwanda*, Kumarian Press, West Hartford.

van de Walle, N (2002), 'Africa's range of regimes', *Journal of Democracy*, vol. 13, no. 2, pp. 66–80.

3 | Authoritarianism and the securitization of development in Uganda

David M. Anderson
and Jonathan Fisher

Introduction

In early 2014, a developing split in Uganda's ruling National Resistance Move-ment (NRM) burst into the open as allies of Prime Minister Amama Mbabazi openly lobbied for his adoption as the party's presidential candidate in the 2016 general election. Though Mbabazi himself – a long-standing ally and disciple of Ugandan president Yoweri Museveni – refused to be drawn further into the intrigue, his wife, Jacqueline, was less circumspect. In a March 2014 interview with the *Daily Monitor* – the country's largest privately owned newspaper – Mrs Mbabazi, herself an NRM official, criticized the 'fascist tendencies' of the Uganda Police Force under the leadership of Kale Kayihura, a man she has previously referred to as 'General Teargas'.[1]

Among a range of allegations levelled at Uganda's security services, the prime minister's wife claimed that they have increasingly become a highly politicized and personalized instrument of state repression – sponsoring informal violent gangs ('lumpens') to intimidate, harass and terrorize perceived opponents of the state, NRM and president. This came less than a year after the high-profile defection of David Sejusa, Museveni's former intelligence chief and senior confidante, who fled Kampala for London, condemning the president's attempt to create a 'political monarchy'.[2] Far from rejecting these criticisms on his apparent militarization of the Uganda Police Force, Kayihura instead asserted that 'I am not going to apologise. I am militarising the police because the situation we are dealing with is militarised'.[3]

Since then, the former prime minister himself – once Museveni's closest and most trusted confidante – has turned against his onetime master, announcing a rival bid for the presidency in June 2015 and warning against the looming threat of Uganda becoming a 'police state' under Museveni.[4] Other former allies of the Ugandan leader (who has been in power since 1986) have also portrayed his regime as an increasingly authoritarian and violent one in the last decade, including his former vice president, Gilbert Bukenya, and former close friend, military advisor and personal physician, Kizza Besigye. Their analysis is shared by a range of monitoring organizations – in 2005, Freedom House scored Uganda's press freedom as 44 out of 100 (with 0 representing most free and 100 least) but this had deteriorated to 57 (on the cusp of 'not free') by 2012.[5] The Committee to Protect Journalists also registered a more than tenfold increase in assaults on journalists in Uganda between 2008 and 2011, with the security forces responsible for more than 90 per cent of such acts.[6] Indeed, the Ugandan regime's response to perceived opposition has become increasingly heavy-handed since 2009 with independent newspapers and radio stations arbitrarily closed (such as the *Monitor* and *Red Pepper* publications and KFM and Dembe FM in May 2013) and protestors fired on by the security services with live rounds, most notably in April 2007, September 2009 and April 2011.[7]

This steady militarization of the Ugandan polity has not occurred, however, without international assistance, particularly from the country's Western donors. This has involved key Western governments not only offering muted or no significant criticism of a range of abuses by the Museveni regime during its tenure but also enhancing its capacity to do so through funding large parts of its budget, training and equipping its military and strengthening its security forces both at home and abroad. Since the mid-1990s, donor officials in Washington, London and Brussels have also increasingly promoted the Ugandan regime to neighbouring states, and within regional and international fora, as a vital provider of counter-terrorism and peacekeeping solutions and have been crucial in facilitating Ugandan troops' military involvement in Somalia, Democratic Republic of Congo (DRC), southern/South Sudan and Central African Republic alone since 2007.

The Museveni regime itself, as this chapter will argue, has played a pivotal role in fostering and sustaining this dispensation. We argue that Kampala has capitalized on major shifts in the international and regional context since 1986 in order to gradually securitize its relations with donors and increase the amount of international support channelled towards its military and security forces. Three key turning points and overlapping periods of securitization will be outlined in this regard – 1986–1995, 1995–2001 and post-2001 – where the contrast between changing global circumstances and a consistent Ugandan approach to donors will be emphasized. Kampala's 'brokering' of these key moments will then be analysed in relation to three regional case studies – Sudan and Congo, Somalia and the fight against the Lord's Resistance Army (LRA). We conclude that donors have been compliant in helping construct and augment a military regime in Uganda through consenting to this gradual securitization of their relationship with the Museveni government. In doing so, they have assisted in the creation of an increasingly militarized, illiberal state.

The Museveni regime and its donors: a brief overview

Yoweri Museveni's National Resistance Army (NRA) captured Kampala, and thus power, in January 1986 following a six-year guerrilla campaign against the increasingly brutal and autocratic regime of Milton Obote (1980–1985) and those of his two short-serving successors, Bazilio Okello (July 1985) and Tito Okello (July 1985–January 1986). Dominated by Ugandans from the west of the country, the NRA/M initially sought to establish a 'broad-based' government as a means both to consolidate its hold on authority and to undermine deep-seated sectarian tendencies within Ugandan politics and society itself. Museveni's first administration, therefore, contained individuals from many regions (including the north, Obote's stronghold) and previous regimes while the re-constituted military included many former rebel soldiers and Obote loyalists (see below; Mutibwa, 1992; Khadiagala, 1995; Kasfir, 2000). The new government also established a novel political system – the 'Movement' system – where individuals stood for office on their own merit and where political parties, associated with Uganda's sectarian past, were banned (Ofcansky, 1996: 60–62; Kasfir, 2000). Driven by a pan-African and left-leaning intellectual programme developed while fighting in the bush, Museveni declared – upon becoming president – that his movement's ascendancy represented no 'mere change of the guard' but, in fact, 'a fundamental change' (Museveni, 1992: 21).

From the beginning, however, the NRM government exhibited three key characteristics that have increasingly come to the fore, leading to the erosion of these principles in practice: firstly, the fusion of the military and political spheres both in the formal state architecture and in policy thinking from the presidency downwards (de Torrente, 2001:184–189); secondly, the heavy personalization and centralization of power in the individual of Museveni himself; and finally the preferment by senior government officials of kinsmen and co-ethnics in the recruiting and promoting of civilian and military personnel within state institutions. As Museveni and the NRM's continued tenure has encountered growing resistance from political opponents, internal challengers and rebel movements since the 1990s, so the regime has fallen back mainly upon these characteristics in its attempts to maintain power (Mwenda, 2007; Tangri & Mwenda, 2010; Tripp, 2010: 39–58).

Thus, Museveni overcame significant international and domestic pressure to retire upon completion of his second formal term as president in 2006, instead securing an abolition of constitutional term limits through bribing parliamentarians voting on the matter (Tangri, 2006: 185–186; Tripp, 2010: 85–86). In February 2014, officials endorsed the Ugandan leader to run for a fifth term in 2016 – a move that would take him into his fourth decade as the party's presidential candidate and (if re-elected) the country's leader.[8]

Formal multi-partyism was restored in Uganda in 2005 (in tandem with the abolition of the Movement system) although – somewhat paradoxically –

69

political pluralism and freedom of speech and association have in fact been steadily more circumscribed since this time. Thus, opposition leaders are now far more frequently harassed and arrested (particularly since the 2011 election) and their supporters, together with protestors motivated by other causes, dealt with increasingly brutally by the security forces and informal para-military groups linked to them (Tripp, 2010: 135–40; *Daily Monitor*, 11 and 15 April 2011). This speaks to one of the wider themes in this volume whereby the introduction of formal democratic competition convinces leaders to enhance their hold on power through increasingly undemocratic means.

In the case of Uganda, however, the Museveni government engineered the reintroduction of multi-partyism itself as a device to entrench its authority. The return to pluralism was included in a portfolio of constitutional amendments (the 'Omnibus Bill') that further centralized executive and presidential power and included the abolition of term limits (Makara *et al.*, 2009). This allowed Museveni to portray the move – domestically and internationally – as the opening of political space where it was in fact part of a package aimed at strengthening his authority and removing the remaining constitutional obstacle to his continuation in office beyond 2006. Moreover, by the early 2000s, internal unity in the NRM was increasingly challenged by the presence of disaffected former cadres (notably Besigye, who produced a highly critical report on the NRM in 1999 and ran against Museveni in 2001) who were technically still NRM members. Thus the restoration of multi-partyism also allowed the ruling party to 'purify' its ranks and to more readily identify, and clamp down upon, political opponents (Makara *et al.*, 2009).[9]

The growing militarization of the Ugandan polity can be seen in the size of the state's formal defence budget, which has risen more than tenfold since 1986, but also in more subtle developments and phenomena (IISS, 1987; 2014). These include Museveni's appointment of military officials to lead a variety of key organizations including the police (since 2001; see Banegas, 2006: 228), intelligence services (since 2005) and interior ministry (since 2013), and the sponsorship and use of non-state violent gangs by regime officials to counter protest and opposition (Mutengesa & Hendrickson, 2008: 63–73; Tangri & Mwenda, 2010: 44–45). Since the late 2000s, the Ugandan leadership has increasingly sought to fund military purchases and enterprises including six Russian fighter jets between 2010–2011 through off-budget means including supplementary budgets and raiding the Bank of Uganda's foreign reserves – evidence also of the growing informalization of authority in Kampala.[10]

While the Ugandan military itself – the Uganda Peoples' Defence Forces or UPDF – has remained at a fairly consistent official strength of between 40,000–45,000 since the early 2000s, its composition has not (IISS, 2003, 2014). As Tripp notes (2010: 52–3), promotions within the UPDF have consistently favoured individuals from Museveni's region (the west) and ethnic group

(Bahima) since the 1990s and periodic purges have removed commanders of questionable loyalty. Their replacements have sometimes been drawn from the presidential family itself – Museveni's son was made the commander of Uganda's Special Forces and overseer of one third of the country's army in 2012 – echoing a phenomenon also seen within State House, where the president's family have largely become his closest advisors since the mid-2000s (Barkan 2011: 9–10; Mwenda 2007; Tangri and Mwenda 2010: 36–40; *AP*, 27/08/12). The centrality of para-military groups, the UPDF leadership and the presidential kinship network in the governing of contemporary Uganda and in the maintenance of NRM/Museveni rule, together with its undemocratic origins and contemporary semi-authoritarian nature, leads us to refer to the Museveni government as a 'regime' in this chapter.

Major Western governments, together with the World Bank, initially approached the Museveni regime with caution and suspicion. Though many within the donor community, particularly the US, had abandoned the Obote regime long before 1986 (Ofcansky, 1996: 129–30), they were not prepared to embrace its eventual successor with any rapidity (Dicklitch, 1998: 95). Ensconced in Marxist thinking, the new rulers of Uganda attempted to establish a planned economy in their first months in power, reaching out to Yugoslavia, Cuba, Libya and North Korea as preferred economic and security partners – to Western powers' dismay.[11] Indeed, in Museveni's second trip to Washington, DC, in 1989, he was upbraided by Ronald Reagan – his first meeting with a US president – for his links to Libya's Moammar Gadaffi. Characteristically, the Ugandan leader defused the situation with humour; Museveni noted that he had previously 'fought against Libya' and had 'taken a battalion' while fighting as part of the rebel Uganda National Liberation Front against the regime of Idi Amin (then financed, in part, by Tripoli).[12]

Kampala formally abandoned socialist economics in 1987 and embraced World Bank economic prescriptions – particularly after 1992 when these reforms began to be implemented with substantial vigour. This *volte-face* was undoubtedly based on pragmatism in part – in his early encounters with UK and US policy-makers in Kampala, London and Washington, the Ugandan leader was informed that his government could expect nothing more than token assistance from Western powers unless it adopted a World Bank Economic Recovery Programme.[13] Moreover, as Ugandan dependence on Western aid has decreased since the later 2000s (see below), the Museveni regime has sought to return to a more interventionary approach to economic governance (Hickey, 2013).

It remains difficult, however, to draw firm conclusions either way. Inflation doubled during Uganda's 1986–1987 socialist experiment and Western diplomats based in Kampala during that period argue that Museveni seemed genuinely open to dialogue on the merits of liberalized markets, becoming convinced following lengthy engagement with donor-commissioned reports and hired experts. He also stood by his decision in the face of substantial opposition from colleagues – telling them that 'they were not rejecting World Bank recommendations but decisions of their president' – and later opined at the UN that 'the greatest structural constraint that has inhibited Africa's growth in the last 35 years [...] has been the phenomenon of sustained state intervention in business' (Haynes, 2001: 239).[14] This may well, however, have all been part of a savvy ploy to convince international actors of his commitment to Bank programmes in exchange for international support. This is certainly the interpretation held by several senior NRM cadres still close to Museveni – although their perceptions are also shaped by NRM mythology whereby the abandonment of Bush war-era economic philosophies by the Movement's chair can only be reconciled through understanding this as an insincere, instrumental sacrifice rather than an authentic change of heart.[15]

Regardless, following this shift in policy, Western donors increasingly came to view Uganda as a potential 'showcase' for largely discredited neoliberal donor prescriptions, with the US, UK and World Bank, particularly, dramatically increasing their aid contributions to the country (Hauser, 1999: 633–634; Djikstra & van Donge, 2001: 843; Whitworth, 2010). They were joined, in this regard, by a range of mid-level donors including Denmark, the Netherlands, Japan, Sweden, Norway and Ireland – as well as the European Community – resulting in a 63 per cent increase in aid flows to Uganda between 1987 and 1995 (from US$303 million to US$812 million; OECD, various years). This enthusiasm and confidence in the Ugandan 'model' led most of these actors (with the exception of the US and Japan) to channel substantial parts of their funding directly into the Ugandan budget from the late 1990s using the new 'General Budget Support' (GBS) modality (Whitworth & Williamson, 2010: 22–26). This meant that, by the early 2000s, over half of Ugandan government spending was provided by donors – and between 50 and 60 per cent of this from only three, the World Bank, US and UK (Fisher, 2011: 114–120).

Kampala's strategic engagement in a range of regional military and peacekeeping activities since the mid-1990s, particularly under the banner of counter-terrorism, has also led several key donors (particularly the US, UK and – since the mid-2000s – the EU) to view it as a vital regional security ally and enhance their support to its military and security services as a consequence (Fisher, 2013a: 11–15). Since 9/11 particularly, for example, the US has made a range of weaponry and training opportunities available to the UPDF under several funding streams and regional assistance programmes and has publicly opposed efforts by some other donors to pressure the Museveni regime into decreasing its defence expenditure (New Vision, 14 November 2002; Fisher, 2012: 416–417; 2013a: 11–15). It has also dispatched its own troops and, in

March 2014, at least four military helicopters to assist and support the UPDF in its military operations in central Africa against the Lord's Resistance Army (LRA) rebel group (Atkinson *et al.*, 2012; Fisher, 2014b).

Most prominently, the US, UK and EU have provided crucial and very substantial funding, training and logistical assistance to the UPDF since 2007 in support of its involvement in the AU peacekeeping mission in Somalia, AMISOM. Perceiving the resolution of the Somali crisis as their major priority in the east African region, officials in London and Washington have privately acknowledged their reluctance to criticize Kampala's domestic abuses in case this compromises its willingness to cooperate in, and on, Somalia (Fisher, 2012: 420–421; 2013b: 481–482). This ambivalence is also frequently reflected in official statements from Brussels, London and Washington on Ugandan governance transgressions. In response to the fatal shooting of protestors by Ugandan security forces in 2011, the UK's minister for Africa gently criticized the Museveni regime's use of 'excessive force', claiming that it 'demeans' the president; the minister was nevertheless quick to praise the Ugandan leader for 'his excellent work […] in counter-terrorism'.[16] Similarly, following Museveni's signing into law of a draconian 'Anti-Homosexuality Bill' in early 2014, a European minister justified the EU decision not to suspend aid by noting that 'Museveni is very important in regional stability – he has all these strategic partnerships on South Sudan and […] in Somalia'.[17]

Some commentators have argued that Uganda's donors should be analytically separated into those focused primarily on security concerns (mainly the US, UK and EU) and those, apparently, without such interests (de Torrente, 2001: 112–118; Tangri & Mwenda, 2010: 46). The latter group, including Sweden, Norway, Denmark, the Netherlands and Ireland, are perceived to be more 'development-minded' and attentive to governance and humanitarian issues – not least by their own number. In a May 2009 interview, for example, a Nordic envoy made clear to one of the authors that the main distinction between their mission's approach to Uganda and those of the US and UK was that theirs had 'no ulterior motive'.[18]

Such stark distinctions are neither accurate nor particularly helpful. Many examples exist of members of this so-called 'Nordic+' group opposing more critical joint donor approaches to governance crises proposed by the US. Prominent European donors, for example, failed to support the US in its attempt to prevent the formalization of the 'no-party' Movement system between 1993 and 1994 (Hauser, 1999). Likewise, Denmark refused to coordinate a united donor condemnation of Museveni's third term bid while chairing a key donor coordination body between 2004 and 2006 (Fisher, 2011: 265–269). Moreover, some of these states have also joined with the US, UK and EU in support of more security-focused enterprises. Denmark and Sweden, for example, have helped fund UPDF activities in Somalia via a UN Trust Fund (Freear & de

Coning, 2013: 7). Furthermore, between 2010 and 2012, Ireland joined the UK in offering training to Uganda's police force.[19]

More generally, though, few donors aside from the World Bank, US, UK and EU have ever provided sufficient aid to Uganda under the Museveni regime to garner particular influence in Kampala in their own right. For most members of the 'Nordic+' group, then, their approach to Uganda has usually been mediated through coordination mechanisms, basket funds and joint donor architectures. This has particularly been the case since the late 1990s as European donors have shifted their support for Uganda towards GBS. Though such fora have often been sites of private disagreement between donor missions, a clear gap between 'security-first' donors and 'development-first' donors is not discernible.

Indeed, European GBS donors rarely appear to have attempted to 'protect' their disbursements from diversion towards security or defence spending on the part of the regime during the 2000s, a particular worry with modalities such as GBS.[20] Major concerns regarding the instrument among these actors have instead arisen more often around corruption-related issues, particularly since c.2008–2009 (Tangri & Mwenda, 2010: 46; 2013). While this chapter will therefore attempt to focus on the actions of Uganda's major donors since 1986 – the US, UK and EU particularly – the general terms 'donors' and 'donor community' will also be employed. This is not to suggest that there have not been differences between donors on many of the issues discussed. We are keen to emphasize, nonetheless, that drawing clear lines between donors in relation to their support for Uganda's militarization is often problematic and misrepresentative of the dynamic and fluid relationship between Kampala and its Western 'partners'.

The securitization of donor–Uganda relations under Museveni

Donor support for the steady militarization of the Ugandan state under Museveni has occurred in a number of phases – most coinciding with important changes in the regional and international environment. We contend, nonetheless, that the Museveni regime has been far from a passive player in this process and has 'brokered' many of these key 'moments' to foster and strengthen the securitization of its relationship with central international patrons. The remainder of this chapter will explore and analyse this 'brokering' and its implications. This will be undertaken in two forms – chronological and case study.

Reconstructing the Ugandan state – and military: 1986–1998 As noted, following its abandonment of socialist-style economic policy in 1987, the Museveni regime received increasingly enthusiastic backing from key Western donors, particularly the World Bank, US and UK. Market liberalization, under heavy donor assistance, characterized Museveni's first decade in government.

74

Aid flooded in as donors rushed to assist in the reconstruction of the state and to foster policies aimed at restoring economic growth (Kuteesa *et al.*, 2010). In the early 1990s, aid rose to more than 20 per cent of GDP, and had only been brought down to 13 per cent by 2000 (OECD, various years). International development assistance (IDA) from DAC donors and multilateral sources totalled an estimated $3.7 billion between 1986 and 2000 (OECD, various years). This was led by the World Bank, US, UK and EU but even mid-ranking donors made substantial contributions to Uganda's reconstruction in these years, with the Swedish Development Agency (SIDA), for example, focusing on health, water, macroeconomic reforms, and human rights, and giving disbursements of US$21 million in 1995, US$12 million in 1996, US$10 million in 1997, and US$12 million in 1998. Though this huge investment led the donors to declare that Uganda's economy was a success in these years, large trade and fiscal deficits remained and were only abated by the increased inflows of aid. Even by 2002, total aid remained significantly greater than the country's export earnings and tax revenues (Weeks *et al.*, 2002: xii, 67–81).

Initially, donors made more limited efforts to influence policy outcomes, but from 1992 they began to demand fundamental economic reforms in return for continued support. In terms of macroeconomic policy, Uganda broadly complied: the currency was devalued, foreign exchange control abolished, the budget system was reformed, and the marketing of cash crops was liberalized (Tumusiime-Mutebile, 2010). This all helped to stimulate a sharp growth rate for the economy, which helped to justify continued donor assistance, but the government of Uganda also willingly embraced the expectations of key donors at this time in regard to poverty reduction (Harrison, 2001). The Uganda Treasury, in particular, became adept at responding to the technical requirements of the World Bank, while also presenting itself as having a strong 'ownership' of its own development policies (Canagarajah & van Diesen, 2011).

A Ugandan-owned Poverty Eradication Action Plan (PEAP) was placed at the centre of government policy, and mechanisms established to allow the Bank and other major donors to contribute directly to Programme funding in key sectors of the economy (Mugambe, 2010). Through this response to 'delivery' on the technical requirements of fiscal policy, Uganda forged ahead in a close relationship with the donors, culminating in 1998 with the country being accepted as a recipient of the HIPC I debt-reduction scheme, enhanced in 2000, allowing the economy to significantly reduce its debt burden (Weeks *et al.*, 2002: 72–81; Kitabire, 2010). Uganda also became the first recipient of GBS during the same period as a consequence of donor trust and confidence in its economic programme and trajectory (Whitworth & Williamson, 2010; Mosley *et al.*, 2012: 64–65).

To a considerable extent, Uganda had by this time become something of a 'showcase' or 'poster child' for the international donor community of a variety of development successes and innovations (Hauser, 1999: 633–634; Harrison, 2001: 672–673).[21] This created an almost symbiotic dynamic to the Uganda–donor relationship, with Kampala keenly aware of the considerable room for manoeuvre this reputation allowed it in its negotiations with development partners. While the Museveni government heavily played upon its economic record into the 2000s in relations with the Bank, US and UK particularly – Kampala's Washington lobbyists promoted Uganda as one of the most 'business-friendly' and 'entrepreneurially spirited' polities in Africa well into the NRM's third decade in power – the central focus of the regime's relations with donors increasingly moved into the peace and security sphere from the later 1990s, as detailed below (Fisher, 2011: 193–194).

This period also saw the Museveni government undertake a range of institutional and practical measures to cement and augment its hold on political and military power. Upon capturing Kampala in January 1986, the new regime, therefore, set about rebuilding the shattered Ugandan state around its own institutions and structures – themselves constructed during its guerrilla campaign against Obote and the Okellos. This included the establishment of the NRM's military wing, the NRA, as Uganda's official army and the steady incorporation of 40,000 rebels and soldiers loyal to previous regimes into the institution between 1986 and 1988 – using the new national army, in Mutengesa's words, as 'a massive depot' for combat-equipped former fighters (Tripp, 2010: 140–141; Mutengesa, 2013: 342). In an effort to establish its authority throughout the country in the face of several regional insurgencies and a limited support base, the new regime rapidly sought to create a large, formidable national military and the NRA quadrupled in size during Museveni's first five years in power – from 14,000 to over 55,000. Military officials – including Museveni himself – also came to dominate the new order established in Uganda with senior serving commanders placed in central positions within the cabinet and legislature (National Resistance Council) (Tripp, 2010: 48–54).

In the midst of their support for its economic reforms, however, donors also called for Uganda to reduce the size of its army, initially financing a US$40 million demobilization programme between 1992 and 1995 aimed at halving the NRA's numbers (Banegas, 2006: 227–228). From the early 1990s onwards, donors also became increasingly insistent that Kampala reduce its ballooning defence budget.[22] These aims were not 'conditionalities' directly linked to aid, however, and the Museveni regime became skilled at apparently accepting donor direction on such matters without actually implementing the intended policies. Threats at home – the activities of the LRA in northern Uganda – and abroad – the 'need' to deploy forces in the DRC in the aftermath of the Rwanda genocide – were used to counter the pressure to demilitarize, with Kampala insisting that 'it had the right to take […] measures in the interest of national security' (Mutengesa, 2013: 353). Military demobilization thus moved notoriously slowly, and in fits and starts, despite external funding for the programme.

Where the regime claimed to have 'demobilized' 36,000 soldiers between 1992 and 1995, in reality many of these individuals were transferred to other state security agencies and to the police (Tangri & Mwenda, 2003); three quarters of Ugandan police personnel had been dismissed in the early NRM years and thus their number needed increasing (Omara-Otunnu, 1987: 178). For the Museveni regime, this represented an early challenge to the maintenance of a militarized polity in Uganda – particularly given the country's acute dependence on foreign aid during this period: but, through a combination of defiance and subversion, Museveni succeeded in evading donor demands to permanently dismantle large sections of the military apparatus while still receiving ever-increasing injections of development assistance. Mutengesa and others have described these strategies in some detail, noting particularly how the regime 'demobilized' soldiers into regime-sponsored armed militia groups and 'home guard' units only to 'remobilize' them later in the face of domestic and regional threats (Mutengesa, 2013: 352–353). On Uganda's part, such strategy was by design, not by accident.

The Ugandan government also dramatically increased its defence spending during this period – from US$58 million in 1988 to US$476 million in 1995 – and vehemently resisted donor demands that it be curtailed or capped. Reluctant to jeopardize Uganda's value to the donor community as a 'success story', donors drew back from threatening aid cuts to secure defence spending reductions (Hauser, 1999: 633–634). Indeed, though donors continued to insist on defence spending cuts throughout the 1990s, they failed to attach aid cuts to these threats until the early 2000s – and even then suspending only token amounts (Banegas, 2006: 229–30; *Daily Monitor*, 18 April 2004; Human Rights Watch, 2000). This allowed Kampala to more than double its defence spending between 1997 and 2004 (SIPRI, 2007: 304). The Museveni regime's experience with donors during this debacle proved to be extremely formative and shaped its subsequent management of relations with this community. The defence spending 'game' played by Kampala, as some former diplomats have labelled it,[23] taught Uganda's diplomats that skilful engagement with the international community could result in increased support even when they needed to simultaneously neuter criticisms and counter threats to the regime's maintenance of its security profile.

The regional hegemon: 1994–2001 The 1994 Rwandan genocide heralded a key moment of change in the approach taken by Western states towards African governments. Coming in the immediate aftermath of the disastrous US military intervention in Somalia, which ended in March 1994, the aftermath of the genocide focused donor minds on the practical and reputational dangers of direct involvement in the continent's affairs and prompted a stepping-back from Africa by many Western governments and UN agencies (Khadiagala, 2001: 261–264). Museveni skilfully brokered this moment by presenting Uganda – and the UPDF – as a potential mediator and regional peacekeeping force that could represent Western interests in the region. Uganda, in effect, became the surrogate force for Western interest (Connell & Smyth, 1998). This represented the start of an important reframing of Uganda's 'value' to Western donors – one that has continued apace to date – with the focus placed on its regional and international role, rather than domestic economic governance.

But surrogacy did not involve the sacrifice of agency. Museveni warmed to this role precisely because it allowed him to further Uganda's regional interests *with* Western support, while also satisfying the domestic need to manage his armed forces. Museveni's former bush comrades, the senior commanders of the UPDF, were happy to see the army being deployed in active roles beyond Uganda's borders, welcoming active service and the economic opportunities that often accompanied such excursions. Having first sent peacekeeping troops into Liberia in January 1994, Uganda therefore put itself forward as a key mediator in the Burundi peace process from 1996, and offered assistance to Rwandan refugees fleeing *genocidaires* (Fisher, 2011: 232–249).

Supported by rhetoric promoting 'African-led [...] peace and stability initia-tives',[24] Museveni adroitly manoeuvred Uganda into the position of the major regional provider of 'African solutions to African problems' within months of the Rwanda genocide of April 1994 (Rosenblum, 2002). Indeed, this was accomplished so successfully and so rapidly that a senior US official from the time recalls relying heavily on Museveni's regional influence in pursuit of US policy goals.[25] Uganda had become indispensable to the security and humanitarian agendas of the West in eastern Africa.

In taking this critical step, Kampala petitioned strongly for increased donor support for its military, especially in relation to equipment and training. Long before AFRICOM was even thought of, Museveni had established the activities that would provide its primary purpose. This military support was willingly provided – particularly by the US, which initiated a programme to 'profession-alize the Ugandan army' in 1997 and invited Uganda to play a leading role in its new regional security framework, and the African Crisis Response Initiative (ACRI) in the same year (US Congress, 1998; Omach, 2000: 84).[26] Seizing the opportunity this new relationship offered, the Kampala regime also offered itself as an African conduit for US support to the Sudanese People's Liberation Army following Washington's fallout with the Khartoum administration in 1993 (Fisher, 2012: 413–414). From here on, Uganda had the blessing of its Western ally to cross the border and interfere in the politics of its northern neighbour. Once again, this came with additional US military assistance, including nearly US$4 million worth of equipment as part of a 'Frontline States Initiative' between 1997 and 1998 and part of a US$20 million transfer of equipment between 1996 and 1997 (US Congress, 1998; Branch, 2007: 197–199).

Domestically, however, the Ugandan military and security services were also playing a key role in cementing the Museveni regime's hold on power during this crucial period. In the north of the country, the UPDF continued its fight against the LRA while showing little interest in guaranteeing the security of local civilians, even rounding up many and transferring them to poorly defended IDP camps from 1996 onwards (Dolan, 2009: 52–56). Likewise, police and security agencies (both legal and – increasingly – extralegal) unleashed a wave of violence and intimidation against opponents of Museveni and the NRM during the 2001 election to ensure a victory for the Ugandan leader, who faced, for the first time since 1986, a serious rival for power (Tangri & Mwenda, 2003: 549). These authoritarian actions were largely ignored by Uganda's allies, and had no discernible impact upon levels of donor support.

Securitization since 9/11 The events of 9/11 represent the final – and most important – moment brokered by Kampala in the incorporation of donor support into its establishing of an authoritarian state. The declaration of a Global War on Terrorism by the US and other Western states in 2001 offered the opportunity to the Museveni regime to present itself as a valuable Western ally in the conflict against Islamist extremism. Having acquired considerable donor military assistance in depicting its proxy war against Khartoum as one against a 'terrorist' state prior to 9/11, Kampala convincingly expanded this label to characterize its engagement in a variety of regional and international theatres including in Iraq, Eritrea and Somalia and counter-insurgency activities in the north and west of the country during the 2000s (Fisher, 2012: 413–422; 2013a: 16–19).

Donor promotion of a counter-terrorism agenda in Africa since 9/11 has permitted the regime to strengthen the Ugandan security services with international support. The passage of an Anti-Terrorism Act by the Ugandan parliament in 2002, for example, was strongly backed by major donors in spite of its conferring sweeping powers upon Ugandan security agencies (Haynes, 2006: 503). Counter-terror legislation has also allowed the Kampala regime to arrest a wide range of putative 'terrorists' since 2002 who in fact have more often been legitimate protestors against government policies – including Baganda, who opposed Kampala's interference in local kingdom politics in 2009.[27]

The most significant type of support, however, has come in the form of military training and funding and provision of equipment, weaponry and technology. Museveni has managed to secure increasing levels of each, particularly from the US, UK and EU, through promoting his government's indispensability as a regional partner in the fight against terrorism and insecurity (Turse, 2015). Kampala consequently became one of only five African states to benefit from a US$100 million Anti-Terrorism Assistance Programme from Washington in 2003 and has received other funding and training packages in relation to specific 'counter-terrorism' missions including against the LRA, Allied Democratic Forces (ADF, an Islamist-leaning rebel movement[28] originating from western Uganda) and, since 2007, in Somalia (Titeca & Vlassenroot, 2012: 167–169; Fisher, 2013a: 4–7).

Indeed, donors have drawn back from providing direct budgetary support to Kampala since 2010 owing to a spate of corruption scandals. These cuts have largely been made to shore up the reputation of Western development agencies at home rather than to apply pressure on the Museveni state – whose budget relies less on international funding now than at any point since the early 1990s (Hickey, 2013; Fisher, 2015). Support to the Ugandan military sector, however, has not been similarly affected. Indeed, donor support to this part of the Ugandan state apparatus has grown steadily and consistently throughout the 2000s and 2010s, as delineated above.

In the last decade, the Ugandan security forces have become a central player in the regime's building of an entrenched, semi-authoritarian polity in the country. Armed units close to the president have secured and now fully control oil fields in western Uganda at Museveni's command – a potentially crucial future patronage resource for him or his successor (Matsiko, 2012; Vokes, 2012). Police and military officials have also become increasingly important as a tool for dealing with domestic regime opponents and critics, with opposition leaders, protestors, journalists and others arbitrarily arrested and harassed with growing frequency since the mid-2000s.

Uganda's security adventures: crises and continuities

The Museveni regime has therefore capitalized on key changes in the international and regional environment to further securitize its relations with donor governments. This has resulted in ever-increasing levels of international support for its security sector both directly and indirectly, allowing it to further entrench and expand the authoritarian and military base of its hold on power. The remainder of this chapter will explore how this dynamic has played out in three key instances since 1986.

The LRA Though less directly associated with injections of international military assistance than, for example, the Somalia mission, Kampala's quarter-century war against the LRA has nevertheless been most frequently and successfully utilized by the Ugandan government to mobilize donor funding since 1987. The shadowy and amorphous nature of the rebel group, together with its unclear ideological underpinnings and unpredictable, brutal manner of warfare, has also provided the regime with numerous opportunities to shape the organization's apparent significance in line with changes in international and regional donor priorities (Fisher, 2013a: 16–19; Titeca, 2013).

During the first period explored above, for example, Kampala consistently rejected donor demands to reduce defence spending by raising the LRA threat. In a 1995 showdown with donors over the issue, for example, Museveni berated Western diplomats for pushing for military cuts when Uganda was 'fighting bandits' and 'criminals' in the north of the country (Channel 4, 1997). Regime officials took donors on *ad hoc*, periodic 'tours' of areas attacked by the LRA during the 1990s to emphasize the apparent importance of maintaining a sizable defence budget (Fisher, 2013b). Sudanese support to the LRA from *c.*1995 also allowed the regime to present itself as a 'frontline state' against Khartoum and consequently benefit from extensive US military assistance and training (Connell & Smyth, 1998).

Following 9/11, however, the Museveni regime skilfully re-packaged the LRA as a 'terrorist' group, particularly in its engagement with the US and UK, and clearly convinced many American officials in this re-labelling with the LRA being designated a 'terrorist group' by the State Department in 2002 and Uganda becoming eligible for a wide range of military assistance programmes, including US$4 million from Washington between 2004 and 2005 to 'counter threats from terrorist organizations such as the LRA' (US Department of State, 2005: 310–311; Atkinson, 2010: 289; Fisher, 2013a: 16–19). The degree of direct military support from donors to tackle the LRA threat since its designation as a terrorist group has not been made clear, indeed has been purposely played down by US and UK officials at times (Branch, 2007: 197–199). It is clear, however, that US and UK military personnel have played an increasingly direct role in facilitating and supporting UPDF operations against the group – particularly since its being forced from Ugandan territory in 2006.

Indeed, in 2011, the US dispatched 100 US military advisors to central Africa to assist Ugandan forces – and other regional militaries – in the fight against the LRA (Atkinson *et al.*, 2012: 371–375). In March 2014, a further 150 advisors were sent, together with a number of CV-22 Osprey military aircraft.[29] Though the advisors have been instructed to not 'engage LRA forces unless necessary for self-defense',[30] this deployment represents the culmination of an extremely successful and well-managed securitization process by Kampala, where its onetime 'bandits' have been transformed into a force perceived by Washington as a threat to 'US national security interests' (*The Guardian*, 14 October 2011; Fisher, 2014b). This process has legitimized ever-closer and increasing collaboration of the US military in particular with the UPDF and the gradual creation of one of the most well-equipped and formidable armed forces on the African continent.

DRC and Sudan In the aftermath of the Rwandan genocide of 1994, the Museveni regime adopted the role of regional policeman as donor agencies and military units withdrew from the continent. With enthusiastic donor support, the UPDF consequently became far more muscular in its provision of 'African solutions to African problems' – notably in increasing assistance to the SPLA from 1995 and invading then Zaire to neuter various insurgencies and, ultimately, depose its leader, Mobutu Sese Seko, in 1996. The former involved extensive transfers of weaponry and logistical support to Kampala from Washington, and the latter, while not associated directly with any military assistance, nevertheless came with the tacit approval of major donors who were keen to see the demise of the Zairian dictator.[31]

Kampala's second Congo invasion in 1998, however, was received with dismay in Western capitals – particularly as the intervention degenerated into internecine warfare with Rwandan forces and economic exploitation by senior Ugandan commanders into the early 2000s (Fisher, 2013c: 551–554). Uganda's continuing military escapades within Sudanese territory during this period – both to pursue the LRA and to assist SPLA operations – were also seen by donors as a considerable barrier to ending the long-running conflict between Khartoum and the southern rebels.[32] Uganda, however, maintained that it would continue to defend and protect itself and its allies, in the interests of regional peace and security, 'with or without' donor support.[33] It also marshalled the 'terrorist threat' posed by the LRA and ADF (both of which it linked to *Al-Qaeda*) to justify its exploits in eastern Congo and southern Sudan (Fisher, 2013c: 553–555). In doing so, Kampala forced donors to decide between supporting or abandoning its key regional proxy.

Whether a bluff or not, this strategy proved successful. Reluctant to alienate one of the key providers of 'African solutions to African problems' and the leading opponents of Islamist fundamentalism in the region, donors ultimately accepted Kampala's transgressions in Congo and Sudan, applying only minor and temporary penalties. Indeed, rather than try to rein in Uganda's regional adventures during the 2000s, donors have instead attempted to legitimize them. Thus, the US, UK, EU and others have lobbied Khartoum and Kinshasa successfully to permit UPDF incursions in pursuit of the LRA within their territory since the early 2000s under a variety of bilateral and regional treaty arrangements (Fisher, 2014b). As noted above, the same donors have also increasingly assisted the UPDF directly in these operations. This is in spite of the fact that senior Ugandan military personnel have steadily formalized their extractive economic enterprises and networks in both Sudan and Congo during the last decade, having established both in the 1990s.

Somalia Uganda's involvement in Somalia since 2007 represents the pinnacle of its successful securitization of relations with donors. Kampala lobbied Washington and London to facilitate its leadership of an African-led peacekeeping mission in the country from 2005 both as an 'African leadership' and 'counter-terrorism' initiative and received their full-throated support by late 2006

(Fisher, 2012: 416–418). Ugandan forces have been the largest contributor to AMISOM since the mission's commencement in 2007 and have also dominated its leadership despite incorporating Kenyan forces into the operation in 2012.

With the stabilization of Somalia having become a major priority for African policy-makers in donor capitals from the mid-2000s, the UPDF has naturally benefited from an unprecedented amount of military assistance and training from major donors since 2007 – including from the EU, which has increasingly sought to position itself as a 'peacekeeping donor' in Africa in recent years (Tardy, 2013). The total extent of this support is difficult to delineate as much of it has been directed by donors to AMISOM overall – and not just the UPDF – bilaterally (US, UK and EU), through a UN Trust Fund established in 2009 (Canada, Denmark, Germany, Sweden and others) or both (UK) (Freear & de Coning, 2013: 7).

Between 2007 and 2013, the US is estimated to have contributed at least US$862 million bilaterally in this regard, the EU at least US$444 million bilaterally, the UK (2007–2011) over US$50 million and other donors (2009–2012) at least US$786 million multilaterally (Global Humanitarian Assistance, 2012: 16; Freear & de Coning, 2013: 7 and 10, notes 7 and 8). Though the UPDF would certainly not have been the sole beneficiary of this more than $US2 billion-strong injection of support, its command leadership of AMISOM since 2007 and contribution of a minimum of 60 per cent of its strength between 2007 and 2012 would undoubtedly have made it the primary recipient.

Ugandan forces have also become major 'trainers' of Somali soldiers since 2010, alongside EU, US and UK personnel based in various military facilities in the country. This EU Training Mission on Somalia has also been supported by other donors including Ireland, Italy and Sweden.[34] Kampala has successfully made use of its presence in the mission to increase and augment the amount of assistance and weaponry it receives from donors, lobbying Western actors to increase their support for the mission and the expansion of its mandate at prominent public fora including the 2010 Kampala Conference and 2013 Somalia Conference in London. Though not always immediately successful, such demands have invariably been met eventually by donors.

The Somalia mission has also enabled Kampala to insulate itself from donor criticisms on governance issues. Since the restoration of multi-party politics in 2005, the Ugandan political system has, as noted above, become steadily more authoritarian, with the security services playing an ever more central role in stifling dissent and with formal democratic institutions being increasingly hollowed out and neutered by the presidency. Officials in London, Washington, New York and Brussels have nevertheless admitted to feeling reluctant to 'push' such issues 'too hard' with the regime for fear of jeopardizing its commitment to staying in Somalia. Such has been the dynamic behind recent aborted donor attempts to 'be tougher' on Kampala over restoring term limits

(2009), reconstituting the Ugandan electoral commission (2009–2010) and post-election violence (2011) (Fisher, 2013b: 478–482).

The degree to which the Museveni regime has capitalized on this 'bind' several key donors find themselves in was demonstrated particularly clearly in late 2012. In the summer of that year, a leaked interim report by a UN Group of Experts (eventually published in November 2012) alleged that Uganda, together with Rwanda, had provided logistical and military support to the M23 militia, a Congolese rebel movement then attacking UN forces in the DRC (UN, 2012). When Western donors failed to immediately disown the report and its conclusions, Kampala threatened to withdraw its troops from AMISOM – arguing that it had been 'maligned' by the UN.[35] Though largely viewing the threat as a bluff as, indeed, it turned out to be, US, UK and EU officials distanced themselves from the report's findings on Uganda (but not on Rwanda) and the next Group of Experts report failed to repeat the allegations (UN 2014).

Conclusion

The Museveni regime is not the first in Uganda's post-independence history to benefit from Western assistance in the consolidation of its hold on power. The UK played a prominent role in supporting the building of independent Uganda's military under the Obote coalition (1963–1965) and first presidency (1966–1971), and British troops directly intervened to quash a mutiny against the country's first government in 1964. Major Western powers were also initially major supporters of the Idi Amin regime, which came to power in a military coup in 1971, and both London and Washington rapidly furnished his government with economic and military aid, along with weaponry and military vehicles, to help entrench the former army commander's new position in Kampala (Ofcansky, 1996: 125–135).

No previous Ugandan administration, however, has been able to maintain such support for any length of time. Obote's flirtation with the Soviet Union – which failed to protect him from overthrow in 1971 – lost him substantial US and UK support during his first period in power while his flagrant human rights abuses during his second put paid to any possible rapprochement with Washington particularly (Ofcansky, 1996: 129–130). Similarly, Western support for Amin was largely withdrawn within a year of his coming to power following his 1972 expulsion of the Ugandan–Asian community and his regime has the dubious honour of being the first to have had 'political conditionality' imposed on its aid disbursements in relation to human rights abuses – more than a decade before this instrument came to be more systematically applied by Western donors in the post-Cold War world.

In the case of the Museveni regime, however, not only has it managed to maintain Western support, military and otherwise, throughout its lengthy tenure, it has seen this support increase and diversify substantially. This has occurred, particularly since the early 2000s, against a background of increasing militarization and authoritarianism on the part of the regime and its steady loss of credibility on the international stage as a result of corruption scandals, repressive legislation, regional military adventurism, democratic backsliding and trigger-happy security forces. Unlike his predecessors, Museveni has been especially imaginative and strategic in incorporating different forms of international support into the overall construction of a militarized state – including through the management of GBS flows, proliferation of external AU/UN peacekeeping missions and seeking training for security services beyond the UPDF, notably the police.

Indeed, we have argued that this situation has not come about by coincidence but through the strategic engagement of the Kampala leadership, particularly the person of Museveni himself, with major Western governments over the course of several decades in the economic sphere (initially) and the international arena. Where other African leaders have been caught unawares by the changing tides of regional and international politics (e.g. Kenneth Kaunda of Zambia, Hastings Banda of Malawi or, eventually, Mobutu Sese Seko of Zaire), Museveni has instead 'brokered' these crucial moments to strengthen and enhance Western support for his increasingly military approach to state-, or perhaps just regime-, building in Uganda. 9/11, then, did not mark so much a change in regional security policy driven by Western concerns. Rather, it presented an opportunity for the further development of strategies already by then embedded in Uganda's foreign policy. What is striking about this is not the disjunctures caused by external shocks – the world events that so dominate the West's analysis – but the strong continuities that mark Ugandan behaviour over a period now spanning over a quarter of a century.

These strategies have played out in a range of regional and international contexts, as this chapter has shown. Uganda's involvement in Somalia since 2007, however, represents perhaps the perfection of Kampala's skilled courting of its Western allies. This is not to say, of course, that US, UK and other donor officials – particularly those posted to Uganda itself – have been blindly 'duped' by Museveni since 1986. Many such individuals, at various levels of seniority, are clearly aware of the particular hold the Ugandan regime has over them when it comes to the Somali mission. Nevertheless, they have yet to try to challenge this state of affairs in their engagement with Kampala; US and UK officials were largely convinced that Uganda's 2012 threat to pull out of AMISOM was a bluff, but were nonetheless unprepared to 'call' the Ugandan leader on this particularly disingenuous piece of diplomacy.

While Western donors may be reluctant to recalibrate their relations with the Museveni regime as long as it fulfils such an important strategic role, the same can less easily be said for Kampala itself. Like its predecessors, the Museveni government has shown little compunction in building ties with non-Western allies; North Korea has been a long-standing provider of military training and equipment to the UPDF and police, as it was to the military of Milton Obote's second administration (Ofcansky, 1996: 134–5; *Daily Monitor*, 12 April 2014). The regime has also fostered closer ties with several 'rising powers' since the late 2000s, to further augment external support for its security sector. In 2011, for example, Beijing pledged US$2.3 million of military aid to support UPDF operations in Somalia while Moscow, which sold six fighter jets to Uganda in the same year, and Iran have also been increasingly courted by Museveni in the security field.[36] In February 2014, in response to Western donors' condemnation of his signing into law of the 'Anti-Homosexuality Bill', Museveni declared: 'I want to work [more] with Russia because they don't mix up their politics with other countries' politics.'[37] Whether this represents a comprehensive change of foreign policy focus on Kampala's part or another calculated bluff remains to be seen. What is clear, however, is that the donor–Uganda relationship has been founded on and sustained by strategic thinking on both sides.

Notes

1 *Daily Monitor*, 9 and 30 March 2014.

2 *BBC News*, 18 June 2013.

3 *Daily Monitor*, 9 March 2014.

4 *Observer*, 26 July 2015.

5 Freedom House, 'Freedom of the Press' entries 2005 and 2012, viewed 30 September 2015, https://freedomhouse. org/report/freedom-press/2005/uganda#. UoaCcpwtZLM and http://www. freedomhouse.org/report/freedom-press/2012/uganda

6 Committee to Protect Journalists, 'Uganda', viewed 30 September 2015, https://www.cpj.org/2013/02/attacks-on-the-press-in-2012-uganda.php

7 *BBC News*, 12 April 2007 and 17 September 2008, *Reuters*, 29 April 2011.

8 *Daily Monitor*, 10 February 2014.

9 Interviews with current and former senior NRM cadres, February 2010 and April 2013.

10 *Daily Monitor*, 23 September 2012. The growing use of supplementary budgets and extra-budgetary funding mechanisms by the regime for regime-maintenance purposes has not only been commented upon by Western diplomats (Interviews, January–April 2011) and Ugandan journalists

(*Independent*, 25 January 2011) but also by a leading Ugandan economic official, Bank of Uganda governor and former chief economic advisor to Museveni, Emmanuel Tumusiime-Mutebile (*Financial Times*, 13 June 2011).

11 Interviews with former Western donor officials based in Kampala during mid-1980s, November–December 2009.

12 Interviews with former US officials, November 2009.

13 Interviews with former Western donor officials based in Kampala during mid-1980s, November–December 2009. Interview with former senior US and UK officials, November–December 2009.

14 *Ibid*.

15 Interviews with senior NRM cadres, April 2013.

16 *BBC News*, 11 July 2011.

17 *Daily Monitor*, 10 April 2014.

18 Interview with Scandinavian diplomat based in Kampala, May 2009.

19 Interviews with UK and Irish officials, November 2010–January 2011.

20 Interviews with European donor officials, May–June 2009, November 2010–April 2011; June–July 2011.

21 See also a 2009 article in *The*

Guardian authored by Alan Whitworth, a British government economist who worked within the Ugandan Finance Ministry between 1990 and 1995, where he argues that 'Uganda has had more influence on current development thinking than any other country' (*The Guardian*, 3 March 2009).

22 Interviews with former Uganda-based donor officials, October 2008–July 2009; November 2009.

23 Interview with former senior donor official, November 2008.

24 *Time*, 1 September 1997.

25 Interview with former senior US official, November 2009.

26 ACRI became African Contingency Operations Training and Assistance (ACOTA) in 2004.

27 *Daily Monitor*, 8 September 2012.

28 Scholars caution against viewing the ADF solely through 'the prism of Islamic terrorism' (Scorgie-Porter, 2015: 192; see also Prunier, 2004) although this is, of course, largely how they have been understood in Kampala and Washington. Formed in 1995 as a coalition of a range of anti-Museveni groups – including, but not limited to, Islamists from the Tabliq group in Uganda – the group received most of its external funding from Islamist networks – and was led, until his arrest in 2015, by Jamil Mukula, an associate of Osama bin Laden who previously received training in Afghanistan and Pakistan. The group has also received domestic support, however, through its integration into the borderland economies and societies of western Uganda/eastern DRC (Scorgie-Porter, 2015).

29 *New York Times*, 23 April 2013.

30 *The Guardian*, 14 October 2011.

31 Interviews with former Western donor officials based in Kampala, London and Washington, June–November 2009.

32 Interviews with former US officials, October–November 2009 and May 2012.

33 *Ibid.*

34 Interviews with EU Training Mission in Somalia personnel, June 2012.

35 *New Vision*, 2 November 2012.

36 *Radio Netherlands Worldwide*, 30 November 2011; *Daily Monitor*, 30 November 2010 and 12 December 2012.

37 *Daily Monitor*, 23 February 2014.

References

Atkinson, R (2010), *The roots of ethnicity: the origins of the Acholi before 1900 of Uganda*, 2nd edition, Fountain Publishers, Kampala.

Atkinson, R, Lancaster, P, Cakaj, L & Lacaille, G (2012), 'Do no harm: assessing a military approach to the Lord's Resistance Army', *Journal of Eastern African Studies*, vol. 6, no. 2, pp. 371–82.

Banegas, R (2006), 'Democracy, security and governance in Uganda: the contradictions of post-conflict reconstruction', in JP Chretien & R Banegas (eds), *The recurring Great Lakes crisis: identity, violence and power*, Hurst, London, pp. 205–32.

Barkan, J (2011), *Uganda: assessing risks to stability*, Center for Strategic and International Studies, Washington, DC.

Branch, A (2007), *The political dilemmas of global justice: anti-civilian violence and the violence of humanitarianism, the case of northern Uganda*, unpublished PhD thesis, Columbia University, New York.

Canagarajah, S & van Diesen, A (2011), 'The poverty reduction strategy approach six years on: an examination of principles and practice in Uganda', *Development Policy Review*, vol. 29, no. s1, pp. 135–56.

Channel 4 (UK) (1997), 'The bank, the president and the pearl of Africa', documentary film, broadcast in two parts.

Connell, D & Smyth, F (1998), 'Africa's new bloc', *Foreign Affairs*, vol. 77, no. 2, pp. 80–94.

de Torrente, N (2001), *Post-conflict reconstruction and the international community in Uganda 1986–2000: an African success story?*, unpublished PhD thesis, London School of

Economics and Political Science, University of London, London.

Dicklitch, S (1998), *The elusive promise of NGOs in Africa: lessons from Uganda*, Macmillan, Basingstoke.

Djikstra, G & van Donge, JK (2001), 'What does the "show case" show? Evidence and lessons from adjustment in Uganda', *World Development*, vol. 29, no. 5, pp. 841–63.

Dolan, C (2009), *Social torture: the case of northern Uganda 1986–2006*, Berghahn Books, London.

Fisher, J (2015), '"Does it work?" – Work for whom? Britain and political conditionality since the Cold War', *World Development*, vol. 75, in print, pp. 13–25.

Fisher, J (2014a), 'When it pays to be a "fragile state": Uganda's use and abuse of a dubious concept', *Third World Quarterly*, vol. 35, no. 2, pp. 316–32.

Fisher, J (2014b), 'Framing Kony: Uganda's war, Obama's advisers and the nature of "influence" in Western foreign policy-making', *Third World Quarterly*, vol. 35, no. 4, pp. 686–704.

Fisher, J (2013a), '"Some more reliable than others": image management, donor perceptions and the global war on terror in East African diplomacy', *Journal of Modern African Studies*, vol. 51, no. 1, pp. 1–31.

Fisher, J (2013b), 'The limits – and limiters – of external influence: donors, the Ugandan electoral commission and the 2011 elections', *Journal of Eastern African Studies*, vol. 7, no. 3, pp. 471–91.

Fisher, J (2013c), 'Structure, agency and Africa in the international system: donor diplomacy and regional security policy in East Africa since the 1990s', *Conflict, Security and Development*, vol. 13, no. 5, pp. 537–67.

Fisher, J (2012), 'Managing donor perceptions and securing agency: contextualizing Uganda's 2007 intervention in Somalia', *African Affairs*, vol. 111, no. 444, pp. 404–23.

Fisher, J (2011), *International perceptions and African agency: Uganda and its donors, 1986–2010*, unpublished DPhil thesis, St Antony's College, University of Oxford, Oxford.

Freear, M & de Coning, C (2013), 'Lessons from the African Union Mission for Somalia (AMISOM) for peace operations in Mali', *Stability: International Journal of Security and Development*, vol. 2, no. 2, art. 23, pp. 1–11.

Global Humanitarian Assistance (2012), *Somalia: international financing investments*, Global Humanitarian Assistance, Somerset.

Harrison, G (2001), 'Post-conditionality politics and administrative reform: reflections on the cases of Uganda and Tanzania', *Development and Change*, vol. 32, no. 4, pp. 657–79.

Hauser, E (1999), 'Ugandan relations with Western donors in the 1990s: what impact on democratisation?', *Journal of Modern African Studies*, vol. 37, no. 4, pp. 621–41.

Haynes, J (2006), 'Islam and democracy in East Africa', *Democratization*, vol. 13, no. 3, pp. 490–507.

Haynes, J (2001), 'Conclusion', in J Haynes (ed.), *Towards sustainable democracy in the 'Third World'*, Palgrave Macmillan, London, pp. 217–41.

Hickey, S (2013), 'Beyond the poverty agenda? Insights from the new politics of development in Uganda', *World Development*, vol. 43, no. 3, pp. 194–206.

Human Rights Watch (2000), 'Uganda', in Human Rights Watch, *Human Rights Watch, World Report 2000*, Human Rights Watch, New York.

International Institute for Strategic Studies (various years), *Military Balance*, International Institute for Strategic Studies, London.

Kasfir, N (2000), '"Movement" democracy, legitimacy and power in Uganda', in J Mugaju & J Oloka-Onyango (eds), *No-party democracy in Uganda: myths and realities*, Fountain Publishers, Kampala, pp. 60–78.

Khadiagala, G (2001), 'The United States and Africa: beyond the Clinton administration', *School of Advanced and International Studies (SAIS) Review*, vol. 21, no. 1, pp. 259–73.

Khadiagala, G (1995), 'State collapse and reconstruction in Uganda', in W Reno (ed.), *Collapsed states: the disintegration and reconstruction of legitimate authority*, Lynne Rienner, Boulder, pp. 33–47.

Kitabire, D (2010), 'Debt management and debt relief', in F Kuteesa *et al.* (eds), *Uganda's economic reforms: insider accounts*, Oxford University Press, Oxford, pp. 264–76.

Kuteesa, F, Tumusiime-Mutebile, E, Whitworth, A & Williamson, T (eds) (2010), *Uganda's economic Reforms: insider accounts*, Oxford University Press, Oxford.

Makara, S, Rakner, L & Svasand, L (2009) 'Turnaround: the National Resistance Movement and the reintroduction of a multiparty system in Uganda', *International Political Science Review*, vol. 30, no. 2, pp. 185–204.

Matsiko, H (2012), 'Guns in oil region', *Independent*, Independent Publications, Kampala.

Mosley, P, Chiripanhura, B, Grugel, J & Thirkell-White, B (2012), *The politics of poverty reduction*, Oxford University Press, Oxford.

Mugambe, K (2010), 'The poverty eradication action plan', in F Kuteesa *et al.* (eds), *Uganda's economic reforms: insider accounts*, Oxford University Press, Oxford, pp. 157–71.

Museveni, YK (1992), *What is Africa's problem?* NRM Publications, Kampala.

Mutengesa, S (2013), 'Facile acronyms and tangled processes: a re-examination of the 1990s "DDR" in Uganda', *International Peacekeeping*, vol. 20, no. 3, pp. 338–56.

Mutengesa, S & Hendrickson, D (2008), *State responsiveness to public security needs: the politics of security decision-making, Uganda Country Study*, King's College London, University of London, London.

Mutibwa, P (1992), *Uganda since independence: a story of unfulfilled hopes*, Hurst, London.

Mwenda, A (2007), 'Personalizing power in Uganda', *Journal of Democracy*, vol. 18, no. 3, pp. 23–37.

Ofcansky, T (1996), *Uganda: tarnished pearl of Africa*, Westview Press, Boulder.

Omach, P (2000), 'The African crisis response initiative: domestic politics and convergence of national interest', *African Affairs*, vol. 99, no. 394, pp. 73–95.

Omara-Otunnu, A (1987), *Politics and the military in Uganda, 1890–1985*, St Martin's Press, New York.

Organisation of Economic Co-operation and Development (various years), *Geographical distribution of financial flows to less developed countries*, Organisation for Economic Co-operation and Development, Paris.

Prunier, G (2004), 'Rebel movements and proxy warfare: Uganda, Sudan and the Congo (1986–99)', *African Affairs*, vol. 103, no. 412, pp. 359–83.

Rosenblum, P (2002), 'Irrational exuberance: the Clinton administration in Africa', *Current History*, vol. 101, no. 655, pp. 195–202.

Scorgie-Porter, L (2015), 'Economic survival and borderland rebellion: the case of the Allied Democratic Forces on the Uganda–Congo border', *Journal of the Middle East and Africa*, vol. 6, no. 2, pp. 191–213.

Stockholm International Peace Research Institute (2007), *SIPRI Yearbook, 2007*, Oxford University Press, Oxford.

Tangri, R (2006), 'Politics and presidential term limits in Uganda', in R Southall & H Melber (eds), *Legacies of power: leadership change and former presidents in African politics*, Nordic Africa Institute, Uppsala, pp. 175–96.

Tangri, R & Mwenda, A (2013), *The politics of elite corruption in Africa: Uganda in comparative African context*, Routledge, London.

Tangri, R & Mwenda, A (2010), 'President Museveni and the politics of presidential tenure in Uganda', *Journal of Contemporary African Studies*, vol. 28, no. 1, pp. 31–49.

Tangri, R & Mwenda, A (2003), 'Military corruption and Ugandan politics since the late 1990s', *Review of African Political Economy*, vol. 30, no. 98, pp. 539–52.

Tardy, T (2013), *Funding peace operations: better value for EU money*, European Union Institute for Security Studies, Paris.

Titeca, K (2013), 'The Lord's Resistance Army in the Democratic Republic of Congo: competing agendas and their effects', paper presented at University of Paris 8, Paris, May 2013.

Titeca, K & Vlassenroot, K (2012), 'Rebels without borders in Rwenzori borderland? A biography of the Allied Democratic Forces', *Journal of Eastern African Studies*, vol. 6, no. 1, pp. 154–76.

Tripp, AM (2010), *Museveni's Uganda: paradoxes of power in a hybrid regime*, Lynne Rienner, Boulder.

Tumusiime-Mutebile, E (2010), 'Institutional and political dimensions of economic reform', in F Kuteesa *et al.* (eds), *Uganda's economic reforms: insider accounts*, Oxford University Press, Oxford, pp. 35–51.

Turse, N (2015) *Tomorrow's battlefield: US proxy wars and secret ops in Africa*, Haymarket, Chicago.

United Nations (2012), *Final report of the Group of Experts on the DRC submitted in accordance with paragraph 4 of Security Council resolution 2021 (2011)*, S/2012/843, United Nations Security Council, New York.

United Nations (2014), *Final report of the Group of Experts submitted to in accordance with paragraph 5 of Security Council resolution 2078 (2012)*, S/2014/32, UN Security Council, New York.

United States Congress (1998), 'Statement of Susan E. Rice, Assistant Secretary of State for African Affairs, before the House International Relations Committee, Subcommittee on International Operations and Human Rights: "Crises in Sudan and northern Uganda", 29 July 1998', Inaugural Address, United States Congress, Washington, DC, 29 July 1998.

United States Department of State (2005), *FY 2006 congressional budget justification for foreign operations*, United States Department of State, Washington, DC.

Vokes, R (2012), 'The politics of oil in Uganda', *African Affairs*, vol. 111, no. 443, pp. 303–14.

Weeks, J, Anderson, DM & Cramer, C (2002), *Supporting ownership: Swedish development cooperation with Kenya, Tanzania, and Uganda*, Department for Evaluation and Audit Internal Audit, Swedish International Development Cooperation Agency, Stockholm.

Whitworth, A (2010), 'Planning and development budget reform, 1990–1995', in F Kuteesa *et al.* (eds), *Uganda's economic reforms: insider accounts*, Oxford University Press, Oxford, pp. 129–156.

Whitworth, A & Williamson, T (2010), 'Overview of Ugandan economic reform since 1986', in F Kuteesa *et al.* (eds), *Uganda's economic reforms: insider accounts*, Oxford University Press, Oxford, pp. 1–34.

4 | Ethiopia and international aid: development between high modernism and exceptional measures

Emanuele Fantini
and Luca Puddu

Introduction

Recent scholarship has highlighted the authoritarian character of the contemporary Ethiopian political regime (Abbink, 2006; Aalen & Tronvoll, 2009a, 2009b), critically assessing the notion of 'revolutionary democracy' advanced by the ruling Ethiopian People's Revolutionary Democratic Front (EPRDF) (Hagmann & Abbink, 2011; Bach, 2011) and its instrumental use of development policies to control rural masses (Lefort, 2010; 2012). In spite of aid-conditionality strategies linking official development assistance (ODA) to recipient countries' performance on good governance and democracy, Ethiopia has managed to attract an increasing amount of international aid in recent years, confirming itself as one of the largest beneficiaries of ODA worldwide.[1] The Ethiopian case is often quoted as paradigmatic of the role of international ODA in sustaining the authoritarian exercise of power. Since the controversial 2005 national elections, the Ethiopian government has enacted restrictive laws and regulations governing the press and civil society organizations, as well as measures to counter perceived terrorist threats implying the restriction of civil and political rights. Not incidentally, in analysing the contemporary Ethiopian political regime, academics have resorted to different categories, from neo-patrimonialism (Abbink, 2006) to electoral authoritarianism (Aalen and Tronvoll, 2009a) or totalitarian 'one-party state' (Tronvoll, 2011).

How can this apparent paradox be explained? Some observers have stressed the Ethiopian government's ability to manipulate official international development discourse, assertively confronting international donors in order to steer ODA to fulfil its political priorities (Furtado & Smith, 2008; Enten, 2010; Feyissa, 2011). Others have pointed to donors' naiveté or ignorance of local political dynamics and real decision-making processes (Vaughan & Tronvoll, 2003). Still other authors have pointed at Western geopolitical priorities in the Global War on Terror trumping the promotion of human rights (Borchgrevink, 2008; Human Rights Watch, 2010; Feyissa, 2011). Other reasons identified refer to the functioning of the international aid apparatus, which has adopted

Ethiopia as a showcase to prove the effectiveness of its work as well as to the moral imperative of aiding a country that, in spite of recent progresses in human development indicators, faces huge humanitarian challenges (Fantini, 2008; Tommasoli, 2014). Most of these interpretations focus on the relationship between international donors and the Ethiopian government. Consequently, they reflect the specificities of the ruling EPRDF's style and practices and emphasize the influence of geopolitical issues on donors' choices. Moreover, this aid relationship is often framed in terms of a negotiation between two coherent and homogeneous actors: the Ethiopian government and the donor(s). In this chapter, while not dismissing this perspective, we would like to distance ourselves from it by highlighting the historic continuities that have existed between foreign aid and authoritarian politics in Ethiopia from the imperial to the current federal government.

We argue that, despite regime changes in 1974 and 1991, important similarities in the way in which relations between foreign donors and Ethiopian rulers are forged can be observed. Firstly, our analysis highlights the continuous importance of what James Scott (1998) has called 'high-modernist' ideology and schemes by successive Ethiopian governments, their ability to frame such discourses in line with the international development *zeitgeist* and the consequent role played by donors in funding, implementing and legitimizing these narratives. Secondly, our chapter demonstrates that international aid cannot be merely understood in terms of a bilateral relationship between donors and recipient governments, but must rather be seen as the result of the interaction of a plurality of heterogeneous actors and competing logics. This leads us to consider the internal divisions and the contradictory logics of the bureaucratic apparatus that have characterized the so-called international donor community in Ethiopia's past and present, but also the role of private companies that act as important 'development brokers' (Lewis & Mosse, 2006) who shape and implement international aid. Thirdly, we draw attention to how government-led modernization programmes and narratives are accompanied by 'exceptional' practices, both by the Ethiopian government and the international donors. Exceptional measures upholding a state of emergency are traditionally associated with humanitarian interventions in response to natural or human-made disasters, such as drought, famine and conflicts (Fassin & Pandolfi, 2010). In this chapter we wish to highlight how high-modernist schemes carried out in the name of 'development' and the bureaucratic apparatus implementing them ordinarily work according to logics of exceptionality, circumventing the rule of law and thereby contributing to the authoritarian exercise of power.

We illustrate our argument with two case studies focusing on imperial and contemporary Ethiopia respectively: the cotton plantation Tendaho Plantation Share Company in the lower Awash Valley (1960–67), and the Gilgel Gibe II hydropower plant in the Omo river basin, south-western Ethiopia (2004–2010).

The empirical material for these two case studies was gathered during archival research in Ethiopia and Great Britain by Luca Puddu between 2009 and 2013 and through several rounds of fieldwork conducted in Ethiopia by Emanuele Fantini between 2007 and 2012, including participatory observation of negotiation processes between the Ethiopian government and international donors.

A short history of international aid to Ethiopia

The historical trajectory of state formation in Ethiopia stands out as an exception in sub-Saharan Africa. Relying on an embryonic state sustained by an intensive system of surplus extraction in the highlands' core of the country, Ethiopian emperors were able to resist European colonialism and expand the territorial borders of the country between the late nineteenth and early twentieth centuries (Zewde, 2001; Donham & James, 2002). Access to external resources, both symbolic and material, was nonetheless critical for preserving independence against aggressive neighbours and consolidating power domestically, especially after World War Two. In this perspective, the relationship between the modern Ethiopian polity and the international system across historical periods has many similarities with that of sub-Saharan Africa: it is 'a history of extraversion', marked by repeated attempts to turn the external environment – including international aid – into a resource in the quest for political supremacy (Bayart, 2000).

After World War Two, Haile Selassie relied heavily on Western economic assistance to sustain the early industrialization and infrastructure development of the country. In 1950, Ethiopia was the first country in sub-Saharan Africa to obtain a loan from the International Bank for Reconstruction and Development (IBRD) for the construction of a highway network, in collaboration with West Germany and the United States Agency for International Development (USAID) (Hess, 1970). The special relationship with the United States and the World Bank, the latter being Ethiopia's main donor since 1968, allowed the emperor to secure a stable supply of hard currency in the form of grants and soft loans. Moreover, in return for the leasing of the army installation of Kagnew Station in Eritrea, Addis Ababa accounted for more than 80 per cent of the overall US military assistance to sub-Saharan Africa between 1951 and 1977 and gained access to the most advanced weaponry available in the continent, such as the F5 'Freedom Fighter' (Lefebvre, 1991). Haile Selassie was able to insert his country within the Cold War competition, playing the Soviet and the Chinese cards in critical moments of the aid relationship. He spoke the language of international development fluently, emphasizing the critical role of Western scientific knowledge, private-sector involvement and government planning (McVety, 2012: 124). Behind the surface of macro-economic orthodoxy, the effective implementation of many modernization projects was nonetheless nurtured by patron–client practices deeply entrenched in the Abyssinian polity. The imperial establishment opposed those aspects of the modernization discourse that could endanger the status quo. By stressing Ethiopian independence in the selective appropriation of modern ideas from abroad, the ideology of development was fused with the 'Great Tradition' of the Solomonic dynasty, turning external assistance into a major resource in the process of political centralization (Kebede, 1999).

In 1974, the imperial regime was overturned by a military junta known as the Derg. After late 1976, the shift of international alliances decided by the 'Red Negus' Mengistu Haile Mariam drove the country towards the eastern bloc. However, the fundamental dynamics of the relationship with international patrons did not change. According to Clapham (1987), the socialist phase in Ethiopia represented one of the clearest examples of the link between access to external resources and the creation of structures of internal control in sub-Saharan Africa. The Soviet Union replaced the role of the United States in providing military equipment and, to a lesser extent, economic assistance: only between 1977 and 1978, in the midst of the Ogaden war, the Derg obtained credit for arms shipments from Moscow worth around 1,500 million US dollars, rapidly gaining the upper hand in a conflict that originally appeared to be irremediably lost (Clapham, 1987: 229). Between 1978 and 1987 the Soviet supplied additional military aid in the region of 7 billion US dollars, making the Ethiopian army the largest and best equipped one in the continent. The Derg also relied extensively on Cuban military advisors, which numbered 12,000 until 1984. Other Eastern countries, notably East Germany, Bulgaria and Czechoslovakia, supplied technical assistance in the agro-industrial sector. In the non-military sector, Western countries and the multilateral organizations continued to play a critical role: in spite of the emphasis nurtured by official propaganda, Soviet contributions accounted only for 22 per cent of total aid figures in the 1980s.

Nevertheless, Soviet high-modernist ideology shaped the planning and implementation phase of some large-scale projects, such as the Melka Wakana hydroelectric scheme and the massive resettlement operation of 1984–85, representing one of the highest phases in the Ethiopian state's attempt to territorialize state power at the periphery (Patman, 1990: 267). Pervasive public intervention in the rural sector through the Agricultural Marketing Corporation, state farms and peasant cooperatives gave the central government an unprecedented power over the peasantry, at the cost of chronic financial losses, which could be managed only by massive reliance on external support (Clapham, 1987: 177). Although proclaiming his faithful adherence to the principles of scientific socialism, Mengistu resisted Soviet attempts to reorganize the Ethiopian political structure in line with the organization of the Marxist-Leninist system. His regime followed the Abyssinian trajectory of one man's rule. Soviet requests to delegate power to a vanguard party led by Moscow-trained cadres were met only in 1984, when Mengistu Haile Mariam's full control over the new institutional architecture was out of the question (Patman, 1990: 270).

In 1991, the EPRDF and the Eritrean People's Liberation Front defeated the Derg at the end of a fourteen-years-long civil war. The regime change did not alter the privileged relationship between Ethiopia and its international partners. Under EPRDF, Ethiopia has confirmed itself as one of the most cherished 'donor darlings', constantly ranked among the top-ten recipients of international aid flows worldwide. Ethiopia is also the largest beneficiary in sub-Saharan Africa if we exclude international flows linked to humanitarian and military emergencies or debt relief.[2] Although the EPRDF government stresses the fact that Ethiopia falls below the regional sub-Saharan average in terms of aid per capita, ODA still remains a major component of the national public expenditure and the overall GDP of the country, covering around one third of the country's annual budget (Alemu, 2009). Such dependence also extends deep into the running of the local administration: only because of the Protection of Basic Services programme, every district (*wereda*) in the country relies on international assistance for 36 per cent of its budget spending in the sectors of health, education, water, agriculture and roads construction (Feyissa, 2011).

The EPRDF's development strategy is based on a hybrid model that keeps together the notion of developmental state with the neoliberal logics of market efficiency. Such dichotomy is not only ideological, but reflects geographical patterns entrenched in the country's recent history. In the highlands, concerns for egalitarian agricultural growth and food security stood behind the launch of the Agricultural Development-Led Industrialisation (ADLI) programme. ADLI is based on the premise that labour-intensive, smallholder agriculture, backed by technological change, improved marketing connections, and state ownership of land, will raise yields without displacing small farmers (Lavers, 2013). On the contrary, in the lowlands where land is deemed to be idle or inefficiently exploited, the government is directly undertaking or indirectly encouraging large-scale investments in commercial agriculture to increase the production of food staples and raw materials. Concerns for food security explain also the EPRDF's decision to abandon its early opposition to resettlement programmes, which are now considered as a viable option to alleviate pressure on drought-prone areas and put uncultivated land into production (Pankhurst, 2012: 140).

The international press and human rights activists have pointed to the instrumental role of international ODA in sustaining the authoritarian exercise of power in Ethiopia, denouncing the complicity by the international donors because of superior geopolitical or economic reasons (Human Rights Watch, 2010; Epstein, 2013; Oakland Institute, 2013). In spite of the poor records in the field of democracy, over the last ten years international ODA to Ethiopia in absolute term has constantly grown. This apparent paradox may be explained by two factors. Firstly, the EPRDF was effective in exploiting the opportunities provided by the US and other countries' concerns with counter-terrorism, representing itself as an oasis of stability within a conflict-prone region surrounded by failed states and crossed by rebel movements linked to global terrorist networks. Secondly, the Ethiopian government has diversified its donors, relying on a wide range of partners to decrease the degree of dependence from one single external source and retaining a relevant leverage in bargaining the content of the aid relationship (Feyissa, 2011).

If USAID, the World Bank, the International Monetary Fund and the European Union have the bigger stake in the aid relationship with Ethiopia, Addis Ababa is increasingly relying on emergent powers such as China and India in the agro-industrial sector, while retaining a close collaboration with countries like Ukraine and North Korea for the supply of military hardware. The Ethiopian government embraced some aspects of the World Bank's neoliberal agenda, but resisted the most radical requests, such as the privatization of land titles, by claiming the necessity to protect lower rural classes. Official narratives of equity and fight against 'rent seekers' are used to justify the pervasive presence of the state within the national economy. The effective implementation of the Productive Safety Net programme (PSNP) in the Amhara and Tigray Regional states is paradigmatic of how concerns for population control and agricultural surplus extraction still dominate over official development narratives (Lavers, 2013). By using the language of foreign donors, the EPRDF has been building a local administrative structure heavily dependent on the party apparatus, with the side effect of extending the authoritarian presence of the state in the rural milieu (Chinigò, 2013: 15).

Ethiopian development: high modernism, brokerage and exception

This section identifies three historical continuities in the relationship between successive Ethiopian governments and its international donors. These concern: *i)* the adoption by different Ethiopian ruling elites of a high-modernist approach drawing on international development narratives; *ii)* internal plurality and contradictions within the international donor community including international private companies involved in development; *iii)* the adoption of exceptional measures in the implementation of international aid programmes. We have identified these elements of continuity by drawing on the literature on the process of state formation in Ethiopia, on the Ethiopian government–donor relationships, on the ethnography of the international aid apparatus and its bureaucratic logics, as well as on participatory observation of the negotiation between the EPRDF government and international donors.

High modernism throughout Ethiopian political regimes Throughout different regimes, Ethiopian ruling classes have pursued state-building strategies by adopting what James Scott defines as a high-modernist ideology: 'a strong, one might even say muscle-bound, version of the self-confidence about scientific and technical progress, the expansion of production, the growing satisfaction of human needs, the mastery of nature (including human nature) and above all, the rational design of social order commensurate with the scientific understanding of natural laws' (Scott, 1998: 4). Development policies, programmes and projects represent the main instruments by which Ethiopian rulers have sought to implement this high-modernist ideology.

By seeking and obtaining international support to achieve their modernist development goals, Ethiopian rulers engaged in contradictory relations with the outside world. On the one hand, the Ethiopian government entered into the donor–recipient relationship as an independent and sovereign state, retaining the power to negotiate its incorporation within the global economy and the structure of international alliances. For Ethiopian ruling classes, including political elites and government officials, donor–recipient relationships have been instrumental in order to reaffirm state sovereignty and the control over its territory and population (Whitfield, 2008), exalting the fact that Ethiopia was the sole African country that did not experience colonial domination (Feyissa, 2011). On the other hand, Ethiopian ruling classes have constantly played what Christopher Clapham has named the 'politics of emulation': the adoption of external models and 'mechanisms of developmental success of countries perceived as having some similarity to their own' (Clapham, 2006: 138) and the hybridization of these models with autochthonous cultural and political repertoires in the organization of state politics and institutions. Following this pattern, Ethiopian intellectuals of the imperial court debated and were inspired by modernization by looking in particular at the lessons of nineteenth-century Meiji's Japan and, later, of the British constitutional monarchy (Zewde, 2002). The Derg military regime followed modernization in the name of revolution and scientific socialism, adhering to the Soviet model (Donham, 1999). The ruling EPRDF crafted contemporary federal Ethiopia by referring to the notions of ethnic self-determination, revolutionary democracy and the developmental state, inspired by the experiences of, among others, East Asian economic successes such as South Korea and Taiwan, and more recently China (Zenawi, 2006; 2012). The pursuit of these three high-modernist approaches, which we can present only schematically here, is marked by several commonalities. First, these high modernisms are inspired by a radical, revolutionary and millennial ethos, translating into centralized top-down planning by a vanguard, enlightened state elite. Second, they aim at incorporating the country's peripheries by dint of development schemes that promote state-building through territorialization, namely the attempt by the central government to delimit and assert control over natural resources and the people that use them in a specific geographic area (Sack, 1986). Third, these high modernisms emphasize moral claims about the improvement of human and national conditions by dint of technology, resulting in a depoliticized narrative that banishes political dissent and upholds authoritarian political practices.

Finally, we would like to drawn attention to the limits and incompleteness of these high-modernist schemes, which are always subject to negotiation, co-optation, appropriation, dissidence and resistance at various scales. These historically contingent interactions among state and non-state actors have been extensively documented within Ethiopian domestic politics (see for instance James *et al.*, 2002). Less explored are the elements that we wish to highlight in the following paragraphs: the plurality and contradictions that exist in the relationship between international donors and the Ethiopian government, as well as within and between their respective internal bodies.

The donors' side: plurality and brokerage Ethiopian elites' high modernism appears in sync with the logics of the international aid apparatus: the millennial and radical ethos of planning inspired by a vision of development as a linear process of transformation and change towards improvement; the adoption of top-down practices of planning and implementation as manifest in negotiations between donors and recipient governments, most of the time taking place at the centre, in the capital; the emphasis on moral imperatives, scientific theories and technical aspects of development and the fight against poverty that officially avoid politics and political issues (Ferguson, 1990; Mosse, 2005).

However, international donors, in spite of sharing most of these logics and often being labelled as a 'community', are not homogeneous or unitary actors. First of all, international donors do not represent a homogenous bloc of countries with a single political agenda. While in the past the donors' plurality was amplified by colonial competition or Cold War divisions, nowadays it is nurtured by a new multipolar global order resulting from 'the rise of the South' and the emerging of 'unconventional' donor countries such as China, India, Brazil, Turkey or South Korea (Mawdsley, 2012; UNDP, 2013). As a result of the growing influence and presence in Ethiopia of such actors, an increasing portion of international aid is channelled through what is technically called 'off-budget assistance', bypassing the formal government–donors aid architecture and the traditional ODA channels recorded by international institutions, statistics and reports. Secondly, a high degree of plurality is also found within the so-called 'traditional donors', mainly the OECD-DAC (Development Assistance Committee) members. While sharing common principles and adopting a similar discourse emphasizing, for instance, good governance, accountability, rights, or aid effectiveness, donors in practice often follow diverging interests and competing agendas as national priorities trump multilateral coordination and harmonization (Borchgrevink, 2008). Thirdly, even in the context of bilateral relations, competing logics, diverging views and conflicting practices between different state bodies or bureaucratic institutions may arise within a single donor country. Discord might erupt between executive and legislative branches, between different government branches – for instance, those in charge of foreign policy and human rights vs those dealing with development or humanitarian issues – or between headquarters and field offices (Schlichte & Veit, 2007).

In particular, the relation between headquarters and country offices appears to be informed by logics of bureaucratic incrementalism (Schraeder, 1994). This notion captures the self-interested nature of bureaucratic agencies and their tendency both to enhance relationships with the host country and to widen the role of their own organization within the metropolitan policy-making establishment. Foreign diplomats and development workers are often subjected to pressures from host governments and subsidiaries of international firms. Furthermore, bureaucratic incrementalism explains why aid workers aim to increase foreign aid budgets of their programmes as it gives them greater possibilities to improve their own position within the administrative hierarchy (Schraeder, 1994: 24). The recourse to image-management strategies aimed at misleading national or foreign masters (Bayart, 2000: 259; Fisher, 2012) is not only a prerogative of recipient countries bargaining their insertion within the international system, but also of diplomats and aid workers who need to 'sell' projects to their respective headquarters. Finally, interventions and interests of different development brokers influence donor–recipient relationships. These brokers might be foreign consultants providing technical assistance to international development organizations and local government institutions, NGOs or private companies, working in the agriculture, infrastructures, oil, mining or manufacturing sectors, often pursuing their commercial objectives aligned with their donor country's 'national interest'. The technical expertise of these actors plays a crucial role in proposing solutions to development 'problems', as well as in depoliticizing development by adopting the allegedly neutral vocabulary of international technical assistance (Ferguson, 1990). The political and professional careers of key individuals behind these high-modernist development programmes often straddle the different domains here identified: national governments, international organizations and bilateral donor agencies, NGOs and local and international corporations.

Development as an ordinary state of exception Both in the past and present the collusion between Ethiopian rulers inspired by high modernism and international donors and companies active in 'development' has materialized in exceptional practices of implementing aid programmes in the country. Making use of Agamben (2003), Toggia (2008) has highlighted how historically different Ethiopian regimes have resorted to a state of emergency to discipline and normalize their respective body politics, invoking the need to ensure 'public order' in the name of the 'consent' or the 'general will' of the population (Toggia, 2008). The normalization of exceptional practices pervades modern Ethiopian regimes' strategies of territorializing state power and disciplining unruly populations in the periphery (Hagmann & Korf, 2012). Commercial companies engaged in infrastructural or agricultural projects may at times reinforce these strategies.

As we will demonstrate in the empirical section of this chapter, in Ethiopia the international aid apparatus has repeatedly legitimized the circumvention of the rule of law by implementing development projects in tune with Ethiopian regimes' authoritarian exercise of power. Donors have been invoking the emergence of exceptional conditions – typically droughts, famines or displacement – to bypass conventional standards of democracy, accountability and transparency. Donors justify the adoption of exceptional measures in different ways that will be illustrated empirically through the two case studies.

First, as Scott reminds us, 'the temporal emphasis of high modernism is almost exclusively on the future' (Scott, 1998: 95). The high-modernist approach works by subtraction, framing issues such as poverty or development as permanent faults in relation to necessary models and desirable objectives set at the international and national levels. Consequently, the negotiation and implementation of development policies and programmes in Ethiopia is marked by a sense of urgency and speed at any cost.

Second, international aid flows to Ethiopia occur within the framework of the rhetoric of necessity that allows ordinary regulations to be bypassed, with the impossibility of distinguishing between the rule and the exception becoming the norm. This applies not only to traditional humanitarian initiatives in response to disaster and emergencies like drought and famines, but also to long-term development programmes. The implementation of the latter constantly refers to a state of necessity justified by moral and political considerations: the need to improve the population's material living conditions, the will to ensure the effectiveness of programmes and initiatives, the imperative of a fast disbursement to abide by national government or international agencies' financial calendars and quantitative targets.

Third, by officially referring to the international development discourse and to the Ethiopian government's narrative of people and country transformation, these practices uphold the authoritarian and coercive exercise of political power. This emerges at the nexus between military and development emergency, 'with an implicit assimilation between war and economy' (Agamben, 2003: 23, our translation) both in symbolic and material terms. Thus the narrative of the 'fight against poverty' is matched with the adoption within development policies of traditional military devices – such as the camp or resettlement policies – or strategies developed by the Derg and EPRDF during the 1977–1991 civil war, such as the fighters' monitoring and sanctioning practice of *gimgema* developed by the TPLF during the civil war and later adopted by EPRDF as an 'account-ability mechanism' within the public administration (Vaughan & Tronvoll, 2003).

The following sections illustrate these theoretical considerations on historical continuity in the relationship between the Ethiopian government and international donors with two case studies focusing on imperial and contemporary Ethiopia respectively: the cotton plantation Tendaho Plantation Share Company in the lower Awash Valley (1960–67), and the Gilgel Gibe II hydropower plant in the Omo river basin, south-western Ethiopia (2004–2010).

The Tendaho Plantation Share Company (1960–1967)

The first case study looks at a cotton development programme undertaken in the Lower Awash Valley between 1960 and 1967, and implemented by the British firm Mitchell Cotts in collaboration with foreign donors. It highlights how dominant narratives of modernization and national progress were appropriated to depoliticize domestic power struggles at the periphery and bypass accountability procedures inherent in foreign aid. By exploiting its connections with higher officials in Great Britain and the United Nations, Mitchell Cotts broadened the imperial regime's extraversion portfolio, providing it with more leverage to negotiate the relationship with donors. Concomitantly, the British firm acted as an auxiliary of the central government in promoting the territorialization of state power along the eastern periphery. Eager to improve their stance within their own organization and vis-à-vis the Ethiopian establishment, concerned British officers justified their action in the name of a developmental paternalism.

High modernism and international aid The Lower Awash Valley lies in the north-eastern corner of Ethiopia at the intersection between the border with Djibouti and Eritrea. Formally incorporated within the Ethiopian empire in 1895, it was still a semi-independent enclave in the 1950s and the presence of the Ethiopian state was limited to a few military garrisons along the strategic routes to Assab and Djibouti (Markakis, 2011). The area was governed by Sultan Ali Mirah. Local prerogatives over land and water access were vested in the local clan structure and the *malaks*, who acted as officers of his sultanate. Having come to power in 1944 and invested with the Abyssinian title of *Dejamatzch* in 1954, Ali Mirah represented the Afar people before Haile Selassie and the Crown Prince Asfa Wossen, to whom he paid an annual tribute. Because of this arrangement, Ali Mirah could bypass the sub-provincial and provincial administrative hierarchy, enjoying direct access to the emperor's offices (Bondestam, 1974; Markakis, 2011). The imperial court followed a typical Abyssinian ruling strategy in the lowlands, aimed at maximizing revenue extraction without incurring the administrative costs associated direct rule (Donham & James, 2002). This strategy was nonetheless contested by a wide range of stakeholders who looked at the sultanate as the *nemesis* of state sovereignty in the Awash

Valley: the emerging rank and files within the imperial bureaucracy and the armed forces; the prime minister's inner circle; the Wollo provincial governor and the Awsa sub-provincial governor (Soulé, 2011).

Centre–periphery relations in the Lower Awash were shaped by the cotton development programme launched in the late 1950s as part of an import substitution strategy by the United Nations. UN consultants detached to the imperial government envisaged the creation of an agro-industrial sector linking cotton farming in the lowlands with the emerging textile industry in urban centres (Nicholson, 1957). The driver of cotton capitalism in the Lower Awash was Mitchell Cotts and Company-Ethiopia, a subsidiary of the British public company Mitchell Cotts Ltd. On November 1960, Mitchell Cotts signed a thirty-three-year agreement with the imperial government to establish a 100,000-hectare cotton plantation, later to be divided into three separate 6,000-hectare units. In 1962, Mitchell Cotts and the Ethiopian government gave birth to the Tendaho Plantation Share Company (TPSC), a joint venture that would promote cotton production and marketing in close collaboration with the parastatal Awash Valley Authority (AVA).[3]

Mitchell Cotts intended to replicate in Ethiopia a successful cotton production scheme it had earlier on implemented in colonial Sudan. Not incidentally, the special advisor enrolled by Mitchell Cotts was Arthur Gaitskell, a former manager at the Gezira scheme.[4] The plantation model reflected the dominant paradigm of agricultural development in the 1950s and early 1960s. UN consultants looked at peasant agriculture as backward and inefficient. Their point of reference was a capital-intensive enclave economy surrounded by a subsistence sector devoted to providing an inelastic supply of labour. In this perspective, the scarcely inhabited and land-abundant lowlands appeared as an ideal site to spread Western agricultural knowledge and grow raw materials for the needs of the textile industry (Congdon, 1961). Irrigation canals and dams would follow soon, generating new economic opportunities for the Afar people and electricity for the country as a whole. TPSC was the vanguard of high modernism, the Awash Valley a *tabula rasa* to be remodelled to spread the seeds of progress. FAO advisors projected into imperial Ethiopia the utilitarian perspective of the state that looks at its territory through the lens of revenue needs. Accordingly, the multifaceted ecological landscape of the Lower Awash had to be simplified for the needs of fiscal knowledge (Scott, 1998: 15). Cadastral surveys and land mapping would help with planning the most rational exploitation of natural resources. In turn, cotton farming would increase fiscal revenues by promoting the monetization of the economy and transforming scattered communities of nomads into sedentary farmers whose surplus could be easily forecast and appropriated.

The Ethiopian government was eager to obtain foreign assistance to finance infrastructural constructions, increase revenues for the public coffers and legitimize itself in face of the younger generations who had acclaimed at the aborted 1960 coup-d'état led by the Imperial Body Guard (Haregot, 2013). Haile Selassie appeased the donors by using the idiom of international development: in 1957, his recently created National Economic Council published the First Five Year Development Plan, promising to turn 'a nation of farmers and pastoralists into a nation of merchants and industrialists' (McVety, 2012: 145). In 1962, the Second Five Year Development Plan marked the commitment towards modernization by appropriating faithfully the basic tenets of Walt Rostow's path towards economic growth: raising labour productivity; improving the rational exploitation of national resources; increasing annual savings to promote investment rates; accelerating the transition from an agricultural economy towards an industrialized one (McVety, 2012: 174–5). Development was not only the language of higher authorities eager to obtain the blessing of Western economists and World Bank officers. With its emphasis on central planning, agricultural extensions and enlightened bureaucracies, modernization could provide the 'centralizers' within the Ethiopian polity with the material and conceptual tools required for political centralization and administrative deconcentration in the Lower Awash (Hagmann & Péclard, 2010). In fact, as much as commercial agriculture, direct rule required technology, infrastructure and knowledge of the territory to overcome the resistance of local elites. Not incidentally, the man who first forecast the benefits of cotton farming in the Lower Awash was not a Harvard-trained intellectual or an advisor of the Ministry of Agriculture, but a lower officer in charge of the Awsa sub-province who inevitably looked at the independence of the sultanate as a growing challenge to his authority. In 1956, the Awsa governor wrote to the governor of Wollo province, recommending the best lands be granted to Dutch investors interested in rice farming. His preference for cash crops was only marginally shaped by the purpose of creating rural employment. By introducing large-scale commercial agriculture, he planned to build a society of easily controllable sedentary agriculturalists, but most of all he hoped to convince the central government to send the long-time requested additional troops to enforce state authority within his jurisdiction.[5]

Donors' internal plurality and private companies' brokerage The cotton programme in the Lower Awash highlights the plurality of interests shaping the outcomes of development projects, as well as the blurred boundary between private and public concerns. In the first years of operations, the fiscal logic of FAO officials and the profit-oriented logic of Mitchell Cotts coincided perfectly. Intelligibility was such that the first plantation manager appointed by the British group was John Congdon, an FAO special consultant to the Ethiopian government for the cotton programme in 1960–1961. Congdon's 1961 report highlighted how concerns of social equity and the necessity to relieve the overcrowded highlands made a joint venture between large estates and small peasants more opportune, suggesting the establishment of an organization responsible for the distribution of inputs to small farmers as well as the collection, processing and marketing of crops (Congdon, 1961). This solution was endorsed by Mitchell Cotts, whose pilot scheme's harvest had not been as successful as expected. Gaitskell suggested to move production around Assayta where land was deemed to be more fertile, and to increase the supply of cotton by providing technical assistance to surrounding outgrowers.[6] Accordingly, in 1962 Mitchell Cotts signed a new memorandum with the Ethiopian government. The firm obtained the effective establishment of AVA, whose creation had been imposed by the British as a critical precondition during the early negotiations in 1960.[7] The agency, supported by a FAO/UNDP programme of technical assistance and composed of a team of Western-trained engineers and economists, would manage the allocation of land and water rights in place of the traditional Afar authorities (Bondestam, 1974). The AVA was also supposed to manage agricultural settlement schemes in the plantation's surrounding areas, both as a tool to compensate displaced Afar pastoralists for the expropriation of their grazing lands (Harbeson, 1978) and to strengthen a system of compulsory marketing cooperatives for the sale of the outgrowers' crop to TPSC. The British firm in turn would enjoy a de facto monopoly over cotton trading and would provide technical assistance, ginning facilities and marketing outlets to surrounding outgrowers.[8]

Mitchell Cotts had a very clear idea of how the empire should deal with the sultanate. The institutional point of reference was the Gezira scheme in Sudan, where the colonial government had played a critical role in the expropriation and successive allocation of land and water rights via the Sudan Plantations Syndicate. Moreover, they feared that Ali Mirah would exploit his influence over Afar subjects to oppose the full allocation of the promised land and water. In fact, the first meeting between Mitchell Cotts and the sultan had been marked by hostility, the sultan having been forced to accept the intrusion of TPSC only after the mediation of the imperial government (Soulé, 2011: 90). Consequently, according to the 1962 agreement the central government had to establish new administrative outposts and police stations at Dubti and Assayta. Contrary to the Awsa governor, powerless in the face of the emperor's refusal to contest the arrangement with Ali Mirah, Mitchell Cotts had good arguments to sustain its demand for stronger state intervention. The British group was firmly entrenched in Ethiopia well before the launch of the cotton project, operating in the import–export of coffee on the Addis Ababa market since the 1950s. One of Mitchell Cotts' general directors in London was Sir Chapman-Andrews, a former foreign officer who had developed a close relationship with Haile Selassie during the 1941 war campaign in Eastern Africa.[9] TPSC had also strong links with the Ethiopian Treasury, which owned a 30 per cent minority share in the joint venture, and the Ministry of Commerce.[10] Finally, the company had the almost unconditional support of the Foreign Office's Africa Department and the British embassy in Addis Ababa. In a report to London, the British ambassador depicted TPSC as 'the sort of scheme which the Ethiopians are crying for', stressing the opportunity that the British Treasury would support it by negotiating an aid package as soon as possible.[11] During the 1960 negotiations, despite the negative response by the British government to the request for financial assistance,[12] the Africa Department suggested the ambassador accompany Mitchell Cotts' managers in their calls with the Ethiopians, 'as it would make us appear more committed than what we really are'.[13]

Development as an ordinary state of exception The British embassy's support of Mitchell Cotts persisted also when the firm's business priorities clashed with the British policy objectives in Ethiopia. The British government was committed to promoting the gradual transition of the imperial system towards a constitutional monarchy. In particular, British officers monitored carefully the evolution of the relationship between the government and the Ethiopian parliament, which had been opened to electoral competition by the 1955 Constitution. In 1966, the British embassy reported with satisfaction the growing political consciousness of Ethiopian deputies, after they rejected an Italian loan agreement in spite of the prime minister and the emperor's blessing.[14] The British ambassador, Russell, did not support the quest for democratization on a mere ideological basis: he was convinced that political liberalization was a critical precondition for a smooth transition in a post-Haile Selassie period.[15] Accordingly, in February 1967 a group of Ethiopian deputies and the president of the Senate were invited to visit the British House of Commons.[16] Conscious of the emperor's attention to his own international posture, the former ambassador to Ethiopia, Douglas Busk, did not hesitate to write an article undercover in the *Economist* to persuade Haile Selassie to delegate more powers to Prince Asfa Wossen, who was considered sympathetic to the idea of a parliamentary Monarchy.[17]

The local embassy's concerns for the democratization of Ethiopia disappeared rapidly in 1967, when London and Addis Ababa engaged in negotiations over the first tranche of the £2 million aid package signed in 1964. The project on the roundtable consisted of the financing of expansion works on TPSC's second plantation unit at Dit Bahari.[18] According to the Imperial Constitution, the parliament had to approve every single project financed by foreign loans. Nonetheless, the similarities between the envisaged Tendaho loan and the Italian aid package rejected by the parliament in 1966 made a negative vote very probable. Ethiopian deputies criticized the high interest rates, the British veto power over the choice of the project, and the idea of using a loan at subsidized interest rates for relending to an overseas commercial firm.[19] Conscious of the situation and in strong need of foreign currency, Minister of Finance Ylma Deressa decided, in consultation with the British embassy, to legally bypass the vote of the Chamber of Deputies.[20] In face of the growing criticism stemming from London against a procedure that clashed with the overall democratization policy, British diplomatic agents and TPSC managers transmitted to the British government a new representation of local events, in order to make their behaviour coherent with the commitments embedded in the aid relationship.

If, some months earlier, parliamentary opposition to the Italian loan had been depicted as 'a promising sign for the future',[21] the pluralism of opinions within the imperial establishment was now perceived as a potential restraint to the progress of the country. When the British Ministry for Overseas Development (ODM) suggested approaching the prime minister and the minister of foreign affairs to obtain support for the British loan, the local embassy insisted on relying exclusively on the Ministry of Finance, whereas the first option would mean a further loss of time and money for TPSC immediately before the sowing season.[22] Concerns from London about the marginalization of Parliament were dismissed on the ground of the irresponsibility of local politicians, who needed to be driven along the correct way to development. When the ODM raised doubts about the unorthodox proposals of the Ministry of Finance, not incidentally rejected by the Ministry of Justice, the British embassy described the reaction of the latter as a mere interministerial squabble 'which frequently bedevils one's work here'.[23]

The fact that the emperor's legal advisor and the parliamentary expert at the American embassy underlined the unconstitutionality of the procedure did not change the picture.[24] Similarly, when the ODM expressed concerns about the opportunity to provide a metropolitan company with subsidized loans via foreign aid, implicitly recognizing the doubts expressed by some Ethiopian deputies, the managers of TPSC insisted that the Dit Bahari scheme was more in the interest of the Ethiopian nation as a whole than of Mitchell Cotts itself.[25] This strategy produced the intended outcome: in autumn 1967, the British government agreed to a joint appraisal study of the project in London, with the participation of Mitchell Cotts and Ethiopian experts. Once the Tendaho loan issue was overcome, local diplomatic agents turned back to the official policy of strengthening the parliament and promoting administrative transparency. Four years later, in 1971, an astonished political officer at the British embassy reported with some criticism to the Foreign Office the anomalies of a parliamentary system where 'the Government can sometimes get around the laws with impunity'.[26]

The Gilgel Gibe II hydropower project (2004–2010)

The second case examines the more recent hydropower project in Ethiopia's south-western Omo Valley. This major infrastructure development has been funded by the Italian government and was implemented by the Italian firm Salini Costruttori contracted by the Ethiopian Electric Power Corporation (EEPCO). Similar to the previous case study focusing on the imperial period, this case study highlights the Ethiopian government's ability to legitimize controversial high-modernist schemes by appropriating international development discourse and to exploit individual donor interests; the brokerage played by private companies, influencing the definition of both the Ethiopian government and the donor's interests by virtue of political links as well as of technical mastering of the issues; and the adoption of exceptional measures upholding authoritarian exercise of power within projects funded by 'traditional' donors like Italy.

High modernism and authoritarianism The Ethiopian government has identified the energy sector, hydropower in particular, as the backbone of its strategy on development and economic growth (Federal Democratic Republic of Ethiopia, 2010). Consequently, it embarked on an unprecedented energy sector development based on large hydropower dams, aiming at quadrupling national energy production by 2015. The biggest – and most controversial – projects are the Great Ethiopian Renaissance Dam (GERD), currently built along the Nile river in the western Benishangul region, close to the border with Sudan, and the complex of three dams and four power plants along the Gibe river, in the south-western Omo Valley in the Oromia region, not far from the Kenyan border. The Ethiopian government presents hydropower as an example of 'sustainable management of natural resources' to cope with climate change, within the national 'climate-resilient green economy strategy' (Federal Democratic Republic of Ethiopia, 2011).[27] Mega-dams are justified by referring to the Ethiopian huge hydropower potential (estimated at 45,000 MW, more than the current power production of the whole of sub-Saharan Africa) and dams' comparative advantages, both ecologically and economically, in respect to other countries in the region. Moreover, hydropower expansion is considered a key element to sustain the steady process of economic growth that earned Ethiopia the title of 'African lion' or 'emerging African country' (McKinsey Global Institute, 2010; Radelet, 2010). Domestic production of low-cost energy is hoped to become a comparative advantage for the growing Ethiopian manufacturing sector, emancipating it from oil imports. In addition, energy development is designed at exporting nearly half of the supply that will be generated in the coming years. Hydropower is also considered a 'social energy', essential to eradicate poverty. In spite of its potential, Ethiopia has one of the world's lowest rates of access to energy services and consumption: in rural areas, where 80 per cent of the population live, less than 5 per cent have effective access to electric power. Annual per capita consumption in Ethiopia in 2009 was 100 kWh against the sub-Saharan regional average of 478 kWh.[28]

As in most cases of large infrastructure development and high-modernist schemes, dams are nowadays at the core of the process of the Ethiopian state building in symbolic and material terms (Gascon, 2008). The development of Ethiopia's hydropower potential is presented as an issue of national sovereignty, defying the obstructions by foreign actors such as the Egyptian government, the World Bank or international environmental NGOs, but also as a prerequisite for poverty reduction and economic growth. Dams tangibly reaffirm the presence of the Ethiopian state, its practices of territorialization and its performance in terms of economic development and re-engineering of rural society. In fact, most of these mega-dams are associated with the development of modern agricultural systems, based on irrigation and market-oriented production that are funded by international private investors. Current strategies of state territorialization through the development of the hydropower sector are in continuity with previous regimes' modernization schemes 'bent on technology-driven "development" and top-down planning at all cost by a self-declared all-knowing state elite' (Abbink, 2012).

Hydropower sector expansion is associated with coercive measures and authoritarian exercise of power. By adopting the depoliticizing and techno-cratic discourse of development (Ferguson, 1990), the Ethiopian government does not allow open and critical debate on projects that are considered to be promoting the national interest and the public good. For instance, Meheret Debebe, CEO of EEPCO, in an interview about the GERD affirmed, 'the dam is not a political issue. Rather, it is a developmental project which determines the bright future of Ethiopia'.[29] Within EPRDF rhetoric, the 'fight against poverty' takes the relay of the 'fight against the Derg': for instance, the construction site of the Great Ethiopian Renaissance Dam was significantly inaugurated on *ginbot haya*, the day that celebrates the military victory by the EPRDF over/against the Derg. In the practices of people mobilization and resources control legitimated by this rhetoric, those who do not align with EPRDF official strategy, like in wartime, are considered dangerous trai-tors and dealt with accordingly (Segers *et al.*, 2008; Lefort, 2012). In spite of their controversial impact in terms of financial sustainability, ecological consequences, social implications and geopolitical tensions along the Nile river basin, these projects have so far generated little public debate in Ethiopia. Critiques come mainly from international observers, human rights activists or co-riparian states, particularly Egypt.

Donors' internal plurality and private companies' brokerage The controversial impacts of Ethiopia hydropower projects and the opacity in their implementation have generated mistrust by international donors, who are reluctant to support such enterprises. An example of such a stance was the long and ultimately unsuccessful negotiation between the Ethiopian government, the World Bank and other Western donors around the funding of Gilgel Gibe III project. The World Bank and other donors withdrew from this process as the Ethiopian government had failed to comply with their requests in terms of social and environmental impact studies, as well as in terms of adherence to international bidding and procurement legislation. Consequently, the Ethiopian government reverted to selected international donors: initially the Italian government and later the Chinese one. These donors proved more flexible in their funding conditions, accepting the Ethiopian government's bypass of international and national bidding norms, and not scrutinizing in depth the projects' social and environmental impact. Later also the African Development Bank and the European Investment Bank funded part of the works, which had been sub-contracted to Salini through competitive bidding procedures in line with national and international legislation. In addition, a significant portion of the investment for these projects was mobilized domestically through government bonds, taxes and funds collection and donations by the population, whose voluntary nature remains questionable. The share of domestic funding seems unique for a low-income country like Ethiopia: it confirms the importance conferred to hydropower development as the 'new national enterprise' (Gascon, 2008).

In this context, the Gilgel Gibe II project is particularly relevant since it pioneered a 'fast-track approach' to planning, funding and implementing hydropower schemes. Exceptional measures and procedures were adopted by invoking the urgency and the necessity to rapidly sustain the processes and the goals of development and economic growth. Once successfully tested with Gilgel Gibe II, these practices have been reproduced and scaled up in more ambitious and controversial infrastructure development projects in Ethiopia such as Gilgel Gibe III, Gilgel Gibe IV, Tana Beles and the GERD.

In April 2004, the Ethiopian government signed a contract with the Italian corporation Salini Costruttori SpA for the construction of the Gilgel Gibe II hydropower plant, with an estimated cost of 400 million euros. The project consisted of a power station expected to generate 420 MW and alimented through a 26km-long tunnel drawing water from the Gilgel Gibe I reservoir, also built by Salini between 1997 and 2003 along the Gibe river. The project was supported by a loan of 220 million euros granted by the Italian government and by a 50 million euro loan from the European Investment Bank. The Ethiopian government provided the rest of the amount with its own funds. Gilgel Gibe II was originally scheduled to be completed in late 2007. However, it was inaugurated only in January 2010 because of engineering problems encountered during the construction.[30]

The reason for adopting a fast-track approach to implementing Gilgel Gibe II was to avoid compliance with conventional project management requirements such as project cycle management, which were reputed to have caused the slow implementation of previous projects, namely Gilgel Gibe I. In contrast, the 'fast-track approach' devised by Salini was adopted, starting all the different project phases – finalization of the design, financing schemes, contracting, construction works – at the same time.[31] This choice was justified by reference to the urgency to rapidly increase the country's energy production capacities, in order to meet a booming demand, and not to jeopardize its promising economic performance. In fact, the low current levels of energy production and consumption, matched with ambitious projections in terms of economic growth, authorize almost all kinds and sizes of hydropower expansion projects.

Gilgel Gibe II contract was awarded to Salini after direct negotiation with EEPCO and without international competitive bidding, which contravenes both Ethiopian and international procurement rules. In addition to urgently increasing the national power-generating capacity, the awarding of the contract to Salini was justified in terms of its unique knowledge of the local territory, namely its prior involvement in Gilgel Gibe I and its assistance in securing international funds. The Gilgel Gibe II project did not figure in the Ethiopian twenty-five-year national energy master plan that was elaborated in 2003. The Gilgel Gibe II project was autonomously designed by Salini and its partner Studio Pietrangeli following the construction of Gilgel Gibe I. It was later proposed to the Ethiopian government as a turnkey project and only then included in the national energy master plan by EEPCO. This strategy was replicated in the following years to integrate new dam projects designed by Salini and Studio Pietrangeli, confirming EEPCO's great flexibility and scarce accountability to other national bodies.

EEPCO is one of the oldest and most powerful parastatal companies, holding monopolistic control of energy production and distribution in Ethiopia. It was transformed into a corporation in 1997. Formally under the supervision of the Ministry of Water and Energy, EEPCO enjoys a high degree of political autonomy and power. It directly and informally reports to the Office of the Prime Minister, with its top management reputed as belonging to the inner circle of former Prime Minister Meles Zenawi. In recent years, by virtue of the large investments in the hydropower sector, it has become one of the champions of the Ethiopian developmental state, interpreting and showcasing EPRDF development strategies and achievements. Thus, Gilgel Gibe II and other dam projects were approved by executive decision bypassing quality checks and control by sector ministries and independent authorities such as the Ethiopian Electricity Agency (EEA) and the Environment Protection Agency (EPA), as well as Parliament and the regional authority that oversees land allocation.

Salini was awarded an Engineering, Procurement and Construction (EPC) contract, negotiated for a lump-sum price in exchange for full completion of the project. This type of contract gives greater authority to the contractor, who, in return, bears greater technical and financial risks. Under this contract, EEPCO's responsibility is reduced to paying the contractor and monitoring the project. However, the fact that Gilgel Gibe II was approved without any feasibility study jeopardized EPCO interests and the capacity to control Salini and hold it accountable.[32] In addition, the Environmental Impact and the Social Impact Assessments were completed almost a year after the beginning of the construction on the site (Hathaway, 2008).

This kind of agreement was also made possible by the peculiarity of Salini Costruttori and Studio Pietrangeli and their history in the country. Both are Italian family-owned companies with a long record of involvement in Ethiopia, dating back to the end of the 1970s, when they built the Legedadi water system to supply the capital, Addis Ababa. Their joint venture currently operates in the construction of Tana Beles, Gilgel Gibe IV and Great Ethiopian Renaissance dams. Salini, in particular, does not merely operate like an international contractor, moving around the globe in search of the most profitable tenders. Rather, it operates like a local investor, assuming its own risks following long-terms interests and a strategy of permanent stay in the country. Thus it was ready to sign a contract worth 10 per cent of the overall Ethiopian federal annual budget in April 2010 and immediately start construction works, even though full financial coverage had not been secured at that point.

Moreover, by mobilizing its connections within the Ethiopian and the Italian governments, Salini acted as a broker to ensure project funding. Negotiations between Addis Ababa and Rome were conducted directly by high-level officers attached to the Ethiopian Prime Minister's Office and the Italian Ministry of Foreign Affairs, with the mediation of Salini. The Italian Ministry of Foreign Affairs-Directorate General for Development Cooperation, as well as the Italian embassy in Ethiopia and its Development Cooperation Office were completely bypassed and informed about the project only once the contract was awarded.[33] They became involved only in the technical appraisal phase once the political agreement was concluded and the contract with Salini already signed. Thus, in spite of energy and water not being included among the priorities and sectors of intervention of the Ethio-Italian Country programme at the time under implementation, the Gilgel Gibe II received a fast track technical appraisal. This led to the signature in November 2004 of a bilateral agreement between the Ethiopian and the Italian governments, with the latter granting a subsidized loan of 220 million euros, the largest in the history of the Italian Development Cooperation Office, in spite of objections raised by the Italian ambassador to Ethiopia, the directorate general for development cooperation of the Ministry of Foreign Affairs and the Ministry of Finance.[34]

The first two criticized the lack of compliance with international procurement norms in awarding the contract and the lack of adequate documentation on the social and environmental impact of the project. The Ministry of Finance raised questions about the sustainability of Ethiopian foreign debt and the plausibility of the repayment back. Ironically, two pages later within the same agreement, the Italian government agreed to annul the whole of the 332 million euros of bilateral debt owed by Ethiopia.

The Italian embassy in Addis Ababa, particularly its Development Cooperation Office, was initially hesitant to get involved in the project. It did so primarily because it was pushed by its superiors; only later on did it take ownership of the project. They were called to manage a 500,000 euro grant for monitoring and evaluation of the project. These funds helped to boost the Development Cooperation Office and to hire technical experts to engage in policy dialogue between the Ethiopian government and the donors in the water and energy sector. By virtue of its endeavour in the hydropower sector, after the beginning of the Gilgel Gibe II works, the Italian Development Cooperation Office affirmed its presence among leading donors in the water sector. In 2006, it become the Chair of the Water Donors Working Group in the country although it has no other commitment in the sector beside the Gilgel Gibe II loan, thus achieving the 'visibility' and 'influence' that international development bureaucracies often seek to obtain.

Development as an ordinary state of exception The Gilgel Gibe II project represents yet another example of exceptional measures adopted in the name of internationally funded development in Ethiopia, this time in the energy/ hydropower sector. Energy is traditionally seen as one of the strategic sectors where the Ethiopian government retains monopolistic control. However, Gilgel Gibe II and other large dam projects show how the expansion of energy development programmes and its modalities were strongly influenced by technical knowledge and private funding provided by non-state actors involving a plurality of interests: private companies, bilateral donors and their bureaucracies. The Ethiopian government, and EEPCO in particular, have been the main architects of this strategy that implies outsourcing the technical and financial aspects of a development strategy to a private actor by virtue of executive, and thus undemocratic, decision. In doing so, they were able to extravert aid resources in the pursuit of what is, ultimately, an authoritarian strategy of state expansion and control over populations and resources in the country's periphery. Gilgel Gibe II was implemented in a scarcely populated area and had relatively little impact in social and environmental terms as it did not necessitate the construction of a large dam and a water reservoir. However, Gilgel Gibe II paved the way for more controversial projects like Gilgel Gibe III, IV or the Great Renaissance Dam. These projects have been supported by the Chinese government, through loans provided by state-owned commercial banks like the Industrial and Commercial Bank of China, following the same exceptional measures of the 'fast-track' approach inaugurated with Gilgel Gibe II. The states of exception that accompany the implementation of all these projects imply that citizen and communities affected by the dams' construction cannot protect their rights and hold accountable an increasingly authoritarian government (CEE Bankwatch Network, 2008; Hataway, 2008; Abbink, 2012; Mains, 2012).

Conclusion

The two cases in this chapter – the cotton production in the Awash in the 1960s supported by the British and the hydropower development in the 2000s funded by the Italian government – highlight important historical continuities in the way in which successive Ethiopian governments and their international donors pursue high-modernist development schemes that contribute to the authoritarian exercise of power in the country. Both cases display strong similarity in the way in which different Ethiopian regimes make use of development to incorporate the periphery as part of state territorialization and social engineering. Ethiopian elites have been effective in appropriating the vocabulary of international development discourse to legitimize these projects and to attract foreign support. Moreover, the presence of a strong central state, displaying higher capacities in terms of policy implementation and territory control in comparison to other African countries, facilitates and perpetuates foreign donors' support to Ethiopia. In this context, a genuine commitment by Ethiopian ruling classes towards transforming and developing the country overlap and coexist with the use of development programmes to uphold and legitimize the authoritarian exercise of political power.

Second, the two cases draw attention to the internal plurality and contradictions among donors. Rather than a homogeneous 'community', international donors appear as competing in an arena shaped by a multiplicity of actors, agendas and conflicting interests. Two elements emerge as particularly significant in reproducing and expanding international aid in support of Ethiopian high-modernist schemes, regardless of their authoritarian nature. On the one hand, bureaucratic incrementalism drives the daily working of the international development apparatus. Consequently, the influence and the effectiveness of donors' agencies and country offices are assessed by looking at the size of their budget and at the rapidity of their disbursement, rather than at the broader political impact and consequences of their work. On the other hand, private companies, which by virtue of their political influence, economic interests and technical knowledge, act as development brokers shaping donors' and recipient government's 'national interest' and development strategies. The straddling of professional careers between national governments, international institutions and private companies contributes to a blurring of the distinctions between these organizations and to the transformation private firms into powerful instruments that implement the *raison d'état*.

Finally, the two cases highlight how, by referring to moral and humanitarian considerations stressing the urgency and the necessity to promote the public interests of development, high modernist development schemes ordinarily work by adopting exceptional measures. The fact that both the United Kingdom and Italy supported and actively contributed to undemocratic practices, challenges conventional assumptions about 'responsible' Western donors devoted to good governance, accountability and transparency while new donors, namely China, are represented as 'irresponsible' powers unbothered by their support for authoritarian rule. This final point highlights not only the nexus between international aid and authoritarian rule in sub-Saharan Africa, but also Western donors' unkept promises in terms of furthering democratic standards in their policies and programmes.

Notes

1 OECD Aid Statistics, http://www.oecd.org/dac/stats/

2 See OECD Aid Development statistics.

3 National Archives of the United Kingdom (thereafter NA), FO 371/138085, VA 1331/6, telegram from Ashe to British embassy (1331/62), 19 December 1962.

4 NA, FO 371/165325, from Joy to Beith, 21 February 1962.

5 National Archives and Library of Ethiopia, Folder 134.45, from Awsa Awraja governor, Felleke Dagne to Dezjamatch Dereje Makonnen, governor of Wollo, 3-1-1949 (EC).

6 NA, FO 371/165325, 1331/62, confidential, telegram from Loy to Foreign Office, 21 February 1962.

7 NA, FO 371/165325,Ja 1331/5, telegram from British embassy in Addis to Boothby, 12 November 1960.

8 NA, FO 371/138085, VA 1331/6, telegram from Ashe to British Embassy (1331/62), 19 December 1962.

9 NA, FCO 31/795, telegram from Alan Campbell, British embassy in Addis Ababa, to Le Tocq, East African Department, 28 June 1971.

10 NA, FO 371/146609, J A 1331/5,60, telegram from UK mission to the UN,

New York, to African Department, 23 November 1960.

11 NA, FO 371/146609, JA 1331/2, telegram from DAH Wright to Foreign Office, 10 October 1960.

12 NA, FO 371/146609, JA 1331/2, letter from Bendall, 3 October 1960.

13 NA, FO 371/146609, JA 1331/3, telegram from Boothby to British embassy in Addis Ababa, 25 October, 1960, confidential.

14 NA, FO 371/190146, Va 1015/34, telegram from Stimson, 21 November 1966.

15 NA, FO 371/190146, VA 1015/25, confidential report from J Russell, 26 May 1966.

16 NA, FO 371/190146, VA 1015/34, telegram from Stimson, 21 November 1966.

17 NA, FCO 31/785, telegram from LeTocq to Campbell, 'Inspired Press Articles on Ethiopia', 5 April 1971.

18 NA, FCO 39/63, UK loan to Ethiopia, first meeting, 15 February 1967.

19 NA, FCO 39/63, Modev 46 from British embassy, Addis Ababa, to Ministry for Overseas Development, 5 April 1967.

20 NA, FCO 39/63, telegram from

British embassy, Addis Ababa, to Ministry for Overseas Development, 21 July 1967.

21 NA, FO 371/190146, telegram 1015/34 from Stimson, 21 November 1966.

22 NA, FCO 39/63,NA, telegram 76, from Ministry Overseas Development to Addis Ababa, 19 April 1967.

23 NA, FCO 39/63, telegram 118 from British embassy, Addis Ababa, to Ministry for Overseas Development, 13 July 1967.

24 NA, FCO 39/63, telegram 60 from British embassy, Addis Ababa, to Ministry for Overseas Development, 12 April 1967.

25 NA, FCO 39/63, note of a meeting with Mitchell Cotts on 25 September in Mr King's room.

26 NA, FCO 31/781, telegram from JS Wall to PB Hall, 19 July 1971.

27 To stress this concern by the Ethiopian government, in the last years former Prime Minister Meles Zenawi has been leading the African delegation to major UN climate change conferences.

28 UNDP and World Bank statistics.

29 *The Ethiopian Herald*, 21 April 2011.

30 Almost two weeks after inauguration, a portion of the tunnel collapsed. The station was shut down and reopened at the end of 2010.

31 A short clip describing the approach is available on the Salini website (http://www.salini.it/en/gruppo/innovazione-ricerca-e-sviluppo/fast-track/ viewed on 30 of October 2013). Significantly, it does not make any explicit reference to feasibility studies, as well as social and environmental appraisals.

32 This was, for instance, evident in the lack of instruments used by the Ethiopian government and EEPCO in particular to challenge the major milestone decisions made in the design of Gilgel Gibe II Tunnel, especially in relation to the geological and geophysical study, and thus avoiding the delays that occurred due to collapse of the tunnel (Kinde & Egenda, 2010).

33 Italian embassy in Addis Ababa, officer, interview with the author, April 2008.

34 Italian embassy in Addis Ababa,

officers, interview with the author, April 2008 and May 2010. On the same issue, see also the report by the environmental activists of the CEE Bankwatch Network (2008).

References

Aalen, L & Tronvoll, K (2009a), 'The 2008 Ethiopian local elections: the return of electoral authoritarianism', *African Affairs*, vol. 108, no. 430, pp. 111–20.

Aalen, L & Tronvoll, K (2009b), 'The end of democracy? Curtailing political and civil rights in Ethiopia', *Review of African Political Economy*, vol. 36, no. 120, pp. 193–207.

Abbink, J (2006), 'Discomfiture of democracy? The 2005 election crisis in Ethiopia and its aftermath', *African Affairs*, vol. 105, no. 419, pp. 173–99.

Abbink, J (2012), 'Dam controversies: contested governance and developmental discourse on the Ethiopian Omo River dam', *Social Anthropology*, vol. 20, no. 2, pp. 125–44.

Agamben, G (2003), *Stato di eccezione*, Bollati Boringhieri, Torino.

Alemu, G (2009), *A case study on aid effectiveness in Ethiopia: analysis of the health sector aid architecture*, Wolfensohn Center for Development, Global Economy and Development at Brookings, Working Paper No. 9.

Bach, JN (2011), 'Abyotawi democracy: neither revolutionary nor democratic, a critical review of EPRDF's conception of revolutionary democracy in post-1991 Ethiopia', *Journal of Eastern African Studies*, vol. 5, no. 4, pp. 641–63.

Bayart JF (2000), 'Africa in the world: a history of extraversion', *African Affairs*, vol. 99, no. 395, pp. 217–67.

Bondestam L (1974), 'People and capitalism in the northeastern lowlands of Ethiopia', *Journal of Modern African Studies*, vol. 12, no. 3, pp. 423–39.

Borchgrevink, A (2008), 'Limits to donor influence: Ethiopia, aid and conditionality', *Forum for Development Studies*, vol. 35, no. 2, pp. 195–220.

CEE Bankwatch (2008), 'The Gilgel Gibe affair. An analysis of the Gilgel Gibe hydroelectric project in Ethiopia', viewed 21 April 2014, http://bankwatch.org/publications/gilgel-gibe-affair-analysis-gilbel-gibe-hydroelectric-projects-ethiopia

Chinigò, D (2013), 'Decentralization and agrarian transformation in Ethiopia: extending the power of the federal state', *Critical African Studies*, vol. 6, no. 1, pp. 40–56.

Clapham, C (1987), *Transformation and continuity in revolutionary Ethiopia*, Cambridge University Press, Cambridge.

Clapham, C (2006), 'Ethiopian development: the politics of emulation', *Commonwealth & Comparative Politics*, vol. 44, no. 1, pp. 137–50.

Congdon JL (1961), *Report no. 1376 to the government of Ethiopia on cotton production*, FAO, Rome.

Donham, DL (1999), *Marxist modern: an ethnographic history of the Ethiopian revolution*, University of California Press, Berkeley and Los Angeles.

Donham, DL & James, W (eds), 2002, *The southern marches of imperial Ethiopia: essays in history and social anthropology*, James Currey, Oxford.

Enten, F (2010), 'Du bon usage des systèmes d'alerte précoce en régime autoritaire', *Politique africaine*, no. 119, pp. 43–62.

Epstein, H (2010), 'Cruel Ethiopia', *The New York Review of Books*, 1 May.

Federal Democratic Republic of Ethiopia (2010), *Growth and transformation plan 2010/11–2014/15*, Ministry of Finance and Economic Development, Addis Ababa.

Federal Democratic Republic of Ethiopia (2011), *Ethiopia's climate resilient green economy strategy*, Addis Ababa.

Ferguson, J (1990), *The anti-politics machine: 'development', depoliticization, and bureaucratic power in Lesotho*, University of Minnesota Press, Minneapolis.

Fantini, E (2008), 'Good governance? Decentramento amministrativo ed elezioni locali in Etiopia', *Afriche e Orienti*, no. 2, pp. 143–49.

Fassin, D & Pandolfi, M (eds) (2010), *Contemporary states of emergency: the politics of military and humanitarian interventions*, Zone Books, New York.

Feyissa, D (2011), 'Aid negotiation: the uneasy "partnership" between EPRDF and the donors', *Journal of Eastern African Studies*, vol. 5, no. 4, pp. 788–817.

Fisher, J (2012), 'Managing donor perceptions and securing agency: contextualizing Uganda's 2007 intervention in Somalia', *African Affairs*, vol. 111, no. 444, pp. 404–23.

Furtado, X & Smith, W J (2008), 'Ethiopia: retaining sovereignty in aid relations', in L Whitfield (ed.), *The politics of aid: African strategies for dealing with donors*, Oxford University Press, Oxford, pp. 131–55.

Gascon, A (2008), 'Shining Ethiopia: l'Ethiopie post communiste du nouveau millenaire', *Autrepart*, no. 48, pp. 141–52.

Harbeson, J (1978), 'Territorial and development politics in the Horn of Africa: the Afar of the Awash valley', *African Affairs*, vol. 77, no. 309, pp. 479–98.

Hagmann, T and Abbink, J (2011), 'Twenty years of revolutionary democratic Ethiopia, 1991 to 2011', *Journal of Eastern African Studies*, vol. 5, no. 4, pp. 579–95.

Hagmann, T & Korf, B (2012), 'Agamben in the Ogaden: violence and sovereignty in the Ethiopian–Somali frontier', *Political Geography*, vol. 31, no. 4, pp. 205–14.

Hagmann, T & Péclard, D (2010), 'Negotiating statehood: dynamics of power and domination in Africa', *Development and Change*, vol. 41, no. 4, pp. 539–62.

Haregot, S (2013), *The bureaucratic empire.*

Serving emperor Haile Selassie, Red Sea Press, London.

Hathaway (2008), *What cost Ethiopia's dam boom? A look inside the expansion of Ethiopia's energy sector*, International Rivers, viewed 21 April 2014, http://www.internationalrivers.org/files/attached-files/ethioreport06feb08.pdf

Hess, R (1970), *Ethiopia: the modernisation of autocracy*, Cornell University Press, Ithaca.

Human Rights Watch (2010), *Development without freedom. How aid underwrites repression in Ethiopia*, Human Rights Watch, New York.

James, W, Donham, DL, Kurimoto, E & Triulzi, A (eds) (2002), *Remapping Ethiopia: socialism and after*, James Currey, London.

Kebede, M (1999), *Survival and modernization: Ethiopia's enigmatic present*, Red Sea Press, Lawrenceville.

Kinde, S & Egenda, S (2010), 'Fixing Gilgel Gibe II – engineer's perspective', March 2010, viewed 25 September 2015, http://www.ethiomedia.com/course/can_gibe_two_be_fixed.pdf

Lavers, T (2013), 'Food security and social protection in highland Ethiopia: linking the productive safety net to the land question', *Journal of Modern African Studies*, vol. 51, no. 3, pp. 459–85.

Lefebvre JA (1991), *Arms for the Horn: U.S. security policy in Ethiopia and Somalia, 1953-1991*, Pittsburg University Press, Pittsburgh.

Lefort, R (2010), 'Powers–mengist–and peasants in rural Ethiopia: the post-2005 interlude', *Journal of Modern African Studies*, vol. 48, no. 3, pp. 435–60.

Lefort, R (2012), 'Free market economy, "developmental state" and party-state hegemony in Ethiopia: the case of the "model farmers"', *Journal of Modern African Studies*, vol. 50, no. 4, pp. 681–706.

Lewis, D & Mosse, D (eds) (2006), *Development brokers and translators:*

The ethnography of aid and agencies, Kumarian Press, Bloomfield.

Mains, D (2012), 'Blackouts and progress: privatization, infrastructure, and a developmentalist state in Jimma, Ethiopia', *Cultural Anthropology*, vol. 27, no. 1, pp. 3–27.

Markakis, J (2011), *Ethiopia: the last two frontiers*, James Currey, Oxford.

Mawdsley E (2012), *From recipients to donors: emerging powers and the changing development landscape*, Zed Books, London.

McKinsey Global Institute (2010), *Lions on the move: the progress and potential of African economies*, McKinsey Global Institute, Washington, DC.

McVety, A (2012), *Enlightened aid: U.S. development as foreign policy in Ethiopia*, Oxford University Press, New York.

Mosse, D (2005), *Cultivating development: an ethnography of aid policy and practice*, Pluto Press, London and Ann Arbor.

Nicholson, GE (1957), *Report no. 728 to the government of Ethiopia on cotton production*, FAO, Rome.

Oakland Institute (2013), *Understanding land investments deals in Africa. Ignoring abuse in Ethiopia: DFID and USAID in the Lower Omo Valley*, viewed 25 September 2015, http://www.oaklandinstitute.org/ignoring-abuse-ethiopia

Pankhurst, A (2012), 'Revisiting resettlement under two regimes', in A Pankhurst & F Piguet (eds), *Moving people in Ethiopia: development, displacement and the state*, James Currey, Oxford, pp. 138–79.

Patman, R (1990), *The Soviet Union in the Horn of Africa*, Cambridge University Press, Cambridge.

Radelet, S (2010), *Emerging Africa. How 17 countries are leading the way*, Center for Global Development, Washington, DC.

Reno, W (1997), 'African weak states and commercial alliances', *African Affairs*, vol. 96, no. 383, pp. 165–86.

Sack, RD (1986), *Human territoriality: its theory and history*, Cambridge University Press, Cambridge.

Schlichte, K & Veit, A (2007), *Coupled arenas: why state-building is so difficult*, Institute for Social Science, Humboldt University, Berlin, Working Paper Micropolitics No. 3.

Scott, JC (1998), *Seeing like a state: how certain schemes to improve the human condition have failed*, Yale University Press, New Haven.

Schraeder, P (1994), *United States policy toward Africa: incrementalism, crisis and change*, Cambridge University Press, Cambridge.

Segers, K *et al.* (2008), 'Be like bees. The politics of mobilizing farmers for development in Tigray, Ethiopia', *African Affairs*, vol. 108, no. 430, pp. 91–109.

Soulé, AH (2011), *Deux vies dans l´histoire de la corne de l'Afrique: les sultans Afar Mahammad Hanfaré et Ali-Mirah Hanfaré*, Centre français d'études éthiopiennes, Addis Ababa.

Toggia, PS (2008), 'The state of emergency: police and carceral regimes in Modern Ethiopia', *Journal of Developing Societies*, vol. 24, no. 2, pp. 107–24.

Tommasoli, M (2014), *In nome dello sviluppo. Politiche di reinsediamento e conflitti in Africa orientale*, Carocci, Roma.

Tronvoll, K (2011), 'The Ethiopian 2010 federal and regional elections: re-establishing the one-party state', *African Affairs*, vol. 110, no. 438, pp. 121–36.

UNDP (2013), *Human development report 2013. The rise of the South: human progress in a diverse world*, United Nations Development Programme, New York.

Vaughan, S & Tronvoll, K (2003), *The culture of power in contemporary Ethiopian political life*, Stockholm, SIDA.

Whitfield, L (ed.) (2008), *The politics of aid: African strategies for dealing with donors*, Oxford University Press, Oxford.

Whitfield, L & Fraser, A (2010), 'Negotiating aid: the structural conditions shaping the negotiating strategies of African governments', *International Negotiation*, vol. 15, no. 3, pp. 341–66.

Zenawi, M (2006), *African development: dead ends and new beginnings*, unpublished paper, viewed 17 April 2014, http://www.meleszenawi.com/wp-content/uploads/2012/11/African_Development-Dead_Ends_and_New_Beginnings_by_Meles_Zenawi.pdf

Zenawi, M (2012), 'State and markets: neoliberal limitations and the case for a developmental state', in A Noman, K Botchwey, H Stein & J Stiglitz (eds), *Good growth and governance in Africa: rethinking development strategies*, Oxford University Press, Oxford, pp. 140–74.

Zewde, B (2001), *A history of modern Ethiopia, 1855–1991*, James Currey, Oxford.

Zewde, B (2002), *Pioneers of change in Ethiopia: the reformist intellectuals of the early twentieth century*, James Currey, Oxford.

5 | Donors and the making of 'credible' elections in Cameroon

Marie-Emmanuelle Pommerolle

Introduction

Cameroon has never been a 'donor darling' like Uganda, Rwanda or Ghana. A good reason for this is that it has never been a model of economic and political liberalization and reforms (Konings, 2011). Nevertheless, the country has benefited from constant financial and political support, briefly questioned at the beginning of the nineties. In 1992, the first multi-party presidential election won by the incumbent Paul Biya (in power since 1982) was indeed hotly contested: his opponents as well as many international observers and some embassies stated that the victory of the opposition candidate John Fru Ndi was stolen. In this debate, Western diplomats strongly disagreed: the US and German ambassadors voiced their discontent and cut aid flows, while France drastically increased its financial support (Ebolo, 1998; Emmanuel, 2010). In 2011, almost twenty years later, Paul Biya was re-elected with 78 per cent of the vote.[1] On that occasion, and amidst harsh criticisms made by NGOs – some funded by donors – and in unofficial conversations, embassies acknowledged that the electoral process was 'acceptable' and sent public messages of congratulation – accompanied by some recommendations and reservations – a few days after the electoral results were proclaimed.[2] Admitting retrospectively that this election suffered from a voter register described as 'worrying' and even 'tarnishing Biya's victory',[3] donors have progressively reached a consensus on the acceptability of the last twenty years of Cameroonian elections. While pushing for reforms since then, constantly negotiating on this issue with a reluctant Cameroonian government, they have been endorsing the consecutive electoral victories of Paul Biya and the Cameroon People's Democratic Movement (CPDM).

The objective of this chapter is to understand why, how and with what effects Western donors have continuously promoted electoral reforms in spite of multiple setbacks, and endorsed electoral results in spite of sometimes strong reservations. The reluctance of the Cameroonian government to follow national or international recommendations on electoral reforms could be easily explained by the economic and political leverage of the Cameroonian government, which was able to 'pick and choose' the projects funded by donors and even its donors. Since the beginning of the 1990s, overseas development assistance had accounted for only 5 to 10 per cent of GNI. Since 2009, with an equivalent volume of around 600 million dollars a year, it accounts for around 2.5 per cent of the country's GNI (World Bank, 2013). Cameroon is thus not financially dependent on donors' funding. Moreover, oil, mining and forest resources as well as the country's positioning as an 'island of stability' in a troubled regional environment give the Cameroonian government additional political leverage (Peiffer & Englebert, 2012). This political leverage may well be illustrated by a 2009 speech by the minister of foreign affairs to diplomatic officials after their criticism of Elecam, the then new independent electoral body. In a short address, he bluntly asked Cameroonian 'partners' to 'be self-disciplined towards Elecam, and to refrain from the temptation of this new form of civilizing mission, which tends to drape under the cloak of a democratic duty to interfere; which does not hesitate to use the national and international media to discredit the national political institutions for non-compliance with the dominant political and cultural models'.[4]

Would this sovereignist reminder be the sign that donors' projects towards electoral reforms are doomed? So why would donors keep pursuing their 'reformist' agenda, even when their financial aid is not a must to the country? This case study, slightly different from the other cases presented in the book because of the little political leverage of donors, underlines that a strategist view of aid relationships does not take into account the complexity of the former. As shown elsewhere with various conceptual tools (Ferguson, 1990; Olivier de Sardan, 2005; Lewis & Mosse, 2006; Whitfield, 2009; Tansey, 2013), foreign donors are not external actors to national politics and the mutual interests of donors and recipients to sustain stable relationships go beyond mere economic or strategic interests. In this specific case, donors interact with Cameroonian political actors in what could be called an 'internationalized political field', referring to Pierre Bourdieu's concept of 'political field' (Bourdieu, 1991). In this internationalized political field, donors are interacting with political parties, state institutions and 'civil society' actors, with unequal material and symbolic resources but each of them trying to impose their perceptions and their rules of the game. All these actors are driven by a shared *illusio*, that is, a shared social interest in playing together in this political field (Bourdieu, 1998): they all believe, want and need this game to be credible, and for this, the electoral process – defined, in democracy promotion programmes, as the main tool and expression of democratization (Dezalay & Garth, 2002) – must be perceived as trustworthy.

The incumbents obviously need the elections to be certified as 'free and fair', as does the electoral administration, which has to demonstrate its capacity to meet its professional objectives. Civil society working on electoral affairs also participates in the process of certifying the elections, but in a more critical way.

Both instances rely on the material or symbolic support of international actors. Since independence, the external recognition of African regimes has indeed contributed to balance their lack of 'empirical legitimacy' (Clapham, 1996), and Cameroon is no exception. NGOs, on their part, have progressively managed to be heard in the national space because of the material and symbolic support of donors. As for the latter, their social interest in participating in electoral affairs is complex. Economic, but also moral and professional, interests keep them pushing for reforms and encouraging the electoral process. Moreover, if some donor officials admit to being regularly confronted with 'donor fatigue', their long history of interactions in this internationalized political field obliged them to take position. Trapped in national politics, but also moved by their own professional and moral conception of democracy diffusion (Petric, 2012), donors have constantly attempted to provide guarantees of electoral credibility.

The analysis of the consequences of this constrained political participation of donors confirms what has been said elsewhere about electoral assistance. The analysis of their day-to-day work points at the same inconsistent policies and lowering 'democratic' standards (Lynch & Crawford, 2011; Brown, 2011). The support of new professional democrats (independent bodies or NGOs) and of electoral technology supposed to guarantee the credibility of the electoral system has been confronted with constant negotiations, changing perceptions of their interests, and professional practices that have contributed to produce distrust between the variety of electoral actors, and between them and Cameroonian citizens.

Indeed, in spite of the formal legitimacy conferred by successive elections, the very weak popular legitimacy of the regime has remained unchanged. Figures of voter registration and voter turnout have been historically low (Abdoulkarimou, 2010); protests are scarce but violent (Amin, 2012); fraud and illegal and exit practices abound (Malaquais, 2001; Albaugh, 2011); cultural expressions of power and dissent are frequent (Nyamnjoh & Fokwang, 2005; Argenti, 2007); demonstrations of loyalty are carefully organized by the regime (Ngaméni & Pommerolle, 2015). Illegitimacy and dissent are, however, until now, not conducive to massive political protestation by parties or associations. Widespread clientelist networks (Bayart, 1985; Socpa, 2000; Hansen, 2010; Manirakiza, 2010) as well as a repressive environment are indeed constraining such voices (Pommerolle, 2008). Be they labelled authoritarian or hybrid, power relations in Cameroon are characterized by an integration of some social groups through clientelist networks and by a pervasive repression (Dicklitch, 2002) that is scarcely addressed by donors.

The aim of the chapter is not to explain the weak popular base of the Cameroonian regime by the actions of donors, but to point out their long implication in the electoral process since the beginning of the 2000s and its effects on a widespread distrust between rulers and ruled. Firstly, I will focus on the internal and historical dynamics of the donor community in Cameroon on the issue of electoral reforms, insisting on the common official language lobbying for change and the actual division of labour between bilateral and multilateral donors. Following their changing interests and perceptions, and related to a tense relationship with the Cameroonian government, bilateral donors tend to withdraw from this issue, leaving multilateral actors, with less political leverage, assuming financial and symbolic costs of electoral reforms. Secondly, I will interrogate the shared social interests of incumbents, opposition parties, civil society and donors in participating in the electoral process and in certifying, even with nuances, its credibility. It is the accumulation of political, economic, professional and sometimes moral interests that explains the institutionalization of the idea of credible elections in Cameroon since the mid-1990s. However, the third part will insist on the unintended effects of this shared *illusio*: with the aim of maintaining the credibility of the electoral process, the concerned actors, and donors among them, produced expectations, technologies and institutions supposed to assert this credibility. However, the debate about the criteria of this credibility and the very functioning of donors' projects such as financing procedures, objectives of success, or fear of instrumentalization have been detrimental to their own goal. Distrust is widespread among actors of the electoral field, and maintains potential voters far from this internationalized political field.[5]

Electoral reforms and the division of labour among donors

After competing on the market of democratic transition (Guilhot, 2005), Western bilateral donors have progressively and discreetly withdrawn from the electoral reformist agenda, some unable to impose their electoral model, others affected by donors' fatigue. Multilateral donors have then taken over this project as 'experts' but with little political leverage.

Negotiations on electoral legislation started in 1991 with popular movements demanding multi-party elections and democracy, followed by the *Conférence tripartite* and the very contested 1992 elections (Gros, 1995; Eboussi Boulaga, 1997; Mehler, 1997). Since then, limited changes of electoral legislation have multiplied, especially on the eve of elections (Olinga, 1998). But claims for structural reforms by opposition parties, civil society actors and donors, such as the setting-up of an independent electoral body or a unique electoral code have constantly been delayed (Olinga, 1998). It was in 2000 that the *Observatoire national des élections* (Onel) was installed. Its mandate was to control the electoral process, but not to organize it (Olinga, 2002). Its members were nominated a few months before each election and were marginalized by the Ministry of Internal Affairs and Decentralization (MINATD) in charge of organizing the elections. Onel was constantly asking for donors' funding and lobbying for its real inclusion in the electoral process (UNOPS/PNUD, n.d.). Donors were supporting the institution by financing training, logistics and electoral observations until they realized, or rather could no longer ignore, that its activities were controlled by the presidency. For instance, the Onel report on the 2004 presidential election was revised and edited by the presidency and released two years after the elections (*ibid.*). Thus, pressure was put on the president to create a more independent body, which became a condition in the Heavily Indebted Poor Countries process. In 2006, Elections Cameroon (known as Elecam) was formally created to answer this request: its mandate is to organize the elections in place of the MINATD. The choice of this institution was the result of intensive lobbying by the Commonwealth and the British High Commission to promote their own electoral model. Although civil society actors, particularly the Peace and Justice Commission of the Catholic Church, had written extensively on electoral reforms and made informed proposals, the Commonwealth ignored local proposals and sold its model to the government.[6] Selecting alternatively a 'francophone' (Onel) and an 'anglophone' (Elecam) model, the government played with its multiple networks, maximizing the rent of extraversion, in a bilingual country (Bayart, 2000; Torrent, 2005). At the beginning, the Commonwealth was willing to support its sister institutions, but was quickly disenchanted. It took the president two years to appoint the governing members of the electoral commission and to make it effective. Moreover, half of them were members of the CPDM, while the remaining were very close to it.[7] This 'original sin' considerably cooled down the relationships between donors and the regime on this particular issue. Eventually, six new members from 'civil society' were appointed in 2010; after the 2011 presidential election, the *Code électoral* was eventually drafted and adopted in 2012. During the same year, a recast of the voter register was decided and the biometric registration of voters completed for the general elections of September 2013. Ironically, this long-awaited revision of voter registration was not financed by donors. While UNDP had attempted to push for such revisions since 2003 and funded some of these attempts, it is on the national budget that this costly reform was eventually paid.

Indeed, donors, in particular bilateral ones, have progressively given up the electoral reform agenda. The ongoing difficulties faced by Elecam, accused of serious inefficiency during the 2011 chaotic presidential elections, have led donors to question their will and capacity to influence the electoral reform process (Transparency International – Cameroon, 2011; RECODH, 2011). At the same time, coordination and mutualization of efforts, through the 2005 Paris declaration, encouraged the multilateralization of aid. Already since 2003, UNDP and the European Union (EU) delegation in Yaoundé had been the main international actors supporting the electoral reform process. Multilateralizing aid on this issue had at least two effects: on the one hand, it technicized the issue because of the neutral or less political mandate of multilateral partners; on the other hand, it gave bilateral actors the opportunity to choose to remain engaged or to disengage from the electoral agenda.

From 2003 to 2010, UNDP has been the main partner of the MINATD in its electoral reform projects and has coordinated the work of donors on the issue. As an intergovernmental organization acting upon the request of the Cameroonian government, UNDP has focused on technical projects such as revising and computerizing the voters' register. As shown by the minutes of the GAPE (*Groupe d'appui aux élections* – Support committee on elections), which coordinated donors' actions on electoral issues from 2003 to 2011, UNDP and other donors have constantly asked for reforms, but also went to great length not to contradict the Cameroonian government. In 2010, as they were discouraged by the political appointments in Elecam and its inactivity, a UN mission sent to evaluate the progress of UNDP-funded projects was delayed several times in order to have the situation settled before its visit.[8] With no political leverage, and progressively abandoned by bilateral actors, UNDP acted as an expert, more than a lobbyist. The UNDP electoral expert present in Yaoundé in 2010 made an interesting diagnosis of the situation: formerly in charge of the 2006 elections in the Democratic Republic of Congo, he stated that the logistical problems he faced there were easier to manage than the 'political obstacles' he was confronted with in Cameroon.[9] In 2011, after the presidential elections and the end of its registration revision project (retrospectively considered as a failure), UNDP put an end to its electoral projects, arguing that, being an international agency, it was only interested in national elections, not in local ones such as the elections held in September 2013.[10]

The second multilateral actor involved in electoral assistance since 2010 was the EU delegation. The two multilateral actors have not coordinated their aid projects on electoral issues, the EU refusing to bring its 2 million euro budget (2010–2013) to the 'basket fund' managed by UNDP. Promoting expertise on electoral issues at a global level as well as in Cameroon, the EU position differed from that of UNDP, as it sometimes adopted critical stances.

This critical stance of the EU translated into tense relationships with the Cameroonian government. In 2009, the Commonwealth issued a very severe communiqué concerning the appointment of the members of the Electoral Council followed by the non-disbursement of a grant by the EU.[11] The government's answer was no less direct, as mentioned in the speech by the minister of foreign affairs quoted in the introduction. In 2011, while the EU delegation engaged in a three-year electoral programme, it has publicly been accused by the government of breaking the law by subsidizing associations defending homosexuals. In 2011, again, during the presidential campaign, an EU-funded NGO was summoned by the Ministry of Foreign Affairs, who accused it of interfering with Elecam's mission.[12] The convocation of the chairman of this association by the MINREX (and not the MINATD) clearly targeted its foreign funding partner. This tense relationship did not, however, halt the 'political dialogue' between the two partners. As stated by the cooperation officer of the EU delegation in Yaoundé: 'It does not work like that in Cameroon.'[13]

EU officials, however, regretted the depoliticization of electoral assistance in Cameroon and wanted to make it clear that the delegation is the only one endorsing the political role that other European countries reportedly would not want to play anymore. The same EU high-ranking official said how 'shocked' he was when, in 2011, Western embassies immediately sent messages of congratulations to President Biya, while everyone knew the 'catastrophic conditions' in which he was elected.[14] At least, he continued, the message of the president of the European Commission had been sent with some delay, and, one might add, contained some cautious recommendations on further reforms.[15] For a former insider of the international development community in Yaoundé, however, the EU in Cameroon, even if more willing to further democratic goals than the UNDP or bilateral donors, has been 'giving up' its democratic ambitions (Courtin, 2011).

The EU's and UNDP's engagement in electoral reforms in Cameroon have left room for bilateral actors to invest in the electoral agenda according to their own interests and perceptions. After a common engagement from 2003 to 2010, especially in the GAPE, most of them disengaged, either financially or politically. If donor fatigue in front of protracted reforms is commonly raised as a reason for this retreat, each donor pursued its engagement through different means. The Germans, who are the second largest bilateral donor, have left aside political diplomacy to focus on the commercial aspect of electoral reform. The German and the Cameroonian press,[16] some government officials, as well as donors and civil society actors[17] mention and condemn the way by which a German firm obtained the contract for the biometrical registration in 2012. Although the German firm was not on the shortlist, it won the tender immediately after a visit by the German secretary of trade and a well-known trade lobbyist. A fellow European diplomat underlines this commercial turn of German foreign policy – which allegedly is not limited to Cameroon.[18] On their side, French and British diplomacies both expected to have their say on national politics because of their colonial pasts but adopted opposite strategies. The effect, however, is the same: giving credibility to the electoral process. Officially supporting EU programmes, French diplomats dismiss Elecam and the biometric voters' registration as mere 'gadgets', suffering, moreover, from their 'anglophone' inspiration.[19] French officials also explain the retreat of French diplomacy from electoral affairs as a way to enhance the credibility of the process. Because of the 'popular fantasy' according to which Paul Biya is the 'French candidate', and, one might add, given the disastrous reputation of France in Cameroon, diplomats have chosen not to intervene publicly on electoral issues.[20] On the contrary, British diplomats have decided, since 2012, to make public their support to Elecam, leaving however the EU to finance the programme, and have thus gained visibility 'at no cost', according to EU officials.[21] On the British side, this overt support is reportedly a way to redress the negative image of Elecam, which has overcome its first difficulties.

Even if not financially engaged, all bilateral donors officially agree with the electoral agenda delegated to the EU and UNDP, and all have, for the last ten years, endorsed the election results. Even if achieved through minimum and sometimes opposite means, the credibility of the electoral process is a necessity shared by donors, incumbents, political parties, and civil society, all acting in the Cameroonian internationalized political field.

Credibility as the illusio of the electoral field

Credibility of the electoral process is thus the common 'social interest' of state institutions, political parties, donors and civil society in Cameroon. It is this shared *illusio* that makes their participation in the electoral process obvious and necessary (Bourdieu, 1998). Against a narrow definition of selfish interest or a naive conception of disinterest, Bourdieu uses the concept of *illusio* to explain why people engage in certain professional or political fields, why they find an interest and a necessity to play a game that may appear incongruous to those who are not socialized to this field. Even if with some distance and criticism, donors, the Cameroonian government, opposition parties, as well as civil society need to believe in the potential credibility of the electoral process. Not accepting electoral results would be denying the legitimacy of the incumbent power, positioning oneself as dissident and possibly being thrown out of the game. Although the boycott of elections did happen in the past,[22] and very severe reports were published,[23] contemporary critics never completely reject the electoral process. Being political professionals – be they elected or expert, domestic or international – each of them needs to be part of the game, in one way or another.

The regime's legitimacy derives partly from the belief in credible elections. Its efforts to impose this belief are thus constant, especially since the mid-1990s. New independent electoral bodies, revisions of voter registration, acceptance of increasing numbers of electoral observers (about 12,000 in the last local and legislative 2013 elections) follow this same goal of giving credibility to the electoral process. In return, opposition parties or civil society actors who question this credibility are accused of bringing disorder. 'Everyone knows the risks posed to our country by those political leaders who have lightly decided to throw away the rules of fair play they have subscribed to. Surely in a democracy, claims are part of the game, but no one would win a bidding war that could lead to all sorts of uncertainties', said the president after his victory in the 2011 elections.[24]

Since 1992 and the first multi-party election, Cameroonian opposition parties have indeed voiced claims about the partiality of the rules of the game. Still popular and supported by some Western donors, they have boycotted the first legislative elections, and the second presidential election. But, as the ruling party proved its capacity to remain and widen its political base, and to integrate opponents in the government through coalitions, opposition parties have progressively chosen to take part in elections (Sindjoun, 2004). Results have been contested in courts, and even by-elections were held, but the final results in favour of the ruling party have always been accepted (Abdoulka-rimou, 2010). Not participating in the electoral game would be synonymous with being ejected from the political field. Even if criticizing the electoral process is constant in their discourse, a minimal credibility is awarded to it, justifying their participation. Opposition parties have indeed been very active in pushing for more institutional guarantees to the electoral process (Olinga, 1998; 2002) before being sidelined by donors and their support for Elecam. Civil society organizations have provided expertise, advocacy, civic education, and observation of the electoral process since 2002, producing harsh criticism but at the same time being more and more included in this political field.

Finally, what is the interest of donors? Why would they constantly try to sustain the credibility of the process? The acceptance of the electoral process and results is, according to donors, a condition to maintaining law and order in Cameroon. Strategic, economic and even professional interests of development workers are protected only if elections are not contested and do not bring about public unrest. What appears to frighten international observers, as well as diplomats or development workers, is a popular mobilization against the current regime. Popular uprisings occurred in 1991 (Eboussi Boulaga, 1997) and, for a shorter period, in 2008 (Amin, 2012; Pigeaud, 2011), questioning the regime's legitimacy and targeting foreign and especially French economic interests. Thus the main objective of international analysts and donors is that 'rules be respected',[25] and 'to ensure that elections are the least contested possible'.[26] 'It is our duty to maintain this stability, that the elections shall not be contested; it can help everyone, including other partners and projects', as one donor official put it.[27] Keeping economic activities and development work safe from popular uprising is one goal, especially in a country surrounded by conflicts in neighbouring Nigeria, the Central African Republic or Chad. This viewpoint might even be strengthened by the political violence that has affected northern Cameroon since 2013 (Pommerolle, 2015). The other objective relates to the everyday work of donor officials: some have specialized in electoral assistance, and need their projects to be considered as successes for them to be maintained in the aid budget.[28] The credibility of electoral reforms is thus an indicator of their projects' success. Because of the short-term posting in the recipient country, donor officials adapt the indicators of their project results to their stay. This short-term perspective has been criticized in the past in the context of electoral observer missions (see Geisler, 1993). But this has also a considerable impact on electoral assistance programmes, and on what donors officials see as success or failure: a programme of sensitization or of observation, a revision of the electoral register completed in a hurry just before the elections, or a new electoral code, even if unsatisfactory, are all valuable outcomes that can justify their work.

Donor evaluations often amount to a positive sanctioning of development activities. In the case of electoral assistance, international actors benefit from the advantage that they are the ones certifying the credibility of the electoral process, and thus the quality of their own work. This 'politics of the [electoral] verdict' (Geisler, 1993) have always been the result of negotiation between international observers and domestic politicians, namely the incumbent regime. Communiqués and observation reports are never the product of mere observation, but a more or less subtle negotiation reflecting the balance of power between donors and the ruling regime. In the case of Cameroon, donors and international actors have validated successive elections, sometimes with reservations, without being able to offer proof of this credibility. Indeed, the Cameroonian regime has constantly managed to discourage international observation, maybe because of the harsh criticism it received in the 1992 elections. In 2002, like in 2004, the government asked for international observation too late, and accreditations were not delivered in time (PNUD/UNOPS, n.d.). Eventually, embassies sent their own personnel, and international election observation consisted of some International Organisation of la Francophonie or African Union observers as well as a few dozen diplomats. The assertions of credibility by donors are thus not informed by their own observations. This underlines how much the appreciation of electoral credibility is not so much linked to facts than to political negotiation.

Searching for credibility and producing distrust

This verdict of 'credibility' is, however, not awarded by donors without attempts to ensure that minimum criteria are met. Independent bodies, NGOs, national electoral observations and controlled processes of registration are all set up, with donors' support, to ensure that rules are respected. These actors and technologies of credibility have, however, suffered from the very functioning of assistance programmes, the ever-changing criteria of 'credibility' as well as the changing balance of power between the Cameroonian government and donors. Mutual distrust in this crowded and competitive electoral field, and distrust from the 'outsiders', namely ordinary citizens, are unintended consequences of this desperate search for credibility.

The establishment of 'independent' bodies has been, everywhere in 'transitional regimes', a prerequisite for 'free and fair' elections (Quantin, 2004).

The credibility of Elecam, which followed the discredited Onel, has long been denied by all the other actors of the electoral field, be they Cameroonian or foreign.[29] Elecam has indeed navigated a narrow pathway since its inception: on the one hand, national institutional partners, and notably the MINATD, which have been deprived of their main *raison d'être* are overtly critical of Elecam's competences; on the other hand, international partners have been condemning more or less severely the political bias of the institution. Both donors and government have contributed to the weakening of the formally independent body.

First, a wide array of political as well as administrative institutions were reluctant to work with this new body. Until the end of 2010, Elecam had difficulties getting its budget voted through by the National Assembly and then disbursed by the Ministry of Finance.[30] CPDM members of parliament have multiplied public criticism against the institution, revealing the anxiety of elites confronted with what they perceive as a threat to their electoral routines.[31] On its side, the MINATD has reluctantly provided the new electoral body with the needed logistics, texts, registers, etc. MINATD agents have been very critical of the recruitment of Elecam staff and their know-how in electoral affairs. Often retired agents of this ministry, former Onel personnel and unemployed university graduates, they directly compete with a powerful *corps* of state agents (Abdoulkarimou, 2010). In the provinces, *préfets* and *sous-préfets* did not support Elecam in its mission during the 2011 elections until a ministerial order was given a few days before the vote in what could have been even more 'catastrophic elections'.[32] On their side, donors, particularly those who had participated in the establishment of this independent body, have been overtly critical of the supposedly political nature of Elecam. Funding was withdrawn in 2009 and scepticism was publicly expressed, namely after the 2011 elections. While Elecam desperately tried to attract foreign funding,[33] most of the 2010–2013 EU election programme was channelled to civil society organizations: Elecam received only 300,000 euros and unofficially but vehemently regrets this low level of financial support.[34] Also, Elecam was not willing to share UNDP funding with civil society actors and refused the money.[35] Relationships between the Elecam and the donors have been tense. Through 'marketing' devices and political 'coups',[36] Elecam tried to overcome this deficit of credibility produced by those who established it.

Facing difficult relationships with the main electoral institution, donors have turned to civil society organizations and asked for the inclusion of civil society members in the electoral process. With the objective of opening the political field, international actors have eventually contributed to divide and polarize the non-governmental space but also to radicalize some of its actors – those left aside by donors' attention – contesting the criteria of credibility agreed upon by the government and 'consenting' donors.

Civil society actors have been active in electoral claims and expertise; in the 1990s and the first years of the 2000s, a few law professors, some NGOs and the Justice and Peace Commission of the Catholic Church were very active in lobbying for reforms. In 2011, the appointment of 'civil society' members and the funding of donors have reinforced competition and distrust, a common feature in Cameroonian 'civil society' (Pommerolle, 2010; Cumming, 2011). One of the most respected electoral activists, a professor of anthropology and former chairman of the Justice and Peace Commission was appointed to the electoral council, endorsing the institutional discourse and giving rise to harsh criticism by fellow civil society activists.[37] Another personality appointed as a 'civil society' member was found to be a 'communication' businesswoman whose firm was in charge of the communication of the president-candidate in the 2011 election.[38] Even though she was dismissed, this episode produced suspicion about the danger of a co-opted 'civil society' and further deteriorated the image of Elecam perceived once more as politically driven.

Moreover, distrust has grown among civil society organizations partly because of donor funding.[39] The capture of aid by some 'happy few' led to suspicion, rumours and division among civil society members.[40] Funding without a 'call for tender' by the EU, as was the case with a 300,000 euro contract awarded to Transparency International – Cameroon, led observers and other associations to question the proximity of this particular NGO to the government (Courtin, 2011). What is perceived as the opacity of aid chan-nelling and preference for established NGOs reinforces a very negative feeling among other NGOs against any electoral reform (Lynch and Crawford, 2011).

Donors' interventions in the electoral process have undoubtedly rendered democratization in Cameroon more complex, as it is no longer monopolized by the state and political parties. This diversity of actors led to a professionalization of the field, in which every participant wants to continue participating. The credibility of the electoral process is thus self-reinforcing. However, changing interests of donors and choices in their support also led to the weakening of some of these actors and to distrust inside the field. Electoral technologies meant to ensure the credibility of the vote have been pushed for as an additional guarantee. The ambivalent support for voter registration, which has been at the centre of donors' attention, led to some unexpected effects, limiting rather than maximizing the credibility of the process.

Since 2003, the revision and reform of the electoral register have constantly been on the electoral agenda. Nevertheless, every election held until the last 2011 presidential election is now considered as biased because of a fraudulent electoral register. The direct contribution of donors to the establishment of such a controversial electoral register is patent: in order to reach 'satisfying' figures of registered voters and to meet the objectives stated in the projects, donors have thus validated fraudulent electoral practices. In 2003, UNDP was asked by the government to support the computerization of the electoral register. As the government did not put in place what was agreed in the 'electoral blue print', UNDP had to change the objectives of its mission and the 2004 presidential election was held without any change to the electoral register. In 2007, before the general elections, the computerization of the electoral register was again planned and financed by UNDP. UNDP's objective was to register 7 million voters. The MINATD, on its side, set an objective of 5 million considering that the last registration, ten years earlier, counted 4 million. The agreed objective was finally 5 million, and, as confirmed by one computer engineer working on this UNDP-funded project, this figure was reached thanks to duplications that were purposely not erased.[41] Again, in 2011, before the presidential election and although donors asked for an update of the electoral list, namely for the suppression of the former register and the creation of a new one, Elecam chose, because of short notice, to clean the existing electoral register, with an objective of 7 million registered voters.[42] Here again, plenty of duplications were kept in the register to reach a figure of 7.5 million.[43] After the 2011 election, Elecam eventually decided to redo the electoral register through biometric registration. This operation diminished the number of Cameroonian voters to 5.4 million but was meant to be much more credible. And, indeed, the alleged credibility of this new biometric register shed a crude light on the falsification of previous electoral lists and on the misplaced satisfaction regarding 'acceptable' elections. This biometric technology itself, designed to ensure an authoritative electoral register, was the subject of suspicion and became a patent sign of the failure of donors and government to make the electoral process attractive, not to say credible.

The ways through which voter registration did take place expresses the great distance between ordinary citizens and the political field: CPDM members, préfets, sous-préfets and chefs de quartiers were more or less officially mobilized to make people register en masse and in some targeted zones. State mobilization as well as ordinary clientelist techniques were used to get people to the registration stations.[44] Resistance and suspicion, sometimes expressed through accusations of sorcery towards registration agents, were common.[45] Civil society actors and even state agents also casted doubts on the transparency of this technology.[46] Technological guarantees as well as the formally inclusive process of registration are not enough to reassure sceptics: they do not believe that duplications of registrations will be eliminated because of what they see as an insufficient centralization and cross-checking of data; some are certain that CPDM entirely supervises the process and marginalizes other parties' representatives; others are convinced that legal flaws allow the ruling party to keep control of the electoral process. This wide popular disaffection and structural distrust among the actors in the political field are partly the results of the enduring engagement of donors relentlessly certifying the credibility of the electoral process even when confronted with blatant evidence of fraud and sometimes indirectly taking part in it.

Conclusion

Recent analysis on elections and democracy in Africa has underlined the ambivalent link between them, questioning the widespread assumption that elections are positively linked with democratization (Lindberg, 2009). According to Bratton (2013), the repetition of elections does not entail democratization. Rather 'bad quality elections enable the durability of autocracy' (*ibid.*: 18). Even if this statement is in line with previous conclusions, it still assumes that democracy can be measured accurately and that the judgement about elections or democracy has no consequence. This position of complete outsider does not tell much about what local political actors think, do and say about elections and their 'quality'. The data collected to judge the 'good' or 'bad' quality of democracy are second-hand: previous research, observation reports and media reports form the basis of an 'objective' judgement. Yet, as mentioned earlier, the 'politics of the [electoral] verdict' (Geisler, 1993) are far from neutral. Moreover, assessing elections from far away, this kind of analysis neglects the fact that national and international actors do produce their own judgements, which themselves have important consequences for local institutional and power dynamics.

This chapter highlights, to the contrary, the need to understand the meanings of national and international actors' discourses and practices and their effects in a very polarized political field. What has emerged is that the establishment of safeguards for 'free and fair' elections, be they supposedly independent actors or sophisticated technologies, are undoubtedly at the centre of power relations, competition and manipulation. They are the results of political negotiations, between national actors and foreign donors, all of them needing to safeguard 'credible' institutions to ensure the country's stability while abiding, even in contested ways, by international criteria of democratic respectability.

What is puzzling in the case of Cameroon, contrary to Uganda or Rwanda for instance, is the particular position of donors. For at least the last fifteen years, they have promoted classic democratic institutions (and not non-partisan democracy like in Uganda or personal rule like in Rwanda), and have not yet had 'economic success' to justify their tenacity. It is this singular relationship between Cameroon and outside actors – leaving little room of manoeuvre to Western donors – that I have retraced in this chapter, but that could be situated in an even longer-term trajectory. Government, opposition and ordinary citizens alike have long enjoyed a very ambiguous relationship with the outside world, translating into a fraught relationship between Cameroon and international actors. As a former mandate and trust territory, Cameroon has always claimed a special status and special relationships with the outside world, especially with the United Nations. Travels to New York, discourses and petitions addressed to the international organization were recurrent during the nationalist struggle of the 1950s, allowing the Union des populations du Cameroun (UPC) to fight French repression (Terretta, 2013).

Postcolonial government and opposition have always been eager to use international resources to fight their struggles (Chouala, 2004), and the Cameroonian government has always tried to bar international assistance to its opponents, who used exile as a refuge (Pommerolle, 2010). Western actors have been expected to play a role in Cameroonian debates, to side with one camp or the other. This involvement of the outside world has assigned donors a role that they find difficult to refuse when confronted with resistance to reforms. Their position is all the more fragile since nationalist claims, another staple of Cameroonian political discourse, are easily put forward against some interventions (Joseph, 1977; Takougang, 2003b). Activated by the government and well received in popular and intellectual spheres, these nationalist claims act as a powerful constraint against democratization pressures.

Notes

1 In between, he was re-elected in 1997 with 92.5 per cent of the vote because of a boycott by opposition parties and in 2004 with 70.9 per cent. Legislative elections were held in 2002, 2007 and 2013. The CPDM won 149, 153 and 148 of the 180 parliamentary seats respectively (see Sindjoun, 1999; Takougang, 2003a; Albaugh, 2011). For the 2013 elections, the reader is referred to the report by national observers (Plateforme des organizations, 2013).

2 'Présidentielle: la position des Etats-Unis et du Commonwealth', *Mutations*, 12 October 2011; 'Rapport: L'Union africaine confirme le faible taux de participation', *Mutations*, 12 October 2011; 'Présidentielle: le club des gentlemen jette un pavé dans la mare', *Mutations*, 14 October 2011.

3 Following the words of, respectively, a British diplomat and a high-ranking civil servant of the Ministry of Internal Affairs and Decentralization (Interviews, 14 and 10 June 2013).

4 See 'Elecam: Le Minrex menace le corps diplomatique', *Mutations*, 20 February 2009.

5 This chapter is based on three periods of fieldwork in Yaoundé, in July 2010 and June and September 2013. Focusing on donors' interventions in political affairs, but also on electoral mobilization and participation, I interviewed the main Western bilateral and multilateral donor officials, Elecam officials (at the headquarters and in the regional and communal offices), electoral officers or experts at the MINATD and civil society actors, and I collected documents on donors' electoral assistance programmes. I also made use of Cameroonian news reports to complement the data collected.

6 Interviews with the head of the Justice and Peace Commission programme on elections and the head of Nouveaux droits de l'Homme, Yaoundé (March 2006).

7 'Elecam: comment Biya a roulé les diplomates', *Le Messager*, 7 January 2009.

8 Interview with a UNDP expert (27 July 2010).

9 *Ibid.*

10 Interview with the UNDP officer in charge of these projects (7 June 2013).

11 'Cameroun-Elecam: la

Commonwealth crie sa colère', *Mutations*, 13 January 2009.

12 Interview with EU officials (10 June 2013) and the director of Transparency International – Cameroon (18 June 2013), see also 'Eyebe Ayissi interpelle Tansparency International sur l'inscription des électeurs par Sms', *Cameroon Tribune*, 23 August 2011.

13 'Ca ne marche pas comme ça au Cameroun' (interview, 10 June 2013).

14 Interview with EU official (15 June 2013); see also 'Les injonctions de l'Union européenne à Paul Biya', 17 November 2011, *allafrica.com*.

15 See also 'Félicitations au chef de l'Etat de José Manuel Durao Barroso, président de la Commission européenne', *Cameroon Tribune*, 15 November 2011.

16 'Marché de la biométrie: le gouvernement impose les Allemands', *Le Messager*, 19 April 2012; 'Soupçons de corruption autour du marché de la biométrie: Elecam crée un scandale en Allemagne', *Le Messager*, 23 October 2012.

17 I have been told about this anecdote several times during my formal and informal discussions in June and September 2013 in Yaoundé.

18 Interview with European diplomat (10 June 2013).

19 Interview with two French diplomats (14 June 2013).

20 A strong resentment against French political or economic actors was expressed, for instance, during the 2008 riots in Douala (Pigeaud, 2011), and in the rumours that France was behind Boko Haram's attacks in North Cameroon (Pommerolle, 2015). This resentment may derive from the memory of the repression against the nationalist movement in the 1950s (Domergue *et al.*, 2011), and the French support to the two postcolonial presidents (Delancey, 1989).

21 Interview with British diplomat (14 June 2013) and with two EU officials (10 June 2013).

22 Parliamentary elections were boycotted in 1992 and presidential elections in 1997.

23 See Ebolo (1998) for the American reports on the 1992 elections, and the Catholic Peace and Justice Commission reports on the 2002 legislative and the 2004 presidential elections.

24 'A la une: Paul Biya, sans surprise', *RFI*, 19 October 2011.

25 *International Crisis Group*, 'Cameroun: les dangers d'un régime en pleine fracture', rapport d'Afrique No. 61, Nairobi/Bruxelles, 24 June 2010, note 117.

26 Interview with UNDP expert (27 July 2010).

27 Interview with donor representative (16 July 2010).

28 Interview with officer in charge of civil society and electoral affairs working at a multilateral institution, previously in charge of the same topic in another country delegation in West Africa (Interview, 16 July 2010).

29 An indication of the widely shared distrust that Elecam suffers from is the remark by a taxi driver when stopping in front of the Elecam headquarters. He laughingly told me: 'Yeah, you are the one frauding the elections!' (Personal observation, July 2010).

30 Interview with a high-ranking Elecam officer (21 July 2010).

31 See for instance the criticism of Elecam voiced by the speaker of the National Assembly in front of diplomatic officials (*Mutations*, 7 March 2012).

32 Interviews with a French advisor in the MINATD and with a high-ranking official in the MINATD (10 and 15 June 2013).

33 'Cameroun: Elecam courtise les bailleurs de fonds', 12 October 2010, available on *camer.be*.

34 Interview with a high-ranking Elecam officer (6 June 2013).

35 Interview with the officer in charge (7 June 2013).

36 Elecam refused to validate two CPDM lists during the senatorial elections in April 2013. Some argue that this was not a sign of independence but a political manoeuvre decided by the presidency.

37 For the negative reactions of his

former civil society partners, see 'Société civile: la pillule "Titi Nwel à Elecam" ne passe pas', 1 September 2011, online publication, copy on file with the author.

38 'Scandale et conflit d'intérêt: Pauline Biyong dans la campagne de Paul Biya', *Mutations*, 26 September 2011.

39 Donors are, however, not seen as solely responsible for such distrust. Cooptation, infiltration and intimidation of activists by the administration during the 2011 electoral campaign have been documented in confidential reports by NGOs.

40 Interview with an NGO leader working on electoral reforms (6 June 2013). For a critique of donors' criteria for allocating funds, see also 'Présidentielle 2011: une Ong accusée de détournement', *Le Jour*, 16 August 2011.

41 Interview with computer engineer (10 June 2013).

42 Interview with high-ranking MINATD official (10 June 2013).

43 Several interviews (June 2013); see also Transparency International (2011) and RECODH (2011).

44 CPDM members of parliament used ordinary tricks like building roads with their personal funds; *préfets* and *sous-préfets* asked the chiefs to mobilize their population (interviews, June and September 2013); see also Mbowou (2013).

45 Interview with an Elecam regional official (June 2013).

46 Various interviews (June and September 2013).

References

Abdoulkarimou, D (2010), *La pratique des élections au Cameroun, 1992–2007. Regards sur un système électoral en mutations*, Editions Clé, Yaoundé.

Albaugh, E (2011), 'An autocrat's toolkit: adaptation and manipulation in "democratic" Cameroon', *Democratization*, vol. 18, no. 2, pp. 388–414.

Amin, JA (2012), 'Understanding the protest of February 2008 in Cameroon', *Africa Today*, vol. 58, no. 4, pp. 21–43.

Argenti, N (2007), *The intestines of the state. Youth, violence, and related histories in the Cameroon grassfields*, Chicago University Press, Chicago.

Bayart, JF (2000), 'Africa in the world: a history of extraversion', *African Affairs*, vol. 99, no. 395, pp. 217–67.

Bayart, JF (1985), *L'état au Cameroun*, Presses de la Fondation nationale de science politique, Paris.

Bourdieu, P (1991), 'Political representation: elements for a theory of the political field', in P Bourdieu (ed.), *Language and symbolic power*, Harvard University Press, Cambridge, MA, pp. 171–202.

Bourdieu, P (1998), *Practical reason: on the theory of action*, Stanford University Press, Stanford CA.

Bratton, M (2013), *Voting and democratic citizenship in Africa*, Lynne Rienner, Boulder, CO.

Brown, S (2011), '"Well, what can you expect?": donor officials' apologetics for hybrid regimes in Africa', *Democratization*, vol. 18, no. 2, pp. 512–34.

Chouala, YA (2004), 'L'action internationale de l'opposition: la transnationalisation de la vie internationale Camerounaise', in L Sindjoun (ed.) *Comment peut-on être opposant au Cameroun? Politique parlementaire et politique autoritaire*, CODESRIA, Dakar, pp. 295–330.

Clapham, C (1996), *Africa and the international system: the politics of state survival*, Cambridge University Press, Cambridge.

Courtin, C (2011), 'Démocratie au Cameroun: l'Europe démissionnaire', *Projet*, no. 324–325, pp. 124–29.

Cumming, GD (2011), 'Good intentions are not enough: French NGO efforts at democracy building in Cameroon', *Development in Practice*, vol. 21, no. 2, pp. 518–31.

Delancey, MW (1989), *Cameroon: dependence and independence*, Westview, Boulder, CO.

Dezalay, Y & Garth, B (eds) (2002),

Global prescriptions: the production, exportation and importation of a new legal orthodoxy, University of Michigan Press, Ann Arbor.

Dicklitch, S (2002) 'Failed democratic transition in Cameroon: a human rights explanation', *Human Rights Quarterly*, vol. 24, no. 1, pp. 152–76.

Domergue, M, Tatsitsa, J & Deltombe, T (2012), *Kamerun! Une guerre cachée aux origines de la Françafrique, 1948-1971*, La Découverte, Paris.

Ebolo, MD (1998), 'L'implication des puissances occidentales dans les processus de démocratisation en Afrique: analyse des actions américaine et française au Cameroun (1989-1997)', *Polis. Revue camerounaise de science politique*, vol. 6, no. 2, pp. 19–55.

Eboussi Boulaga, F (1997), *La démocratie de transit au Cameroun*, L'Harmattan, Paris.

Emmanuel, N (2010), 'Undermining cooperation: donor-patrons and the failure of political conditionality', *Democratization*, vol. 17, no. 5, pp. 856–77.

Ferguson, J (1990), *The anti-politics machine: 'development', depoliticization, and bureaucratic power in Lesotho*, University of Minnesota Press, Minneapolis.

Friedrich Ebert Stiftung (2013), *Prévenir et lutter contre la fraudes électorales au Cameroun*, Friedrich Ebert Stiftung, Yaoundé.

Geisler, G (1993), 'Fair? What has fairness got to do with it? Vagaries of election observations and democratic standards', *Journal of Modern African Studies*, vol. 31, no. 4, pp. 613–37.

Gros, JG (1995), 'The hard lessons of Cameroon', *Journal of Democracy*, vol. 6, no. 3, pp. 112–27.

Guilhot, N (2005), *The democracy makers: human rights and the politics of global order*, Columbia University Press, New York.

Hansen, KF (2010), 'Inside electoral democracy: gift-giving and flaunting in political campaigning in Cameroon',

Journal of Asian and African Studies, vol. 45, no. 4, pp. 432–44.

Joseph, R (1977), *Radical nationalism in Cameroon. Social origins of the UPC rebellion*, Clarendon, Oxford.

Konings, P (2011), *The politics of neoliberal reforms in Africa: state and civil society in Cameroon*, Langaa, Bamenda.

Lewis, D and Mosse, D (eds) (2006), *The ethnography of aid and agencies*, Kumarian Press, Bloomfield, CT.

Lindberg, S (2009), *Democratization by elections: a new mode of transition*, Johns Hopkins University Press, Baltimore.

Lynch, G & Crawford, G (2011), 'Democratization in Africa 1990–2010: an assessment', *Democratization*, vol. 18, no. 2, pp. 275–310.

Malaquais, D (2001), 'Arts de feyre au Cameroun', *Politique africaine*, no. 82, pp. 101–18.

Manirakiza, D (2010), 'Football amateur au Cameroun: entre clientélisme politique et échanges mutuels', *Politique africaine*, no. 118, pp. 103–22.

Mbowou, CJ (2013), *Etre sans papier chez soi. Identification, visibilité, invisibilité dans les marges camerounaises du Lac Tchad*, Masters' dissertation, Université Paris 1 – Panthéon Sorbonne, Paris.

Mehler, A (1997), 'Cameroun: une transition qui n'a pas eu lieu', in JP Daloz & P Quantin (eds), *Transitions démocratiques en Afrique*, Karthala, Paris, pp. 95–138.

Ngaméni, N and Pommerolle, ME (2015), 'Fabrics of loyalty: the politics of international women day's wax print cloth in Cameroon', *Africa*, vol. 85, no. 4, in print.

Nyamnjoh, FB & Fokwang, J (2005), 'Entertaining repression: music and politics in postcolonial Cameroon', *African Affairs*, vol. 104, no. 415, pp. 251–74.

Oisín, T (2013), 'Internationalized regimes: a second dimension of regime hybridity', *Democratization*, vol. 20, no. 7, pp. 1169–94.

Olinga, AD (2002), L'Onel. Réflexion

sur la loi camerounaise du 19 décembre 2000 portant création d'un Observatoire national des élections, Pucac, Yaoundé.

Olinga, AD (1998), 'Politique et droit électoral au Cameroun. Analyse juridique de la politique électorale', *Polis. Revue camerounaise de science politique*, vol. 6, no. 2, pp. 31–53.

Olivier de Sardan, JP (2005), *Anthropology and development. Understanding contemporary social change*, Zed Books, London.

Peiffer, C & Englebert, P (2012), 'Extra-version, vulnerability to donors, and political liberalization in Africa', *African Affairs*, vol. 111, no. 444, pp. 355–78.

Petric, B (ed.) (2012), *La fabrique de la démocratie. ONG, think-tank et organisation internationale en action*, Edition de la MSH, Paris.

Pigeaud, F (2011), *Au Cameroun de Paul Biya*, Karthala, Paris.

Plateforme des organisations de la société civile appuyées par l'Union européenne (2013), *Mission d'observation électorale. Rapport final*, Yaoundé.

Pommerolle, ME (2015), 'Les violences dans l'extrême-nord du Cameroun: le complot comme outil d'interprétation et de luttes politiques', *Politique africaine*, no. 138. pp. 163–77.

Pommerolle, ME (2010), 'The extraversion of protest: conditions, history and use of the "international" in Africa', *Review of African Political Economy*, vol. 37, no. 125, pp. 263–79.

Pommerolle, ME (2008), 'La démobilisation collective au Cameroun: entre régime postautoritaire et militantisme extraverti', Critique internationale, no. 40, pp. 73–94.

Pommerolle, ME & Machikou, N (2015), 'Fabrics of loyalty: the politics of international women's day wax print cloth in Cameroon', *Africa*, Vol. 85, no. 4, pp. 655–75.

Quantin, P (ed.) (2004), *Voter en Afrique. Comparaisons et différenciations*, L'Harmattan, Paris.

RECODH (2011), *Election présidentielle du 9 octobre 2011. Rapport d'observation*, Yaoundé.

Service national Justice et Paix (2005), *De la souveraineté du peuple camerounais en question. Rapport de synthèse sur l'observation de l'élection présidentielle du 11 octobre 2004*, Yaoundé.

Service national Justice et Paix (2003), *Les élections municipales et législatives 2002 au Cameroun: la loi, le crime, la justice*, Yaoundé.

Sindjoun, L (ed.) (1999), *La révolution passive au Cameroun*, CODESRIA, Dakar.

Sindjoun, L (ed.) (2004), *Comment peut-on être opposant au Cameroun? Politique parlementaire et politique autoritaire*, CODESRIA, Dakar.

Socpa, A (2000), 'Les dons dans le jeu électoral au Cameroun', Cahiers d'études africaines, vol. 40, no. 157, pp. 91–108.

Takougang, J (2003a), 'The 2002 legislative election in Cameroon: a retrospective on Cameroon's stalled democracy movement', *Journal of Modern African Studies*, vol. 41, no. 3, pp. 421–35.

Takougang, J (2003b), 'Nationalism, democratisation and political opportunism', *Journal of Contemporary African Studies*, vol. 21, no. 3, pp. 427–45.

Tansey, O (2013), 'Internationalized regimes: a second dimension of regime hybridity', *Democratization*, vol. 20, no. 7, pp. 1169–94.

Terretta, M (2013), *Nation of outlaws, state of violence. Nationalism, grassfields, tradition and state building in Cameroon*, Ohio University Press, Athens, OH.

Torrent, M (2005), 'Cameroun/ Commonwealth (1995): itinéraire et bilan', Outre-Terre, no. 11, pp. 95–113.

Transparency International – Cameroon (2011), *Rapport final de la mission d'observation électorale*, Yaoundé.

UNOPS/PNUD, *Processus électoral du Cameroun. Contribution du Programme des Nations Unies pour le

Développement. Synthèse documentaire 2003-2004, Yaoundé.

Whitfield, L (ed.) (2009), *The politics of aid: African strategies for dealing with donors*, Oxford University Press, Oxford.

World Bank (2013), 'Indicators', World Bank, Washington, DC, http://data.worldbank.org/indicator

6 | Foreign aid and political settlements: contrasting the Mozambican and Angolan cases

Helena Pérez Niño
and Philippe Le Billon

Introduction

Four decades after the end of Portuguese colonial rule, two decades after the end of the Mozambican civil war and over a decade after the end of the Angolan civil war, the expectation of post-conflict, post-socialist democratization has not yet materialized in Mozambique or in Angola. The obfuscation of the line dividing the state and the ruling parties, the use of the state apparatus and resources to consolidate the party in power, and the restriction and at times open harassment of critics, journalists and the opposition imply that both countries are best described today as 'competitive authoritarian' regimes than as semi-democracies (Levitsky & Way, 2002). However, there are important differences in the type of regime and the material and political sources of power in each case.

For reasons discussed in this chapter, Angola never went on to become a significant recipient of foreign aid and its relations with traditional donors have been tense at best. It was also one of the few countries in the region that was never subjected to a structural adjustment programme (de Oliveira, 2007). In brief, the international actors who invested in promoting democratization and the good governance agenda did not have much purchase in Angola and those actors that did have leverage were never too bothered with the liberal peace package.

The trajectory of Mozambique is more intriguing in the light of a strikingly different post-war story. Western diplomats were pivotal to the negotiated agreement that brought the war to an end, and third-party mediation and inducements sustained peace-building and laid the foundations for the multi-party system. Already a darling of some Western donors during its wartime socialist period, Mozambique remains one of the most aid-dependent econo-mies in the region (Oya & Pons-Vignon 2010; Manning & Malbrough, 2012). The contemporary democratic deficit in Mozambique has not come about for want of the donors' insistence on good governance.

The undisputed control of Angola's enviable oil rent by the People's Movement for the Liberation of Angola (MPLA) is routinely blamed for providing the material foundations for the consolidation of a tightly centralized one-party state that is fully under the control of President dos Santos and the *Futunguistas*, the group of key advisors from the upper echelons of the party. A critical interrogation of this consensus goes beyond the remit of this chapter and has to an extent been discussed elsewhere (Pérez-Niño & le Billon, 2013). However, if the MPLA has sustained its position on the basis of patronage, co-option and disciplining mechanisms funded directly or indirectly on natural resource revenues, then how to account for the Mozambique Liberation Front's (Frelimo) similarly solid grip of the Mozambican state and seemingly authoritarian practices in the absence (at least until very recently) of significant sources of revenue?

This chapter contends that official development assistance (ODA) in Mozambique has *functionally* sustained Frelimo's undemocratic practices. This is not to say that aid funds have been used as a currency of patronage (see Auty, 2007). Rather, as the chapter will show, Frelimo has been able to craft a political and economic order that benefits disproportionately a powerful minority of domestic accumulators and some foreign investors. This crafting was made possible by the relative stability created by the substantial contribution of donors to the social expenditure in health services, education and social provision. Such contribution has become a core dimension of what Mushtaq Khan (2010: 1) defines as a 'political settlement': a stable order emerging 'when the distribution of benefits supported by its institutions is consistent with the distribution of power in society, and the economic and political outcomes of these institutions are sustainable over time'. The resilience of this political settlement rests in large part on the donors' continued willingness to pick up a substantial share of the social expenditure bill that has so far provided Frelimo with a buffer against the likely social and political backlash of its socially or environmentally regressive policies. While many donors have been interested in exerting influence in the state's social protection and poverty reduction strategy, we suggest that they contributed or at least failed to react to developments in the fiscal, investment and natural resource strategies that reinforced the regressive character of the Mozambican economy. The chapter proceeds as follows: the first section discusses the progress and pitfalls of post-conflict democratization in Mozambique and Angola. The second section traces the very divergent ODA trajectories, explaining briefly the implications of Angola's resource rents-based alternative to traditional donors' funding and technical assistance. The third section proposes linkages between the sources of funding – aid in Mozambique and natural resource rents in Angola for a contrast – and the ensuing effects on the different political settlements and authoritarian features of each regime.

Sources of finance and democratic governance through war and peace Mozambique and Angola share a common history as the largest colonies Portugal had in Africa. Both territories are vast and the Portuguese administration only belatedly managed to extend its effective presence beyond the cities of the coast and along the main transport corridors. A long history of uneven colonial penetration, coupled with the effects of forced labour and juridical forms of racialized stratification engendered social inequalities and regional cleavages that exploded in both cases in the aftermath of the liberation struggle.

Both civil wars were inscribed in the geopolitical order created by the liberation struggles in the continent, the immediate challenges and pitfalls of independent statehood, the struggle against apartheid and the pressures and interests of the Cold War. Admittedly, the forces at play were different in either case, with the Angolan civil war more decisively inserted in the sphere of Cold War politics and the Mozambican civil war fuelled by the advocates of minority rule in Rhodesia and South Africa. But they were similar in that both conflicts revealed the often violent beginnings of state-building with regional power holders vying for dominium and survival and different political orders coexisting in tension.

The financial costs of waging war in Angola (1975–2002) posed substantial challenges for the MPLA substantial challenges early on in the post-independence years. Aware that the only viable source of revenue was the oil rent, a young MPLA, made cohesive by the military challenge of the competing independence parties (Unita and FNLA), opted early on for a pragmatic strategy: to refrain from nationalizing the sector but to excel at managing it. By 1976, Angola had regained the pre-independence production levels, and, even during the war, oil revenues accrued to the state grew from US$1.5 billion in 1992 to 40 billion in 2012. Sonangol, the national oil company, is hailed for its management of the oil rent in a way that allowed Angola to capture an important share of the revenues. This, Angola achieved through concentrating scarce capacity in the oil sector and through the alignment of the interests of highly skilled technocrats and the MPLA regime (de Oliveira, 2007; Thurber et al., 2011; Heller, 2012). Angola thus came to dispose of the means for a 'developmental neo-patrimonialism' (Kelsall, 2011), one that would combine the central management of rents (through effective institutions of rent capture) with a long-term outlook (via institutions of rent allocation, but more on this below).

In order to pay for war, the MPLA approved a series of oil-backed private loans that built up into considerable indebtedness at the end of the war. In the post-war period, Angola and the IMF negotiated credits and adjustment without success. Demands for fiscal constraints and giving IMF access to the oil accounts were not palatable to post-war MPLA (Shaxson, 2007; Heller, 2012). But, in 2003, Angola and China negotiated a series of loans to finance reconstruction. As a consequence of this alternative approach, the engagement of Western donors and creditors in Angola remained marginal also after the war (Bäautigam, 2011; Corkin, 2011).

The Mozambican civil war had its origin in a campaign by anti-Frelimo armed militias, supported by the government of Zimbabwe-Rhodesia in the aftermath of the Mozambican independence. These groups formed the Mozambican National Resistance (Renamo) and extended its presence in central Mozambique with this financial and military assistance until the signature of the Lancaster House Agreement in 1979. Thereafter, the role of the main supporters passed on to South Africa's apartheid regime. With such support also waning as a consequence of a non-aggression accord between Mozambique and South Africa in the mid-1980s, Renamo unleashed a territorial strategy that relied more on the exaction and coercion of the population in their controlled areas, in contrast with their original tactics of attacks on public infrastructure, schools and health posts (Vines, 1995; Young & Hall, 1997). Throughout the early 1980s, Mozambique went into deep economic crisis, fuelled by the war and by the contradiction of a highly statist economic model, with a thin bureaucracy and weak productive base. Burdened by the crisis, Frelimo began relaxing centralized planning and moved away from the socialist economic model. Samora Machel, a deft diplomat, masterminded the reestablishment of relations with the West. Foreign aid and international funding by Western donors, the IMF and the World Bank was conditional on Frelimo's implementation of a structural adjustment programme (Macamo, 2006).

Third-party mediation through negotiations, inducements and humanitarian aid was central to fostering the peace negotiations that eventually led to the general peace agreement of 1992. Italy became a critical facilitator, particularly through the Catholic community of Sant'Egidio. By the early 1990s donors were well versed in Mozambican politics and the humanitarian challenges ahead and keen to engage in the peace-building effort despite their diverse political agendas (Manning & Malbrough, 2010). The United Nations, multilateral agencies and bilateral donors effectively used both positive and negative inducements to support the peace-building effort.

An early difference between the two countries was MPLA's ability to protect the oil sector from the rigours of war and to use oil as a means to leverage finance to ultimately win the war and finance reconstruction. Frelimo did not have access to such resources and the need to find financial and political support against Renamo saw the Mozambican state, headed by Frelimo, appealing for external assistance, not least from Kaunda in Zambia and Nyerere in Tanzania. As Mozambique progressively turned towards the West, it established diplomatic relations and benefited from international cooperation in a way that was denied to Angola. In reaction to the failed Angolan peace process of 1991, Western donors became ever more invested in crafting and sustaining the contemporary peace process in Mozambique.

Sustained diplomatic linkages and determined involvement in bringing an end to the war resulted in a very different post-conflict role for donors in the two countries. Stark differences in the quantity of ODA disbursed in each country are underscored by the different aid modalities and channels used. But beyond quantitative and qualitative characteristics of development assistance, the political drivers of the relationship between donors and recipient countries played a major role. The historical trajectory and the different sources of finance in the post-war period determined the role of the international donors in both countries as well as their comparative weight and influence in domestic politics.

Natural resources and foreign aid provide very different foundations for financing post-war reconstruction and state-building and they also entail different risks. It is therefore not surprising that, in the post-war period, Angola and Mozambique have diverged in terms of the political settlements that sustain MPLA and Frelimo in power. The main challenge when it comes to natural resources is the need to have a beneficiation strategy with a long time-horizon. In the post-structural adjustment period, lax fiscal regimes and poor negotiation of royalties and profits have condemned natural resource-rich countries to a depletion of their endowments with only minor beneficiation. But even if extraction arrangements are in place to ensure local beneficiation, the challenge still lies in the strategic and transparent use of resource revenue to ensure the socialization of national wealth as well as to fund productive diversification and broad-based growth. In the post-war decades, Angola has emerged as an illiberal state with impressive performance in the field of securing command over its oil rent. In the virtual absence of development assistance, most social provision is funded through the budget and ultimately with funds that come from the exploitation of oil and gas resources. However, Angola's achievements in terms of socializing the benefits of mineral wealth and funding the transition to a diversified economic structure have proved far more limited, with a regime that shows no intention of opening space for democratic competition (Ovadia, 2012).

Aid-dependent economies face different challenges: foreign assistance can cover for public services and provision in contexts in which the domestic economy is weak and fiscal structures are fragile. But donors are less adept at financing the type of reforms that can structurally upgrade the productive apparatus to generate broad-based growth. This ultimately compromises the recipient country's prospects of gaining independence from foreign aid. Both natural resource rents and aid can introduce great volatility via price fluctuation or sudden changes in disbursements (Fielding & Mavrotas, 2005). However, donors allow recipient countries less autonomy in the management of aid disbursements than resource revenue. As a consequence, aid-recipient countries have less space for leveraging resources into the restructuring of the productive base. Challenges for aid-dependent countries revolve around securing donors' commitment to stable transfers, remaining in control of the development agenda and conquering greater autonomy and manoeuvrability. However, the ultimate challenge is to leverage rents for a sustainable transformation of the productive structure.

Unlike Rwanda or Ethiopia, countries studied in this volume, Mozambique did not formulate an ambitious state-led developmental strategy (Hagmann & Abbink, 2011; Ansoms & Rostagno, 2012). Long before the end of the civil war, Frelimo acquiesced with opening the space for privatization and hoped for market-led growth, a turn that was supported by donors at the time, either directly because this was conducive to what was deemed 'sound macroeconomic policy' or because their agenda rather emphasized good governance, democratization and, later on, decentralization, none of which were seen at the time as conflicting with liberalization and privatization.[1] Mozambique's inability to bring about a transformation of the productive structure and the creation of sources of domestic funding meant that social provision, particularly in health and education, remained extremely dependent on external funds (de Renzio & Hanlon, 2007; Manning & Malbrough, 2012). Therefore, the effect of foreign aid has been that of sustaining an otherwise unviable status quo.

When a country depends heavily on a particular rent – be it natural resource, revenue or foreign aid – there is a risk that political institutions become more preoccupied with managing and sustaining these rent flows rather than developing a more productive and diversified national economy. This can lead to distorting the institution-building process. The prominence of Sonangol as a core locus of Angolan politics and economy is an example of this (de Oliveira, 2007; Ovadia, 2012). The vast resources and time devoted by the Mozambican state institutions in order to comply with donors' planning and execution of resources is another example (Macamo, 2003; Macamo & Neubert, 2003; Castel-Branco, 2008; Oya & Pons-Vignon, 2010).[2] But here, too, differences emerge. On the one hand, the effective mobilization of natural resource rents depends wholly on becoming managerially efficient, whereas in the case of aid allocation a host of geopolitical and strategic interests weigh heavily. On the other hand, the presence and influence of donors in Mozambique have directed the negotiation with the Mozambican government towards issues of governance and democratization. The more limited leverage of traditional donors in Angola meant that similar issues were absent from policy debates.

Overseas development aid to Angola and Mozambique Angola and Mozambique had different relations with donors and creditors from the time of independence in 1975. Throughout the period and until the end of the Mozambican war in 1992, ODA flows to both countries were growing year-on-year. However, Mozambique was better at attracting ODA. In 1992 Mozambique received US$1.4 billion compared to US$343 million for Angola. During the following decade, total ODA to Mozambique stabilized at around US$1 billion per annum (excluding debt-related operations), whereas ODA to Angola – at war until 2002 – also stabilized but around a lower average of US$300 million. Since the end of the Angolan war, the trajectories have further diverged, with ODA to Angola contracting to US$200 million (or about US$10 per capita) in 2011, while flows to Mozambique expanded rapidly to reach a peak of US$2 billion in the same year. (US$87 per capita) (OECD-DAC, 2013).[3] Furthermore, not only has Mozambique received roughly ten times as much foreign aid as Angola, but Mozambique receives more aid than other countries in the region with similarly poor human development indicators.

Angola's alternative finance mechanisms

The importance of oil rents in Angola stands in sharp contrast with that of foreign aid. Since 2006, a key change in terms of oil profit-sharing agreements resulted in a remarkable growth of revenue for Angola, resulting in a reduction of the total share of ODA as a percentage of GDP, which went down to less than 1 per cent. A very low contribution of aid as a percentage of GDP, which rarely exceeded 10 per cent, has resulted in a more limited presence and influence of aid agencies, even at the height of the humanitarian effort between 1992 and 2003. Competing Angolan independence parties invited Cold War sponsors to take sides, but it also detracted from gaining widespread support for the MPLA government, even from some of the more 'neutral' donors such as Norway. Most Western countries followed the distant, if not hostile stance of the US vis-à-vis the MPLA. Divisions extended at times within donor governments, as in the case of the French government during the early 1990s, with both ideological and opportunistic motives guiding support for UNITA or the MPLA. The MPLA expelled many foreign aid workers after the 1977 coup attempt, on the suspicion of sympathies with the 'putschists', but demand rose for foreign assistance in the 1980s as oil revenues declined and government military expenditure increased. Cuba and Sweden provided most of the ODA. Domestic NGOs were first allowed in 1989, in the main UN humanitarian aid programme – the Special Relief Programme for Angola – launched in 1990, yet until the Bicesse Accords in 1991, most people had to rely on domestic mutual assistance for relief.

By 1992, NGOs and ODA-funded projects in Angola were geared towards a massive reconstruction effort. Yet this agenda was quickly shelved and superseded by humanitarian priorities as the war restarted in 1992, and again in 1998 after the collapse of the 1994 Lusaka Protocol. Throughout that period, UNITA tightly controlled humanitarian and developmental assistance, which had until 1993 been limited to a few humanitarian organizations (ICRC and MSF-France) and CARITAS, while access to UNITA-controlled areas after 1998 became almost impossible. Foreign assistance briefly increased following the death in combat of Savimbi in February 2002, but remained focused on humanitarian and demobilization issues. The low priority put on the transition and democratization agenda was further compromised by the sharp decline in donor funds after 2003, as well as low levels of coordination activities and support for local NGOs and public services (Serrano, 2009).

In a now decade-old review of foreign aid to Angola, Ostheimer concluded that '[n]either humanitarian actors nor the donor community question the existing structures within Angola. Humanitarian actors mainly abstain from a critical approach for security reasons and the fear of governmental harassment [...]. The international community placed Angola high on the donor agenda

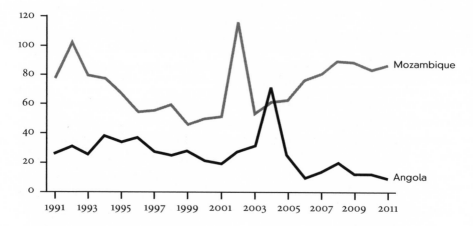

Figure 6.1 ODA per capita (US$), comparative Angola and Mozambique
Source: OECD-DAC (2013).

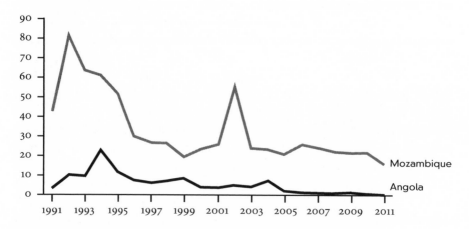

Figure 6.2 ODA as a percentage of GNI, comparative Angola and Mozambique

Source: OECD-DAC (2013).

but concentrated mainly on curing symptoms and not the underlying causes' (Ostheimer, 2000: 134). In bypassing or substituting for the state, aid agencies would have further undermined state resilience, which combined with the privatization and commercialization of social services, likely contributed to 'social exclusion and the further hollowing-out of public sector legitimacy' (Sogge, 2009: 20). According to Ostheimer, aid agencies had 'played a critical role in the privatisation of the Angolan state and its de-linkage from society' (*ibid.*).

The return to war in 1992 and 1998 meant that most aid agencies focused on humanitarian priorities rather than development projects with greater potential to strengthen local and national institutions. Furthermore, most humanitarian organizations sought to work outside state structures, which they often distrusted, and in effect replaced local state institutions, while heavily relying on 'traditional authorities' to reach beneficiaries without much consultation or consideration for power relations within communities (Serrano, 2009).[4] After 2002, humanitarian agencies did seek to strengthen community and state-level institutions, and linkages between them; yet these efforts largely failed as a result of the rapid disengagement of international agencies and lack of coordination with other key actors.[5]

For some observers, the last major development policy push by traditional donors dates back to the 2003 push for the Angolan government's Anti-Poverty Strategy Paper (*Estratégia de Combate a Pobreza*) and the creation of an 'observatory' of the government's anti-poverty work, which has remained dormant (Hilhorst & Serrano, 2010). Western donors' turn-away from Angola in 2004 was compounded by the continuous rise of oil revenues and the new massive loans from China, which in contrast to the numerous oil-backed loans passed with Western banks included a clear political agenda shaped around post-war reconstruction and infrastructure development, notably with the aim of demonstrating the 'peace dividend' of the MPLA's victory and consolidating popular support for the ruling party in view of elections then scheduled in 2008.

Mozambique and Western donors

At critical points of the Mozambican post-conflict transition to a multiparty democracy, it was the coordinated action of donors that activated the necessary lever to keep both parties in the game, pushing through stalled legislative debates and providing guarantees in the 1994 presidential elections, which Afonso Dhlakama, Renamo's long-standing leader, threatened to boycott. Of these incentives, the most influential was the creation by the UN and bilateral donors of two trust funds to support the emergence of opposition parties. Under this programme, seventeen emerging political parties received $150,000 each, with Renamo receiving at its peak a monthly stipend of $300,000 (Manning & Malbrough, 2010).[6]

This coordinated intervention had two effects: it reassured donors that they were on the right track, giving way to portrayals of Mozambique as a case of aid effectiveness, which in turn legitimized foreign missions in the eyes of their superiors and national constituencies. On the other hand, by having the donor community intervene to solve political deadlocks, international mediation progressively became institutionalized in Mozambican politics, while Renamo and Frelimo found it hard to use democratic mechanisms and build mutual trust.

The decade following the 1994 elections was a period of accommodation in which Frelimo officials learned to navigate donor relations while complying with the agenda of structural adjustment. The emphasis of the first decade of development assistance was on the consolidation of democratic mechanisms. Support was given to the state at the national level. But the presidency of Chissano was marred by serious accusations of corruption and by crimes such as the murder of journalist Carlos Cardoso. Donor disenchantment with institution strengthening led, in the second decade, to a greater emphasis on decentralization and good governance (Manning & Malbrough, 2012).

Mozambique became one of the largest recipients of ODA by Western donors and qualified for debt relief through the Heavily Indebted Poor Countries and the Multilateral Debt Relief Initiatives. In the two decades since the end of the conflict, most of the key policy discussions in Mozambique have had a substantial input from donors. Underpinning the relationship between donors and the state, financial assistance was increasingly channelled directly to the general budget; and assistance has since been conditioned to a continuous cycle of planning and performance evaluation by donors (de Renzio & Hanlon, 2007).[7]

General budget support aimed at reconciling donor and national agendas in the framework of the budget and PRSP cycles. By pooling donor funds, it was expected that there would be a reduction in the time officials spent addressing ODA-related requirements. But budget support did not reduce bureaucratic overload in Mozambique and observers have noted that, with donors becoming the main counterparts of negotiations with the state, the weakening of the domestic mechanisms of oversight and participation was left unaddressed (de Renzio & Hanlon, 2007; Manning & Malbrough, 2012).[8] Budget support and the relative shift from project to programme aid signalled a degree of trust of the donors in Mozambique political institutions and was congruent with the period's emphasis on ownership and harmonization. Macamo noticed, however, that programme aid required an ever-growing bureaucracy at central state level and that this gave an inordinate advantage to whichever party is in power. The large budget support programme gave Frelimo more autonomy and more control over expenditure, while at the same time creating administrative positions that were used for patronage (Macamo, 2006). Therefore, as Manning and Malbrough observed, 'the unintended consequence of strengthening state capacity has been to strengthen the ruling party's grip on the state' (2012: 21).

This was the result of the state increasingly functioning on the basis of foreign assistance funds and Frelimo turning social provision and public employment into mechanisms to strengthen the party.

Angola and Mozambique ODA channels and modalities compared

There are manifest differences between Angola and Mozambique not only in terms of the total magnitude of ODA but also in its composition. At a lower level, Angola receives a similar proportion from multilateral institutions and DAC donors. In Mozambique, DAC donors' contribution has far exceeded the disbursements by multilateral institutions. Furthermore, DAC donors provided the basis of the expansion of ODA inflows to Mozambique in the last decade. However, a 2008–2009 hiatus in aid (see Figure 6.1) and a recent announcement about severe reduction of programme aid forecast for the 2015 general budget indicate that it is unlikely that past levels of support by Western donors will be sustained in the remainder of this decade.[9] The impact of this financial contraction will be felt disproportionately in the Mozambican public sector, the main channel of aid delivery in Mozambique. Between 2007 and 2011, 53 to 70 per cent of total ODA went to the public sector in Mozambique, and 10–12 per cent to civil society and NGOs. In Angola, the proportion channelled through the public sector and civil society has been roughly on par. In 2011, for example, civil society organizations received US$95 million against US$82 million allocated to the public sector. The differences extend to the modality of foreign aid as Mozambique pioneered a budget support programme that saw ODA represent 51.4 per cent of the general budget in 2010 and 39.6 per cent in 2012 (ECDPM, 2012); in 2010, 41 per cent of total ODA was allocated to budget support (OECD-DAC, 2013). In contrast, budget support has been marginal in Angola, representing 3 per cent of total ODA in 2011 while in that same year 81 per cent of total ODA in Angola went to fund projects. With an ODA composition that has over the last decade emphasized budget support, Mozambican public revenue is disproportionately exposed to changes in aid inflows. A similar contraction in Angola would not affect the general budget.

Mozambique's public sector vulnerability to changes in aid inflows is also a consequence of the proportional contribution that these funds make to total public revenue. ODA represents around 20 per cent of GNI in Mozambique,[10] whereas in Angola it represented less than 10 per cent of GNI before 2004 (see Figure 6.2). Since then, the growth of oil revenue has reduced ODA's contribution to GNI to about 1 per cent. Differences in this respect could be attributed to Angola having commercially exploited its oil deposits for a longer period than Mozambique its own gas and coal deposits. As will be shown below, the differences transcend the mere presence of natural endowments and are closely related to the political processes underpinning the design of fiscal regimes to capture and channel resource revenues into state income.

But if Mozambique is vulnerable to fluctuations in aid disbursement, Angola is not less protected from changes in oil prices. The 2008 financial crisis caused an accelerated slump in global oil prices that exposed the extent of Angola's dependence on the oil rents. After hovering around US$130 per barrel in July 2008, prices fell down to US$40 in December and would only recover by the end of 2009. The 2009 budget exercise had to be revised downward mid-way through the year to accommodate for the shortfall. Revenue from oil taxes in 2009 fell to US$14.6 billion, only two thirds of the revenues obtained in 2007 (Jensen & Paulo, 2011). Before the crisis, oil-related revenue was estimated at around 80 per cent of total state revenue. In 2009, it fell to 59 per cent (Global Witness & OSISA, 2011). As a consequence of the crisis, the Angolan government fell behind in debt repayment, which it tried to compensate for in part by accepting a Stand-by-Agreement with the IMF that resulted in a US$1.4 billion loan in 2009.

An important difference between Mozambique and Angola, however, is the greater degree of autonomy and manoeuvrability allowed by Angola's sovereignty over the oil rent. Although Mozambique has stepped up the tax collection exercise by the Treasury and deployed other strategies to mitigate the foreseeable diminution of ODA, the latter still remains an important component of state revenue over which the government has only limited control.

Unpacking authoritarianism in Angola and Mozambique In Angola and Mozambique, democratic and authoritarian institutions and practices coexist and sometimes enter into contradiction. However, the foundations of the political settlement are different enough to postulate that the two countries exemplify different types of competitive authoritarian regimes. While MPLA's dominance in Angola is characterized by a personalized power structure tightly controlled by dos Santos and a close group of political allies, Frelimo's power is exerted by a more fragmented and heterogeneous group representing different and autonomous business interests. Within Frelimo, different factions cohere around the fundamental direction of public policy but do not always align politically. Notably, unlike Angola, the business interests linked to the leadership are more loosely articulated and do not owe their position to a single centralized source of patronage. Factions in Frelimo seem to exert more leverage than in the MPLA (de Oliveira, 2011; Ovadia, 2012; CIP, 2013b).

Bearing in mind the different sources of funding and the trajectories of the parties through war and peace, it could be argued that the MPLA first became cohesive and monopolized the oil rent, then succeeded in neutralizing the opposition and only later was in a position to use patronage to co-opt allies. In contrast, Frelimo first created the conditions for the emergence and consolidation of a national bourgeoisie, but the leadership needs to permanently stoke an internal coalition to remain in power (Hanlon & Mosse, 2010).

ANGOLA: A CENTRALIZED AND PERSONALIZED REGIME At the time of independence in 1975 different groups in Angola vied for political control of the state. The MPLA had established credentials in the liberation struggle as one of three competing national independence parties born in the 1950–60s. It distinguished itself by its urban roots in Luanda and cross-ethnic constituents, including a large number of mestiços. This basis, together with a closer affinity to the post-Caetano Portuguese (Marxist military) regime and the backing of Cuban military, ensured its dominance in Angolan politics from 1975 onwards, but compromised its legitimacy. The MPLA could not claim to be representative and its legitimacy was limited.

War broke out in the immediate aftermath, and in hindsight it helped consolidate a cohesive and disciplined MPLA. Its relative weak position in the contest for national legitimacy underscored the importance of controlling the oil rent. It has been observed that the war had the paradoxical effect of freeing the MPLA from facing political opposition and shifting all its efforts to the military front. This meant that during the war the MPLA had no need to negotiate policy-making and developed a state apparatus that had no room for other parties (Thurber *et al.*, 2011). This modus operandi would strongly influence the way the MPLA conceived its political role even after the formal adoption of the multi-party system.

Moreover, also internally, the MPLA leadership has been rarely challenged, with the exception of the failed 1977 coup attempt led by hard-liner Nito Alves. The regime evolved from a one-party socialist regime into a pragmatic, incrementalist and highly centralized regime controlled by the president and his entourage (Chabal & Vidal, 2008). Some forms of dissent do occur within the party, but are rarely public or directly affect the party's grip on the state. State power rests on a highly centralized and personalized patronage system, ensuring that access to political seats, official functions and the largest business opportunities rest within the remit of presidential approval (Vines & Weimer, 2011).

The military victory that put an end to the civil war further debilitated UNITA. Thus, from a fragile territorial presence throughout the 1980s and 1990s, the MPLA regime moved on in the post-war decade to a decisive extension of state presence on the basis of military strength and oil revenues. This highly centralized top-down approach is evident in the presidential control over nominations for provincial governments and in the somewhat disorderly use of political practices and policies that go from the state-driven and developmental to the provision of services in remote areas being outsourced to private contractors (Soares de Oliveira, 2013: 165). The MPLA was able to survive and come out of the difficult 1990s as a prosperous and unchallenged ruling party, whose official legitimacy was boosted through two rounds of elections, in 2008 and to a lesser extent in 2012.

The strength of the Angolan state, however, remains precariously rooted in the centralized control and limited handouts of a party state, rather than on the legitimacy of inclusive governance or the effectiveness of a developmental state. Angola's impressive trajectory in terms of managing the oil rent to its advantage has not been matched with an efficient strategy to redistribute the benefits of oil wealth. The socio-economic prospects for a large part of the Angolan population remain grim.[11] It is generally agreed that the oil rent flows into the general budget. To an extent, it is elsewhere that the opportunities for corruption and oil-based patronage are to be found, for example in the selection of local partners in joint ventures and in the array of business opportunities and contracts created through stringent local content provisions (Heller, 2012).

Angola is still far from leaving behind its reputation for petro-despotism. Nepotism and shady deals in the design of a sovereign wealth fund have attracted recent criticism, as well as delays in rent transfers from Sonangol to the budget, blurred accounting and reports of misappropriation (Global Witness & OSISA, 2011). The oil rent is the bedrock of the MPLA's continued stability. However, it is noteworthy that the oil patronage in Angola has not bred conflicts that threaten the stability of the political accommodation and that it has not prevented the creation of efficiency and capacity in the technical management of the sector. Thurber *et al.* (2011) attribute Sonangol's comparative efficiency to its centralized management, the long time-horizon of the implementation of a management strategy (a by-product of Dos Santos' long tenure) and the fact that the 'points of engagement' (i.e. the opportunities for oil-based patronage) are also centralized and tightly controlled, but to an extent limited to local content contracts and ancillary services. In this way, oil patronage does not interfere or preclude managerial efficiency.

It is necessary to examine the workings of a political settlement that has achieved remarkable stability in a context where a small entrepreneurial elite reaps the benefits of immense oil wealth while the majority of the population lives in poverty (67 per cent under US$2 (PPP) in 2009).[12] It is the rent management architecture in Angola that seems to explain in part the durability of the MPLA regime. A tight administration of opportunities and contracts linked directly and indirectly to the oil sector has worked to reward economic interests and sectors aligned with the higher echelons of the MPLA. In the process, political allies can become strong business players in their own right but also, importantly, sectors in the opposition are excluded from the only source of patronage available.

This has resulted in the formation of interest groups that derive their economic position from their links to the MPLA and in whose very own interest it is to remain on good terms with the regime and to contribute to sustaining the status quo. This is in line with the argument by Levitsky and

Way (2002) that elites who calculate that they stand to win in the future if the regime stays in place contribute to regime durability.

MOZAMBIQUE: A FRAGMENTED BUT STABLE SETTLEMENT Frelimo's ability to monopolize power and channels of patronage in Mozambique is more limited than the MPLA's. Mozambique does not have a single substantial source of potential revenue of the magnitude of oil deposits in Angola and opposition parties have a more prominent role in Mozambique, notably as a result of the mediated peace agreement and substantial donor support for opposition parties during the peace-building period.

Mozambique is not resource-scarce, but its mineral and energy resources are of lesser value and their exploitation involves some formidable logistical challenges. The resource rents will be available in an advanced stage of the consolidation of Frelimo's hegemonic rule, whereas in Angola the consolidation of the MPLA went hand in hand with the development of resource rents. Democratic mechanisms do not always prevail in Mozambique, but legitimation and authority, as well as party cohesion, have been constructed differently than in Angola. ODA in the form of financial resources and the presence of donors as a source of political legitimacy play an important role.

Many of Mozambique's largest domestic business groups have links of one kind or another with Frelimo, but Frelimo is a far cry from the MPLA's monolithic block. Unlike the MPLA, Frelimo cannot rely solely on patronage and repression. Its strategy to prolong hegemony rests on upholding the creation of a national bourgeoisie as much as on sustaining the loyalty of its bases through patronage (Sumich, 2010). Unlike Angola's at times statist development strategy, Mozambique embraced a decisive liberalization that saw the widespread privatization of state enterprises in the 1990s (West & Myers, 1996; Pitcher, 2002). Large fortunes have been made through concessions, tenders and outsourcing contracts in service provision, the licensing of telecommunications, public–private partnerships and the rapid expansion of the domestic banking sector (CIP, 2013a; IESE, 2013). Domestic accumulators are prominent in all these segments. Some of the country's largest domestic business conglomerates are headed by Frelimo's strongmen (and women) and other business groups are in close proximity to the party. President Guebuza's business group has documented stakes in some of Mozambique's most profitable sectors. This is true of other political dynasties such as the Machels, the Chissanos as well as other Frelimo heavyweights from different provinces (Hanlon & Mosse, 2010). This dynamic gained momentum after the discovery and commercial redevelopment of substantial coal and gas deposits in northern Mozambique during the late 2000s. Domestic capital does not have the financial muscle to operate in the extractive industries but can operate around it and reap the benefits.

With former President Joaquim Chissano (1986–2005) and more decisively under Guebuza after 2005, Mozambique has conditioned the state to support large-scale investors. Attracting foreign investment and supporting domestic capitalists have been at the centre of public policy. Mozambique is now host to a set of mega-projects exploiting the country's endowments (electricity, heavy sands, coal and soon gas too). However, the post-conflict fiscal regime was designed to provide incentives to attract investment but lacked mechanisms to secure revenue collection (Bolnick, 2009). Although a new Code of Fiscal Benefits introduced in 2002 redressed what was agreed to be a fiscal regime with excessive tax incentives, the Mozambican state still provides ample benefits in contracts negotiated on a case-by-case basis, and taxation and royalty rates remain low in comparative terms. Fiscal incentives contribute to make the Mozambican economy extremely porous, with mega-projects that do not create jobs and have no meaningful linkages with the economy.[13]

As a result of this strategy, Mozambique had one of the lowest levels of tax revenue as a share of GDP in the world. Between 1993 and 1999, tax revenue represented 11.4 per cent of GDP and only after considerable reform reached 14.4 per cent in 2006 (Bolnick, 2009). Such a low fiscal base constrains both the capacity and the autonomy of the state and reinforces aid dependency, confirming the hypothesis that links aid dependence and low tax revenue.

Similarly, the thrust of infrastructural investment has been focused on the transport and energy demands of the mega-projects. This unbalanced development strategy has become a fertile ground for social discontent and political instability. Spikes in the rise of transport, utilities and food prices have sparked massive riots in the past years and in 2012 Renamo has threatened to return to an all-out war. In the same period, municipal elections were marred with irregularities. Frelimo is investing its resources and rallying its regional bases in an attempt at containing the rapid expansion of support for the opposition Democratic Movement of Mozambique (MDM) – particularly in Sofala, Zambezia and Nampula. MDM is a splinter of Renamo but led by the son of a former Frelimo vice president, and is now the second largest party in Mozambique. It draws support from the traditional Renamo strongholds of central Mozambique and increasingly also among disenchanted urban dwellers and the youth in Maputo and Matola.

In summary, Mozambique could be on the edge of major political instability. So far, a crucial element helping to keep the whole system together has been the social buffer of foreign aid that flows through the budget and through development projects, providing a lifeline to public service delivery, particularly in health and education. The argument here is that aid-funded social provision has created conditions in which Frelimo can maintain a macroeconomic policy that is skewed in favour of rapid rents and unproductive accumulation without facing the full social and political consequences of such a strategy.

This confirms Manning and Malbrough's (2012) observation that aid had helped cement *partidarização* – the 'partization' of public administration and blurring of the separation between state institutions and the ruling party – during the first post-independence decade, but it expands it by examining the more structural consequences and the function of aid within Mozambique's political settlement.

Conclusion

The relationship between foreign development aid and political regimes in recipient countries is not straightforward. It is shaped by a combination of multiple factors acting on each other and changing over time. On the one hand, there are international doctrines around the role of aid and ways in which effectiveness, accountability and harmonization are operationalized in different periods. Post-conflict reconstruction in Mozambique and Angola took place in a period that saw changes in emphasis and narratives, from market-led growth and liberalization to the good governance agenda, from project aid to programme assistance, even to general budget aid. But Western donors' strategies and decision-making processes require disaggregation: from the sheer diversity of donors' agendas and interests, to the different character of the bilateral relations and the widely diverse economic interests of donor country firms in the recipient country. All these factors interact with the type of political settlement in place and the trajectory and specific challenges of different state-building projects, particularly in the Lusophone countries in which liberation movements waged a protracted anti-colonial struggle, conquered power but were soon thereafter engulfed in civil wars, and where opposition parties have had a tumultuous transit from armed opposition into credible electoral competitors (Pearce, 2010).

This chapter has contrasted the very restricted interaction of donors and the state in Angola, with the long-standing, deep and extensive footprint of Western donors in the post-independence political process in Mozambique. The availability of the oil rent prevented the formation of strong dependence on Western donors in Angola with some notable ramifications. In the face of a military victory, a weak civil society and political opposition, the restricted space for liberal diplomacy and foreign policy meant that there was nothing standing in the way of the consolidation of an authoritarian regime under MPLA. Few mechanisms are in place to make MPLA accountable and to open up the space for democratization in Angola. But, on the other hand, exempted from a structural adjustment programme that was a condition for joining the international aid and financial architecture, Angola managed something significant. It created a national oil company that resisted war and post-conflict liberalization and that, in spite of corruption and clientelism, operates efficiently, remains state-owned and is the main source of public revenue. It is this contribution to public expenditure that funds the Angolan health and education systems and infrastructure and diversification investments.

Angola and Mozambique's human development indicators are roughly on a par. But the financial sources of social provision are strikingly different in the case of Mozambique. Donors had a prominent role in providing assistance for post-war reconstruction as well as in forging a new economic order based on the privatization of state assets, trade and financial liberalization and the adoption of massive fiscal incentives in order to attract foreign investment. In the meantime, the substantial post-conflict effort to build a multi-party democracy in Mozambique became derailed as a result of Renamo's clumsiness and Frelimo's continued co-option of the state. The provision of foreign aid can be judged successful in that a relapse to war was largely prevented and elections have been regularly held. But the reorganization of the Mozambican productive structure resulted in the emergence of investment enclaves that do not contribute to the national economy via job creation or taxation. Foreign investors and national business groups alike have benefited from fiscal incentives. Frelimo builds its support partly on those groups and Western donors have not forcefully opposed this regressive macroeconomic policy either because they endorse these ideas of market-led growth as the main channel for poverty reduction or because they face the pressures from their own national firms, which compete in Mozambique for tenders and concessions and benefit from the fiscal and investment regime. Despite decades of impressive GDP growth, poverty is on the rise and Mozambique is still one of the world's least developed countries. One factor preventing the Mozambican social powder keg from exploding is the sustained support received in the form of foreign aid, which until 2014 represented most of the funding available for social provision.

To conclude, if Angola provides a fascinating example of the advantages and pitfalls of restricted engagement with donors (Jahn, 2007), Mozambique exemplifies the ambiguous effect of foreign aid on domestic politics as one-party rule becomes institutionalized and the regime becomes more authoritarian.

Notes

1 Both Memoranda of Understanding between the GoM and PAP (The Programme Aid Partners) – the group of donors providing programme aid – mention the implementation of 'sound macroeconomic' policy and poverty reduction as underlying principles for the provision of programme aid and budget support respectively (GoM/PAP, 2004; 2009). One problem with the way poverty reduction was internalized in the MOUs and the relation between the GoM and donors is that it relied fully on insisting that *expenditure* was transparent and prioritized poverty reduction. However, poverty reduction is not simply about the correct execution of budget funds, but about aligning the fiscal, investment, monetary, infrastructure and production strategies to broad-based growth. This explains, in part, the paradox that characterizes Mozambique in the past

decade: rapid GDP growth, growing aid disbursement and growing poverty (Cunguara & Hanlon, 2012).

2 Macamo (2006) pointed out that the creation of a large bureaucratic architecture to manage programme aid risked becoming a parallel state apparatus. It was estimated that civil servants' activities related to liaising with donors took an average of two months' work per year.

3 Angola's population is estimated at 19 million against Mozambique's 23 million (UNSTATS, 2010).

4 There were important exceptions: ADRA, an Angolan NGO, worked with local state administration and emerging community organizations to integrate relief, social infrastructure and institutional capacity building (Serrano, 2009).

5 Humanitarian aid first tripled between 2001 and 2003, but then declined from US$197 million to US$26 million in 2006, while the number of registered INGOs and National NGOs dropped from 195 and 365, to 57 and 68 between 2001 and 2006 (OECD-DAC, various years; Serrano, 2009).

6 Mozambique has had regular presidential and parliamentary elections. Renamo obtained the majority of the votes in central Mozambique in the 1994 presidential election, but, as a result of its very troubled transition into a political party, it has since lost an important proportion of the vote. Increasingly elections in Mozambique are marred by Frelimo's undemocratic practices. While there is no overt violent repression of opposition, Frelimo has abused its majority in the electoral commission to tamper with the regulation in order to prevent Renamo, but increasingly the opposition Democratic Movement of Mozambique (MDM), from running and winning the vote. Fraud was documented particularly in the 2009 presidential elections and the 2014 elections for municipal councils (Macamo & Neubert, 2003; Manning, 2010).

7 Mozambique received budget support since the early 1990s, but it was in 2000 that a coordination mechanism including a group of donor countries contributing to programme aid was set up. In 2004, the relation between the GoM and these donors was formalized in a Memorandum of Understanding.

8 A telling example of this is the planning of the annual budget and the poverty reduction strategy papers that have been negotiated between the government and the donors prior to being presented in Parliament. According to Macamo (2006), such sequence restricts the participation of the opposition and civil society in policy dialogue and reinforces the advantages that Frelimo derives from being in government at the instance of foreign development assistance.

9 During 2012, the contribution of most bilateral donors to Mozambique was reduced (OECD, 2013). The total amount received increased to US$1.264 billion in 2012, up from US$1.156 in 2011 on the back of multilateral institutions transfers. Among others, disbursements from the US, the UK, Sweden, Portugal, Spain and the Netherlands decreased in relation to previous years (O Pais, 2013b). According to the Ministry of Finance, despite committing to a support programme equivalent to 41.4 per cent of the 2012 budget, due to disbursement shortfalls on the part of donors, BSP amounted only to a 27 per cent of total execution (O Pais, 2013a). During 2014 a number of donors announced a restructuring of their strategy in Mozambique and some are pulling out of budget support altogether. A press statement by the G19 (the group of programme aid partners) raised alarms by announcing in June 2014 a severe reduction in aid pledge for budget support in 2015. Overall programme aid will increase from US$270 million to US$289 million, but key sectors of education and health face important cut-backs (Hanlon, 2014).

10 Down from 30 per cent in 2004 (Oya & Pons-Vignon, 2010).

11 Socio-economic indicators for

Mozambique generally still lag behind those of Angola, though they are improving faster except for the maternal mortality rate.

12 World Development Indicators.

13 The International Poverty Centre's country study of 2007 went as far as to characterize the mega-projects as operating an enclave economy (Virtanen & Ehrenpreis, 2007).

References

Ansoms, A & Rostagno, D (2012), 'Rwanda's vision 2020 halfway through: what the eye does not see', *Review of African Political Economy*, vol. 39, no. 133, pp. 427–50.

Auty, RM (2007), *Aid and rent-driven growth: Mauritania, Kenya and Mozambique compared*, United Nations University, Helsinki, UNU-WIDER Research Paper No. 2007/35.

Bolnick, B (2009), *Investing in Mozambique: the role of fiscal incentives*. USAID, Maputo.

Bräutigam, D (2011), *The dragon's gift: the real story of China in Africa*, Oxford University Press, Oxford.

Castel-Branco, CN (2008), *Aid dependency and development: a question of ownership? A critical view*, Instituto de Estudos Sociais e Económicos, Maputo, Working Paper No. 01/2008.

Chabal, P & Vidal, N (2008), *Angola: the weight of history*, Columbia University Press, New York.

CIP (2013a), 'Elite política moçambicana à "caça" de contratos de prestação de serviços na indústria extractiva', Centro de Integridade Pública, Maputo, *Serviço de Partilha de Informação*, no. 13.

CIP (2013b), 'Potential revenues from Rovuma. Implications of the 2006 contracts for government income', Centro de Integridade Pública, Maputo, *Serviço de Partilha de Informação*, no. 7.

Corkin, L (2011), 'Uneasy allies: China's evolving relations with Angola', *Journal of Contemporary African Studies*, vol. 29, no. 2, pp. 169–80.

Cunguara, B & Hanlon, J (2012), 'Whose wealth is it anyway? Mozambique's outstanding economic growth with worsening rural poverty', *Development and Change*, vol. 43, no. 3, pp. 623–47.

de Renzio, P & Hanlon, J (2007), *Contested sovereignty in Mozambique: the dilemmas of aid dependence*, University College Oxford, Oxford, Global Economic Governance Programme.

ECDPM (2012), 'Africa at a turning Point? The case of Mozambique', *Great Insights*, vol. 1, issue 10, European Centre for Development Policy Management, Maastricht.

Fielding, D & Mavrotas, G (2005), *The volatility of aid*, World Institute for Development Economics Research, Helsinki, UNU-WIDER Discussion Paper No. 2005/06.

Global Witness & OSISA (2011), *Oil revenues in Angola: much more information but not enough transparency*, Global Witness and Open Society Initiative for Southern Africa-Angola, London, viewed 1 October 2015, www.globalwitness.org/library/oil-revenues-angola-much-more-information-not-enough-transparency

Hagmann, T & Abbink, J (2011), 'Twenty years of revolutionary democratic Ethiopia, 1991 to 2011', *Journal of Eastern African Studies*, vol. 5, no. 4, pp. 579 –95.

Hall, M & Young, T (1997), *Confronting leviathan. Mozambique since independence*, Hurst, London.

Hanlon, J (2014), 'Mozambique: news reports and clippings', Number 262, 13 June 2014, available at tinyurl.com/mozamb

Hanlon, J & Mosse, M (2010), 'Mozambique's elite – finding its way in a globalized world and returning to old development models', paper presented at the UNU-WIDER conference on the role of elites in economic development, Helsinki.

Heller, PRP (2012), 'Angola's Sonangol: dexterous right hand of the state', in MC Thurber, R Hults David & DG Victor (eds), *Oil and governance: state-owned enterprises and the world energy supply*, Cambridge University Press, Cambridge, pp. 836–82.

Hilhorst, D & Serrano, M (2010). 'The humanitarian arena in Angola, 1975–2008', *Disasters*, vol. 34, no. 2, pp. 183–201.

Jahn, B (2007), 'The tragedy of liberal diplomacy: democratization, intervention, statebuilding (part II)', *Journal of Intervention and Statebuilding*, vol. 1, no. 2, pp. 211–29.

Jensen, SK & Paulo, FM (2011), *Reforms of the Angolan budget process and public financial management: was the crisis a wakeup call?*, Chr. Michelsen Institute, Bergen, CMI Report No. 2011:7.

Kelsall, T (2011), 'Developmental patrimonialism? Rethinking business and politics in Africa', Overseas Development Institute, London, Africa Power and Politics Programme, Policy Brief No. 2.

Levitsky, S & Way, L (2002), 'The rise of competitive authoritarianism', *Journal of Democracy*, vol. 13, no. 2, pp. 51–65.

Khan, MH (2010), *Political settlements and the governance of growth-enhancing institutions*, School for Oriental and African Studies, London, Working Paper, viewed 1 October 2015, http://eprints.soas.ac.uk/9968/1/Political_Settlements_internet.pdf

Macamo, E (2006), *Political governance in Mozambique*, Report for the UK Department for International Development, June, viewed 1 October 2015, http://www.open.ac.uk/technology/mozambique/sites/www.open.ac.uk.technology.mozambique/files/pics/d70313.pdf

Macamo, E & Neubert, D (2003), 'When the post-revolutionary state decentralizes: the reorganization of political structures and administration in Mozambique', *Cadernos de Estudos Africanos*, vol. 5, no. 6, pp. 51–74.

Manning, C (2010), 'Mozambique's slide into one-party rule', *Journal of Democracy*, vol. 21, no. 2, pp. 151–65.

Manning, C & Malbrough M (2012), *The changing dynamics of foreign aid and democracy in Mozambique*, United Nations University, Helsinki, UNU-WIDER Working Paper No. 2012/18.

Manning, C & Malbrough M (2010), 'Bilateral donors and aid conditionality in post-conflict peacebuilding: the case of Mozambique', *Journal of Modern African Studies*, vol. 48, no. 1, pp. 143–69.

Massingue, N & Muianga, C (2013), 'Tendências e padrões de investimento privado em Moçambique: questões para análise', in L Brito, C Castel-Branco, S Chichava e A Francisco (eds), *Desafios para Moçambique*, Instituto de Estudos Sociais e Económicos, Maputo, pp. 125–48.

O Pais (2013a), 'Incumprimento dos doadores faz cair dependência externa', *O Pais*, 22 February.

O Pais (2013b), 'Governo diz que o desempenho dos doadores caiu', *O Pais*, 5 May.

OECD-DAC (various years), *Aid statistics* (database), Organisation for Economic Co-operation and Development, Paris, http://www.oecd.org/dac/stats/

OECD (2013), *African economic outlook 2012/2013: country notes*, Organisation for Economic Co-operation and Development, Paris.

Ostheimer, AE (2000), 'Aid agencies: providers of essential resources?', in J Cilliers & C Dietrich (eds), *Angola's war economy: the role of oil and diamonds*, Institute for Security Studies, Pretoria, pp. 115–40.

Ovadia, JS (2012), 'The dual nature of local content in Angola's oil and gas industry: development vs. elite accumulation', *Journal of Contemporary African Studies*, vol. 30, no. 3, pp. 395–417.

Oya, C & Pons-Vignon, N (2010), 'Aid, development and the state in Africa', in V Padayachee (ed.), *The* political economy of Africa, Routledge, Abingdon, pp. 172–98.

Pearce, J (2010), 'From rebellion to opposition: UNITA in Angola and RENAMO in Mozambique', in W Okumu & A Ikelegbe (eds), *Militias, rebels and islamic militants: human insecurity and state crises in Africa*, Institute for Security Studies, Pretoria, pp. 365–88.

Pérez Niño, H & le Billon, P (2013), *Foreign aid, resource rents and institution-building in Mozambique and Angola*, United Nations University, Helsinki, UNU-WIDER Working Paper No. 2013/102.

Pitcher, MA (2002), *Transforming Mozambique. The politics of privatization, 1975–2000*, Cambridge University Press, Cambridge.

West, HG & Myers, GW (1996), 'A piece of land in a land of peace? State farm divestiture in Mozambique', *Journal of Modern African Studies*, vol. 34, no. 1, pp. 27–51.

Serrano, M (2009), 'Humanitarian aid and local institutions in Angola: strengthening institutions or institutionalising weaknesses?', in N Vidal & P Chabal (eds), *Southern Africa: civil society, politics and donor strategies: Angola and its Neighbours – South Africa, Namibia, Mozambique, Democratic Republic of Congo and Zimbabwe*, Media XXI and Firmamento, Luanda and Lissabon, pp. 63–76.

Shaxson, N (2007), 'Angola's homegrown answers to the "resource curse"', in J Lesourne & WC Ramsay (eds), *Governance of oil in Africa: unfinished business*, Institut français des relations internationales, Paris, pp. 51–102.

Soares de Oliveira, R (2013), 'O governo esta aqui: post-war state-making in the Angolan periphery', *Politique Africaine*, no. 130, pp. 165–87.

Soares de Oliveira, R (2011), 'Illiberal peacebuilding in Angola', *Journal of Modern African Studies*, vol. 49, no. 2, pp. 287–314.

Soares de Oliveira, R (2007), 'Business success, Angola-style: postcolonial politics and the rise of Sonangol', *Journal of Modern African Studies*, vol. 45, no. 4, pp. 595–619.

Sogge, D (2009), *Angola 'failed' yet 'successful'*, Fundación para las Relaciones Internacionales y el Dialogo Exterior, Madrid, FRIDE Working Paper No. 81.

Sumich, J (2010), 'The party and the state: Frelimo and social stratification in post-socialist Mozambique', *Development and Change*, vol. 41, no. 4, pp. 679–98.

Thurber, MC, Hults, DR & Heller, PRO (2011), 'Exporting the "Norwegian model": the effect of administrative design on oil sector performance', *Energy Policy*, vol. 39, no. 9, pp. 5366–78.

Vines, A (1995), *Renamo: from terrorism to democracy in Mozambique*, James Currey, London.

Vines, A & Weimer, M (2011), *Angola: assessing risks to stability*, Chatham House, London.

Virtanen, P & Ehrenpreis, D (2007), *Growth, poverty and inequality in Mozambique*, International Poverty Centre, Brasilia, Country Study No. 10.

Conclusion: democracy fatigue and the ghost of modernization theory

Nicolas van de Walle

Introduction[1]

The development community appears to be undergoing what might be called African democracy fatigue, and a process of rehabilitation of African authoritarian governance is emerging. A backlash has emerged in recent years against democracy promotion (Carothers, 2006). The limits and failures of African democracies are increasingly emphasized and a developmental advantage is claimed for countries that do not have multi-party electoral politics, whether under the banner of the 'Beijing Model', or of 'the developmental state'. This turn of events is surprising, given the growing optimism concerning Africa's developmental potential. The democratization wave that swept the region a quarter of a century ago left in its wake significant political liberalization, even if the number of regimes that might actually be defined as liberal democracies has not exceeded a dozen at any one time, and the region's modal regime is now electoral autocracy, in which the regular convening of nominally competitive elections is combined with most of the attributes of authoritarian rule.

Still, there is no gainsaying that the region today enjoys a higher level of political competition and popular participation than at any time since independence. This democratic era has coincided with a general reduction in the number of violent conflicts in the region (Wallensteen & Sollenberg, 2001; Themnér & Wallensteen, 2012), and a considerably faster rate of economic growth. Economic growth has climbed spectacularly in Africa, from 1.7 per cent in the 1980s, to 2.5 per cent in the 1990s, and over 5 per cent annually in the first decade of the new century. The latest numbers suggest an average GDP growth of 5.2 per cent in 2012 and 5.6 per cent in 2013 (World Bank, 2014).

The real significance of these positive developments in economic growth and security are well worth pondering, but it remains a puzzle that so many influential voices in academia and the policy world are choosing this moment to criticize the developmental impact of democracy and/or to herald the developmental virtues of authoritarian rule. In this chapter, I will argue that the growing disillusion with democratic governance in low-income countries is actually a return to attitudes within the policy community that have been dominant for most of the existence of foreign aid, and which were only displaced temporarily in the late 1980s, when the governance failures of authoritarian rule had become too egregious to ignore, and the optimism unleashed by the region's democratization wave managed to temporarily displace long-standing attitudes.

Modernization theory in the 1950s first provided an intellectual justification for favouring authoritarian rule, which comforted both foreign policy objectives and the bureaucratic logic of foreign aid. These dynamics are being reasserted in the current era, at least in part abetted by the very public failures and limitations of the democracies that emerged during the third wave of democratization (for instance Bratton & van de Walle, 1997; Crawford & Lynch, 2012; Cheeseman, 2015). Having said that, the current fatigue has generated some useful academic debates about the relationship between economic growth and political regime type as well as a number of claims about the relative merits of authoritarian governance that should be considered seriously.

In the next section, I deconstruct the current fatigue with democratic governance within the public policy community, and more specifically the foreign aid community. A second section traces the intellectual origins of the current backlash and links them to the ideas of modernization theory. A third section then examines the central claims being made for an authoritarian advantage in the development process. I conclude with some implications of the argument, cautioning against the current enthusiasm for authoritarian-led economic growth on the African continent.

Democracy fatigue

The chapters in this book identify a number of different explanations for the growing dissatisfaction with democratic politics in the foreign aid community. A first category of factors can be viewed as conjunctural. One should not exaggerate the depth and breadth of the commitment to democracy within the aid community, as commercial, bureaucratic and foreign policy concerns have always been the key aid allocation mechanisms (Alesina & Dollar, 2000; Collier & Dollar, 2002), and have consistently weighed more than governance or democracy considerations (Crawford, 1997; 2001). Still, the end of the Cold War is often held to have resulted in an increase in political conditionality by the donors in Africa, as it signalled a lower opportunity cost for donors to assert the importance of democratization and improved governance (Dunning, 2004). Many donors explicitly made progress on governance a criteria for aid allocation; the US actually established a completely new aid agency, the Millennium Challenge Corporation (MCC), in part to more assiduously employ political conditionality to allocate aid (Radelet, 2003; Carbone, 2004).

In recent years, however, other foreign policy concerns have once again begun to crowd out this concern with democracy and good governance. Since September 2001, and with the rise of the war on terror in Africa, most Western donors have been more complacent about the governance failures of states like Uganda, Ethiopia, Chad or Burkina Faso that have proved willing to offer troops, logistical support or even just diplomatic support (Birdsall, 2008; van de Walle, 2010; see also Anderson and Fisher in this volume, on the case of Uganda). For the US, the political conditionality criteria of the MCC have been watered down, to allow additional recipients that have been useful allies of the US, despite being authoritarian states, such as Rwanda, Uganda and Burkina Faso. More generally, as Abrahamsen argues in her contribution to this book, security concerns have powerfully conditioned the donor support for good governance and democracy.

The emergence of major new actors in the region, most notably China, has proven to be another significant factor in shaping Western donor attitudes in recent years. China has made a series of highly visible loans to the region for large infrastructural projects, partnerships with African governments and other general economic development activities. The Chinese government's carefully balanced rhetoric of not imposing political conditionality on its aid, and not interfering in internal African affairs, has put some pressure on Western countries to do the same (Woods, 2008). It was thus no accident that Secretary of State Hillary Clinton's first trip to Africa in August 2009 targeted countries like Angola, which were hardly democratic, but had received much attention from China (Sheridan, 2009).

The extent to which the war on terror and the emergence of the BRICS countries (Brazil, Russia, India, China and South Africa) as other sources of development finance for African governments have changed the Western donor's political conditionality on behalf of democratic consolidation to the region can be debated. What is not debatable is the extent to which these developments have lessened the leverage of the west in the region. Conditionality has become less effective in changing the practices of African governments, which today have broader and more diverse access to development finance. Indeed, the improved economic health of the region has had largely the same effect. With access to private capital, lower levels of public debt and higher growth rates, dependence on public aid from the West has signally declined in recent years, and with it the willingness to listen to Western advice. This decline in leverage almost inevitably has meant a greater reluctance to apply political conditionality on the part of Western governments.

In addition to these conjunctural factors, democracy fatigue is increasing in part because of what one might call the *sausage factory effect*, in allusion to the phrase variously attributed to both Bismarck and Mark Twain, that it is better not to see how both laws and sausages are made. Participatory multi-party electoral politics has now been the default political system for two decades across the region. Even if many of these regimes are not really democratic, the everyday practice of what looks like democracy is rarely elegant, and the observing of it can lead one to disillusion with competitive and participatory politics.

Debates in the legislature are rarely particularly distinguished and elections are even less occasions for careful debate about complex policy choices than they are in older democracies. Instead, they are vulgar affairs characterized by simplistic slogans, blatant pandering to voters, and vote buying. Similarly, corruption may or may not increase after a transition to democracy, but clearly talk about corruption increases, as a freer press and the opposition publicize every scandal by the state elite. An independent judiciary is also more likely to prosecute corruption cases, keeping them in the media. The inevitable result is the appearance of greater corruption than in the good old authoritarian days when state elites got away with corrupt practices far away from the public eye. In sum, the gap between the rhetoric of democracy and its implementation inevitably leads to disappointment.

The technocratic culture embedded within the aid community also results in a limited patience with participatory processes. Much of the current aid regime, in the sense of its modalities, institutions, rituals and procedures, was first set up in the 1950s and 1960s, when most recipient states were not democratic, and there was little political participation and virtually no civil society. Centralized economic planning was in vogue, even if few states had the capacity or discipline for its implementation. This led to the emphasis on planning out a set of aid activities exclusively with the executive branch of government, with no accountability or transparency. Twenty years ago, few donor officials had ever set foot in an African legislature, or talked to an African journalist. Decision-making on aid issues took place entirely within the executive branch. Today, this aid regime deals uncomfortably with the increasingly participatory politics in Africa, in which more active media, opposition parties, legislatures and civil societies have some kind of say in policy-making, challenging technocratic principles that favour executive implementation (see Chapter 4 on Ethiopia in this book). The new veto points slow down decision-making and implementation, introduce new variables in the policy process about which the donor officials are ill-informed, and push them into contact with more local agents who do not have higher economics degrees from Western universities. The culture shock can be intense.

The last decade has been marked by a series of innovations in the aid community, from Sachs' Millennium Villages (Munk, 2014), to the increased reliance on experimental forms of evaluation (Banerjee et al., 2011), and 'Cash on delivery' and other results-based aid modalities (Birdsall & Savedoff, 2010). These reforms are not without merit, but what strikes is their emphasis on top-down expertise and planning. Each emphasizes technical capacities within the executive branch of the recipient government, or within the donor agencies themselves, that are in practice needed to palliate the weakness of the local administration. None of these reforms address the perhaps key dynamic in recipient countries, their political liberalization over the last quarter century, with its attendant rise of more powerful mechanisms of accountability and participation.

The modal African country is not democratic so much as an electoral autocracy in which multi-party elections are regularly scheduled and the regime adopts the language and rituals of democracy, but remains profoundly authoritarian, with unaccountable executive branches of government, politicized judicial systems and various human rights abuses. One of the ironies of the current era is that many observers attribute the ills of these electoral autocracies to democracy, and their deficiencies are held to result from their democratic façade rather than their authoritarian core. A perfect illustration of this is electoral violence, and how it is often discussed. A number of scholars have argued that democratic elections cause a spike in political violence that poses special dangers for democracies in low-income poorly institutionalized political systems. Collier, for instance, is categorical: discussing a set of mostly African countries, he writes, 'at low incomes, democracy increased political violence' (Collier, 2009: 22; also Snyder, 2000; Chua, 2004). To be sure, there are cases of electoral violence in fledgling low-income democracies, and there is no denying that elections are discreet events that heighten political tensions. Still, many of the cases of violence cited take place during the actual political transition to democracy, and should be causally linked to the process of democratization rather than to the democracy regime type. Indeed, regime transitions are inherently unstable and dangerous moments for many countries.

Moreover, a careful recent study of electoral violence in Africa is insightful on this issue; when it takes place before elections or on election day, it is almost invariably conducted by forces linked to the incumbent regime. When it occurs after elections, it is invariably undertaken by opposition groups protesting unfair elections (Bekoe, 2012; Straus & Taylor, 2012). It seems analytically wrong to blame democracy for the violence of authoritarian leaders who do not want to lose elections they have been constrained to convene, but the conflation is typical of the current era, in which the practice of electoral autocracy serves to undermine support for democratic governance, rather than to make the case for democratic deepening. The current democracy fatigue should be understood in the context of a much longer intellectual history that shapes attitudes within the public policy and academic communities. I now turn to this issue.

The ghost of modernization theory

It should be said at the outset that the econometric literature offers little statistical support for the notion that the relationship between economic growth and regime type favours authoritarian regimes, at least since the end of World

War II. On the contrary, that a weak but positive relationship exists between democracy and growth is the most likely conclusion, given the balance of evidence from the several dozen econometric studies on the subject, which typically find either a democratic advantage, or at least the absence of a difference between regime types (for a more complete discussion, as well as Africa-specific data, see Masaki & van de Walle, 2014). In sum, the cross-national statistical literature offers little compelling evidence for an authoritarian advantage.

To be sure, a very small number of authoritarian governments have enjoyed records of very rapid and sustained economic growth. Almost all of them have been found in East Asia, suggesting that region-specific factors have been at play. The literature bestowed on these countries the moniker of 'developmental state(s)' and has sought to explain why they have been so much more successful than other low-income countries (Johnson, 1982; Haggard, 1990; Woo-Cumings, 2002; Kohli, 2004). But these states are exceptional, representing a very small proportion of the total number of low-income authoritarian regimes, many more of which tend to have mediocre to disastrous developmental growth records.

Still, there is no gainsaying that the view that authoritarianism has a developmental advantage has a long tradition in the public policy of economic development. Why is this? First, traditional economic growth theory has long had an anti-democracy bias deeply embedded into its DNA. Growth is understood to result from savings and investment, which require the deferral of current consumption. Economists long believed that greater investment would occur under governments that could quell the natural tendency of citizens to prefer current to future consumption. That such governments would naturally tend to be authoritarian was viewed as an article of faith, so that a prominent economist such as Jagdish Bhagwati could write in a 1966 introductory textbook that there was a 'cruel choice' between democracy and economic growth (Bhagwati, 1966: 204). Though he eventually would change his views on this (Bhagwati, 1995), it remains a popular view among economists.

The resulting bias against democratic forms of governance is, moreover, reinforced in part by efficiency considerations. Having to deal with the additional veto points that are the hallmarks of participatory politics has the disadvantages of both slowing down decision-making and preventing technocratic principles from necessarily carrying the day. From interest group pressures (Olson, 1982) to the political business cycle (Nordhaus, 1975), a large literature warns us about the anti-growth effects of political participation. Invariably, the solution is to insulate economic technocrats, who will require neither competition nor accountability to promote the public good and sustainable economic growth (Williamson, 1994).

Much of the early economic growth literature was influenced by modernization theory, according to which democracy is not compatible with lower levels of national income. For scholars in the 1950s and 1960s, such as Huntington

(1966) or Lipset (1956), the favoured sequence of development was to promote economic growth first, which would help bring about the strengthening of political institutions, and the changing of individual attitudes in a way that would eventually favour political democratization. Barrington Moore (1966) enhanced these arguments by pointing to the importance of social structure, and in particular the size of the middle class in shaping political institutions. He argued that the social alliances forged between elites shaped the nature of political outcomes. Thus, to the economics argument about the need to defer current consumption, the sociologists and political scientists of the modernization school added an argument about the endogeneity of institutions and political attitudes to the level of economic activity. Because political behaviour was derived from economic activity, rather than the other way around, the logical policy sequence was to worry first about economic growth, and only subsequently about political institutions.

The arguments of the modernization school were particularly attractive to the foreign aid community because they justified continued and even increased aid to countries in which fledgling democracies were overturned by the various military coups in the years following independence, particularly when the latter adopted anti-communist rhetoric. In foreign policy terms, modernization theory offered a convenient rationalization to continue to support these low-income countries. But the subsequent dramatic failures of most authoritarian regimes in the 1970s and 1980s undermined the confidence in the predictions of the modernization school, and increasingly the donor community began to criticize the poor governance of these regimes and advocate their democratization, as a way to improve their governance.

The theory and empirical evidence for modernization theory came under scrutiny in other ways as well. The sequence theory of development, according to which all countries throughout history have to go through the same stages of development, came to be much criticized (Gerschenkron, 1962). Dependency and world systems theorists problematized the external impact of the global economy on development (see Hadenius, 1992; Randall & Theobald, 1998). Late industrialization in developing countries came to be understood to follow a different path, as economies were able to skip steps, and political scientists came to ask whether a similar 'speeding up' of political processes was an option for late developers. At the micro level, the survey evidence on democratic attitudes in poor countries suggested that their citizens did not actually have a radically different understanding of democracy than those in older, richer democracies (Bratton et al., 2005).

Today, modernization ideas appear more attractive again. Democratization and the routinization of multi-party elections across the region did not turn out to be magic bullets, although the evidence suggests that democratic norms and institutions are strengthening, albeit unevenly and slowly, across a wide variety of countries (Posner & Young, 2007). As I suggested above, the messy practice of imperfect democracy in the region has made many people forget the disaster that was authoritarian Africa in the earlier era. Once again, the donor community is receptive to ideas from modernization theory, and, indeed, the apparent success of a small number of well-publicized cases, notably Angola, Ethiopia and Rwanda, seems to offer renewed vindication of an authoritarian advantage, particularly in comparison to such feckless democracies as, say, Nigeria, Malawi or Benin.

The new literature on the authoritarian advantage

The current democracy fatigue has been buttressed by an academic literature that makes the case for an authoritarian advantage, typically with four sets of key claims, which regularly appear in a loose and diverse set of relatively like-minded papers, reports and books, many of which have been sponsored by, and are influential within, the donor community. These arguments deserve to be properly, if briefly, assessed.

Argument 1: Elections are problematic in low-income countries and are likely to result in a decline in the quality of policy-making. The echoes of Huntington are striking when Booth and Cammack (2013: 87), for instance, assert that 'the trouble with democracy [...] is that its effectiveness depends on social and economic conditions which are not yet enjoyed in most developing countries'. In the African context, they assert, 'what wins elections is not sound development planning but a popular public policy gesture or two accompanied by targeted handouts to particular key clients' (Booth & Cammack, 2013: 88). Similar claims can be found in the work of Khan (2012), Kelsall (2013) or Collier (2009), as well.

The link to the modernization theory argument about sequencing is clear. Yet, there is little evidence of a necessary historical sequence, with a large number of economic and institutional prerequisites for electoral democracy. As Carothers has argued convincingly (2007), the lesson of the last fifty years is certainly not that authoritarian government does a better job of achieving these prerequisites for successful democratic practices. Indeed, the call for democratization in these countries was greater than in, say, China or South Korea, at least in part because in the vast majority of authoritarian countries the regime was doing a horrendous job of providing either institutional or economic development.

Assertions about the dangers of elections are often based on the premise that the power of societal forces is greater in Africa's low-income countries, and the capacity of states to process social demands is lower, making the public policy apparatus vulnerable to pressures that increase in electoral cycles. Kelsall (2013) and Booth and Cammack (2013) refer to 'competitive clientelism' to capture this idea of participatory politics leading to cycles of increasing distributive spending. In fact, there is some evidence of a political business cycle, in which spending is increased during African elections (e.g. Block, 2002), but it has also been found in Western democracies (Nordhaus, 1975; Hibbs, 1977) so its relationship to levels of income does not appear strong. Indeed, management of fiscal matters in Africa remains fragile and prone to deficits, but most experts point to dramatic improvements in the last two decades, and the region continues to exhibit much lower levels of debt than in the 1970s and 1980s (e.g. IMF, 2014).

Moreover, in political systems with histories of inattention to service delivery and largely inadequate social service provision, the spur of elections to increase transfers to citizens might actually constitute a step in the right direction in the form of investments in human capital (van de Walle, 2014). Stasavage (2005), for instance, offers compelling evidence that democratization in the region has resulted in an increase in education spending. De Gramont's (2015) review of the municipal governance of Lagos, Nigeria, offers a more mitigated but on the whole positive assessment of the impact of local democracy.

On the other hand, the notion of a weak state battling powerful societal forces and losing control of policy to popular distributive demands fails to convince. Low-income states are inevitably smaller than high-income states, both in fiscal and in organizational terms. Civil society and interest group organizations are also considerably smaller, due in part to their repression during the previous decades of authoritarian rule, and in part to the fact that structural factors such as lower levels of urbanization and income militate against the existence of a substantial and powerful civil society. There is also little evidence in various surveys, such as the Afrobarometer, to suggest that democratization has fuelled a participatory explosion in recent years. It is true that ethnic heterogeneity complicates politics in some African states, and there are a small number of cases in which ethnic violence marred multi-party elections, but the evidence that democracy has unleashed a participatory explosion that overwhelms governments is not compelling. Much more violence can be associated with authoritarian rulers who are unwilling to leave power – from Burkina Faso to Togo or Zimbabwe.

Argument 2: What matters to economic growth is not the type of regime that prevails, but rather the nature of the relationship between states and the holders of capital. To scholars like Kelsall (2013), Khan (2010) or Gray and Whitfield (2014), when the business–state relationship is productive, growth ensues. To paraphrase Barrington Moore (1966), 'no bourgeois, no economic growth' is the message. This productive relationship can occur whether or not a regime is democratic, though these scholars suggest it is more likely to happen under authoritarian regimes.

That economic development requires this productive relationship between state and capital is probably axiomatic, and is an idea that features prominently in a huge political science literature, at least since Moore's work (1966). The recent literature argues that the key is an appropriate 'political settlement', in which the national commitment to economic growth is signalled by the balance of power between state and social elites (Khan, 2010). Political settlements are clearly not necessarily based on formal deals, since plenty of countries have formal agreements that do not result in economic growth; South Africa, for instance, clearly enjoyed a fairly explicit deal at the end of the apartheid era between the African National Congress (ANC) and the white holders of capital, and yet it remains the slowest growing country in Africa that is not in a state of war (from two very different perspectives, see Marais, 2001; and Handley, 2008: 62–100). At the same time, Rwanda's relatively rapid growth today could hardly be claimed to have resulted from a formal political settlement since the minority RPF fought its way to power following civil war and an ethnic genocide, and probably does not enjoy much support within the majority Hutu population (Reyntjens, 2013).

Political settlements should thus be understood in the informal sense that the relationship between state elites and business elites favours growth. Twenty years ago, Evans (1995) had argued that an enormous variation exists in the relationship between states and capital in low-income countries, which seems likely, given widely different economic results across space and time. Some low-income states have actively preyed upon the private sector, skimming off profits and in effect racketeering firms, while only a small minority of states have sought to nurture business and discipline it, in order to promote indus-trialization. Evans described the productive relationship as one of 'embedded autonomy', where state elites were autonomous from societal interests, but also close to them, but he did not precisely explain what factors resulted in these kinds of productive situations.

At some level, the political settlements thesis is little more than the banal claim that economic outcomes are largely determined by the interplay of social forces. It is hard to imagine anyone disagreeing with this claim. To give the claim analytical muscle and policy implications, a specific argument has to be made regarding how and when this productive relationship comes about. Otherwise, the political settlements claim suffers from being largely circular, as these authors do not present independent indicators of the state–business relationship apart from a successful economy. It is thus hypothesized that growth results from a productive relationship between capital and the state, and such a relationship is said to exist because there has been economic growth. Without a more explicit description of causal mechanisms, and a way to measure the settlement independently of outcomes, the claim is largely non-falsifiable. For these claims to have public policy implications, moreover, we need to much better understand the factors that produce a pro-growth political settlement. Otherwise, it is not clear how this information is useful. Since it clearly does not exist in a majority of authoritarian states, in any event, it does not help to explain a putative authoritarian advantage.

Argument 3: The East Asian developmental state model can be exported to Africa. The claim is increasingly made that the East Asian experience, China in particular more recently, provides a viable development model for Africa, which could bring sustainable double-digit growth to the region, if adopted. Recent policy initiatives in countries like Rwanda and Ethiopia are similarly lauded for following this east Asian developmental model (Bräutigam & Xiaoyang, 2011; Booth & Golooba-Mutebi, 2012).

The success of authoritarian state capitalism in China over the last couple of decades is one of several factors that have conspired to make a 'Beijing Model' of development fashionable today. Its proponents claim a stark contrast with the 'Washington Consensus', which they invariably criticize, instead insisting on the viability of a substantial and activist role for the state in development, a focus on industrialization and export-led growth, even when short-term comparative advantage is missing, and a focus by foreign aid on the productive sectors of the economy, rather than the social sectors (Chang, 2002; Lin, 2012; Noman and Stiglitz, 2012; Gray & Whitfield, 2014).

This is not the place to discuss the details of development models and blueprints, but several points can be made in the context of the themes of this book. First, it is odd that a literature that often rightly chides Western donors for trying to impose a Western development model on African countries today (for instance, Chang, 2002) is so insistent that Asia is an apt model for the region, given its very different history, state traditions and structural factors such as population density, historical human capital levels and neighbourhood dynamics. It seems more likely that Africa's structural transformation will have to be suited to the realities of specific countries in the region, with their own historical legacies and various geographic and human characteristics, adapted to the world of the twenty-first century (Kelsall, 2008).

Finally, it should be said that the proponents of the Beijing model invariably overstate the emphasis of Western donors on governance and democracy, which is typically presented as monolithic, excessive and all encompassing, and contrasted unfavourably with Chinese pragmatism. At best, the good governance agenda being implemented in Africa is 'overly ambitious and complex' and thus a case of 'making the pursuit of the best the enemy of the good' (Noman & Stiglitz, 2012: 33). This is rhetorical overkill: until the mid-1990s, very little aid included a governance component, and the allocation of aid generally did not take into account governance issues. In fact, more corrupt governments appeared to receive more aid, not less (Alesina & Weder, 2002). This appears to have improved modestly since then (see the introduction of this volume, as well as Wright and Winters, 2010), but there remains little agreement within the donor community about what a governance strategy should look like, or regarding how to employ governance conditionality (Crawford, 2001).

Moreover, whatever the ambitious declarations emanating from headquarters and annual donor meetings, the reality at the ground level is almost always more accommodating to local governance deficiencies. As Brown (2011) has argued, it seems much more likely that bureaucratic dynamics and individual incentives conspire to lead local donor officials to exaggerate the quality of governance and democracy and its progress over time, and to argue against enforcing conditionality. Pommerolle's chapter in this book about the donors' curiously uncritical stance vis-à-vis electoral exercises in Cameroon illustrates this dynamic nicely.

Proponents of the Beijing model assert, finally, that citizens in low-income countries value economic growth and security more than they do good governance, much like citizens in East Asia. The demand within African countries for democratization and better governance is significant, however, even if many of the ideas about these topics are not purely indigenous, and even if donors have pushed for them fitfully and inconsistently. In survey after survey, African citizens demonstrate their attachment to the principles of liberal democracy and their desire for more accountable and effective governments. This attachment can at times and in certain countries be more instrumental than intrinsic (Bratton & Mattes, 2001), and it can compete with other values for Africans, but its importance in the region should not be underestimated.

Argument 4: Good governance may delay structural transformation and economic growth, because rent seeking by the private sector with the help of the state can generate the excessive profits needed to generate endogenous growth. This is potentially an important insight into the process of late development, and it appears to have some salience to economic growth processes in the East Asian tigers in the past (Kang, 2002). Of all the claims for an authoritarian advantage, it offers the most arresting and counterintuitive argument. The implication is that democratic countries are less able to generate these profit margins, at least some of which will require semi-legal deals to fashion and maintain private monopolies (for instance Khan, 2012: 120–21). But is this the case in Africa? This is an empirical hypothesis that is far from self-evident. For instance, Mauritius offers a case of a long-standing democracy in which pro-growth state elites have actively cooperated with business, and have provided key fiscal advantages to business (Bräutigam, 1999; Subramanian & Roy, 2003). Mauritian voters rewarded the governments who orchestrated rapid economic growth by re-electing them, suggesting this model is not incompatible with democratic politics.

In addition, cosy crony capitalism has only rarely produced structural transformation (Kohli, 2004). For every South Korea, there are ten low-income countries in which 'straddling' strategies by state elites and generous deals to business have only resulted in white elephants and an inefficient private sector. After all, rent seeking has a bad name precisely because, in the vast majority of cases, it ensures a far from optimal use of productive inputs and generates less than adequate economic growth. Again, we need more detail on the special circumstances that can make rent seeking productive.

Another related argument is that corruption in East Asia's success stories has been the equal of corruption in Africa and yet did not prevent growth, so the Western obsession with corruption is unhelpful and the focus should instead be only on the governance issues that are directly helpful to growth processes themselves (for instance, Khan, 2012). Other, more general improvements in governance as well as democratic reforms can be delayed until later in the development process, since 'democracy should not be confused with the more difficult task of creating governance capabilities for supporting growth' (Khan, 2012: 121).

Scholars like Khan are probably correct that good governance may be as much the product of development as its cause. The empirical literature is fairly contradictory on the endogeneity of governance (Mauro, 1995; Sachs *et al.*, 2004; Kaufmann *et al.*, 2007; Kurtz & Schrank, 2007), but some proponents of governance have undoubtedly exaggerated its likely impact on growth, particularly in low-income economies with many other constraints on economic growth.

The comparison of governance weaknesses in Africa with East and South East Asia is also useful. Khan is almost certainly right that different types of corruption can have varying effects on growth, though we need more specific empirical categories than the ones he proposes to gain analytical leverage on the issue. But the argument that corruption is no worse or more dysfunctional in Africa than anywhere else goes too far. The cross-national literature on corruption does indicate higher levels and more systematic breakdowns in governance in low-income African economies (Mauro, 1995; Kaufmann *et al.*, 2007). Peter Lewis's (2009) careful comparison of Nigeria and Indonesia captures well the far more pernicious and comprehensive failures of governance in the former.

Conclusion

I have argued that the foreign aid predilection for authoritarian forms of government finds its origins in both the modalities of aid as they developed after World War II, and in the intellectual apparatus of modernization theory. The postcolonial crisis of development that came to a head in the 1980s, followed by the third wave of democratization, which profoundly shocked political institutions, led foreign aid away from this bias for an authoritarian advantage, but it was only a matter of time before the older framework reasserted itself. A number of scholars have supported this bias, in a way that strikingly demonstrates the continued intellectual influence of modernization theory.

The economic and military support of authoritarian rulers has had a deeply ambiguous effect in Africa since independence. Although some authoritarian rulers proved able to temporarily spur economic growth and institutional development, in time, authoritarian governments have not proven to be developmental. Indeed, in Africa, a striking correlation exists between the degree of openness of political institutions and development. Botswana and Mauritius, the two most successful democracies of the region, also have had the best developmental records. In addition, the reasonably non-repressive single-party regimes of countries such as Côte d'Ivoire and Kenya enjoyed better records than the more repressive regimes of personal dictatorships such as Toure's Guinea or Mobutu's Zaire.

Will this historical disadvantage for authoritarian regimes in terms of bringing about development/fostering development reverse itself? Are the claims now made for Rwanda, say, or Ethiopia a harbinger of more systematic turn to developmental states in the region, and should these regimes thus be more actively supported by the donors? Perhaps, but a number of factors call for considerable caution. Both states are post-conflict states with substantial ethno-regional cleavages that historically have destabilized them, and one wonders whether the current stability is sustainable (Reyntjens, 2013; Abbink & Hagmann, 2013). While both countries have undergone substantial growth, albeit from an exceedingly low base, neither state has shown much capacity for structural transformation so far. Both face daunting problems based on their geography, human capital constraints and unresolved ethnic conflicts. Finally, both records are exceedingly dependent on the leaderships of single men, and one wonders what happens after they have been, inevitably, replaced. Indeed, Ethiopia now faces this question, directly. And where are the other cases? The least one can say is that to put all of the burden of a putative authoritarian advantage on the thin reed of these two cases is not auspicious for the argument.

Given their tragic pasts, one hopes the current regimes in Rwanda and Ethiopia are truly developmental today. Ultimately, though, plenty of other African countries strike me as having a greater developmental potential, from Ghana and Senegal to Zambia and even Nigeria. These countries are not necessarily model democracies and the stench of the democratic sausage being made on a day-to-day basis can be hard to ignore. But these countries have regimes that better reflect the sensibilities and dynamism of young people and of an increasingly educated and urbanized population. With more capital and purchasing power in the region today, a dynamic private sector finally has a better chance to emerge. Regular multi-party elections and term limits make their leaders slightly more accountable and limit the damage a single leader can do. I believe these countries are more likely to figure out the development puzzle, though some may not right away. Foreign aid should devote more resources and energy to figure out how to help them do so.

Note

1 I thank Pierre Englebert, Tobias Hagmann, Filip Reyntjens and Pablo Yanguas for useful comments on an earlier draft.

References

Abbink, J & Hagmann, T (eds) (2013), *Reconfiguring Ethiopia. The politics of authoritarian reform*, Routledge, New York.

Alesina, A & Dollar, D (2000), 'Who gives foreign aid to whom and why?', *Journal of Economic Growth*, vol. 5, no. 1, pp. 33–63.

Alesina, A & Weder, B (2002), 'Do corrupt governments receive less foreign aid?', *American Economic Review*, vol. 92, no. 4, pp. 1126–37.

Banerjee, A, Banerjee, AV & Duflo, E (2011) *Poor economics: A radical rethinking of the way to fight global poverty*, Public Affairs, New York.

Bhagwati, JN (1995), 'The new thinking on development', *Journal of Democracy*, vol. 6, no. 4, pp. 50–64.

Bhagwati, JN (1966), *The economics of underdeveloped countries*, McGraw-Hill, New York.

Birdsall, N (ed.) 2008, *The White House and the world: a global development agenda for the next U.S. president*, Center for Global Development, Washington, DC.

Birdsall, N & Savedoff, W (2010), *Cash on delivery: a new approach to foreign aid*, Center for Global Development, Washington, DC.

Block, SA (2002), 'Political business cycles, democratization, and economic reform: the case of Africa', *Journal of Development Economics*, vol. 67, no.1, pp. 205–28.

Booth, D (2012), *Development as a collective-action problem. Addressing the real challenges of African governance*, Overseas Development Institute, London.

Booth, D & Cammack, D (2013), *Governance for development in Africa: solving collective action problems*, Zed Books, London.

Booth, D & Golooba-Mutebi F (2012), 'Developmental patrimonialism? The case of Rwanda', *African Affairs*, vol. 111, no. 444, pp. 379–403.

Bratton, M & Mattes, R (2001), 'Support for democracy in Africa: intrinsic or instrumental?', *British Journal of Political Science*, vol. 31, no. 3, pp. 447–74.

Bratton, M, Mattes, RB & Gyimah-Boadi, E (2005), *Public opinion, democracy, and market reform in Africa*, Cambridge University Press, New York.

Bratton, M & van de Walle, N (1997), *Democratic experiments in Africa: regime transitions in comparative perspective*, Cambridge University Press, New York.

Bräutigam, D (1997), 'Institutions, economic reform, and democratic consolidation in Mauritius', *Comparative Politics*, vol. 30, no. 1, pp. 45–62.

Bräutigam, D & Xiaoyang, T (2011), 'African Shenzhen: China's special economic zones in Africa', *Journal of Modern African Studies*, vol. 49, no. 1, pp. 27–54.

Brown, S (2011), '"Well, what can you expect?": donor officials' apologetics for hybrid regimes in Africa', *Democratization*, vol. 18, no. 2, pp. 512–34.

Carbone, M (2004), 'The Millennium Challenge Account: a marginal revolution in US foreign aid policy?',

Review of African Political Economy, vol. 31, no. 101, pp. 536–42.

Carothers, T (2007), 'The "sequencing" fallacy', *Journal of Democracy*, vol. 18, no. 1, pp. 12–27.

Carothers, T (2006), 'The backlash against democracy promotion', *Foreign Affairs*, vol. 85, no. 2, pp. 55–68.

Carothers, T (2002), 'The end of the transition paradigm', *Journal of Democracy*, vol. 13, no. 1, pp. 5–21.

Chabal, P (2009), *Africa: the politics of suffering and smiling*, Zed Books, London.

Chang, HJ (2002), *Kicking away the ladder: development strategy in historical perspective*, Anthem Press, London and New York.

Cheeseman, N (2015), *Democracy in Africa: success, failures and the struggle for political reform*, Cambridge University Press, New York.

Chua, A (2004), *World on fire: how exporting free market democracy breeds ethnic hatred and global instability*, Doubleday, New York.

Collier, P (2009), *Wars, guns, and votes: democracy in dangerous places*, Harper, New York.

Collier, P & Dollar, D (2002), 'Aid allocation and poverty reduction', *European Economic Review*, vol. 46, no. 8, pp. 1475–1500.

Crawford, G (2001), *Foreign aid and political reform: a comparative analysis of democracy assistance and political conditionality*, Palgrave, Basingstoke.

Crawford, G (1997), 'Foreign aid and political conditionality: issues of effectiveness and consistency', *Democratization*, vol. 4, no. 3, pp. 69–108.

Crawford, G & Lynch, G (eds) (2012), *Democratization in Africa: challenges and prospects*, Routledge, New York.

de Gramont, D (2015), *Governing Lagos: unlocking the politics of reform*, Carnegie Endowment for International Peace, Washington, DC.

Dunning, T (2004), 'Conditioning the effects of aid: Cold War politics, donor credibility, and democracy in Africa', *International Organization*, vol. 58, no. 2, pp. 409–23.

Evans, PB (1995), *Embedded autonomy: states and industrial transformation*, Princeton University Press, Princeton.

Gerschenkron, A (1962), *Economic backwardness in historical perspective*, Frederick A. Praeger, New York, Washington and London.

Gray, H & Whitfield, L (2014), 'Reframing African political economy: clientelism, rents and accumulation as drivers of capitalist transformation', paper presented at the African Studies Association Annual Meeting, Indianapolis, November 2014.

Hadenius, A (1992), *Democracy and development*, Cambridge University Press, Cambridge.

Haggard, S (1990), *Pathways from the periphery: the politics of growth in the newly industrializing countries*, Cornell University Press, Ithaca NY.

Handley A (2008), *Business and the state in Africa: economic policy-making in the neo-liberal era*, Cambridge University Press, New York.

Hibbs, DA (1977), 'Political parties and macroeconomic policy', *American Political Science Review*, vol. 71, no. 4, pp. 1467–87.

Huntington, S (1968), *Political order in changing societies*, Yale University Press, New Haven and London.

IMF (2014), *Regional economic outlook: sub-Saharan Africa: fostering durable and inclusive growth*, International Monetary Fund, Washington, DC.

Johnson, C (1982), *MITI and the Japanese miracle: the growth of industrial policy: 1925–1975*, Stanford University Press, Stanford.

Kaufmann, D, Kraay, A & Mastruzzi, M (2007), 'Growth and governance: a reply', *Journal of Politics*, vol. 69, no. 2, pp. 555–62.

Kang, DC (2002), *Crony capitalism: corruption and development in South Korea and the Philippines*, Cambridge University Press, Cambridge.

Kelsall, T (2013), *Business, politics, and the state in Africa: challenging the orthodoxies on growth and transformation*, Zed Books, London.

Kelsall, T (2008), 'Going with the grain in African development?', *Development Policy Review*, vol. 26, no. 6, pp. 627–55.

Khan, M (2012), 'Governance and growth challenges in Africa', in A Noman (ed.), *Good growth and governance in Africa: rethinking development strategies*, Oxford University Press, Oxford, pp. 114–39.

Khan, MH (2010), 'Political settlements and the governance of growth-enhancing institutions', School for Oriental and African Studies, London, Working Paper, viewed 1 October 2015, http://eprints.soas.ac.uk/9968/1/ Political_Settlements_internet.pdf

Kohli, A (2004), *State-directed development: political power and industrialization in the global periphery*, Cambridge University Press, Cambridge.

Kurtz, MJ & Schrank, A (2007), 'Growth and governance: models, measures, and mechanisms', *Journal of Politics*, vol. 69, no. 2, pp. 538–54.

Lewis, P (2009), *Growing apart: oil, politics, and economic change in Indonesia and Nigeria*, University of Michigan Press, Ann Arbor, MI.

Lin, JY (2012), *New structural economics: a framework for rethinking development and policy*, World Bank, Washington, DC.

Lipset, SM (1959), 'Some social requisites of democracy', *American Political Science Review*, vol. 53, no. 1, pp. 69–105.

Marais, H (2001), *South Africa: limits to change: the political economy of transition*, Palgrave Macmillan, Basingstoke.

Mauro, P (1995), 'Corruption and growth', *The Quarterly Journal of Economics*, vol. 110, no. 3, pp. 681–712.

Masaki, T & van de Walle, N (forthcoming), 'The impact of democracy on economic growth in sub-Saharan Africa, 1982–2012', in C Monga & JY Lin (eds), *The Oxford handbook of Africa and economics: context and concepts*, Oxford University Press, Oxford.

Monga, C (2012), 'Shifting gears: igniting structural transformation in Africa', *Journal of African Economies*, vol. 21, suppl 2, pp. ii19–ii54.

Moore, B (1966), *Social origins of dictatorship and democracy: lord and peasant in the making of the modern world*, Beacon Press, Boston.

Munk, N (2014), *The idealist: Jeffrey Sachs and the quest to end poverty*, Anchor Books, New York.

Noman, A (ed.) 2012, *Good growth and governance in Africa: rethinking development strategies*, Oxford University Press, Oxford.

Noman, A & Stiglitz, J (2012), 'Strategies for African development', in A Noman (ed.), *Good growth and governance in Africa: rethinking development strategies*, Oxford University Press, Oxford, pp. 3–50.

Nordhaus, WD (1975), 'The political business cycle', *Review of Economic Studies*, vol. 42, no. 2, pp. 169–90.

Olson, M (1982), *The rise and decline of nations. Economic growth, stagflation and social rigidities*, Yale University Press, New Haven and London.

Posner, DN & Young, DJ (2007), 'The institutionalization of political power in Africa', *Journal of Democracy*, vol. 18, no. 3, pp. 126–40.

Radelet, S (2003), *Challenging foreign aid: a policymaker's guide to the Millennium Challenge Account*, Center for Global Development, Washington, DC.

Randall, V & Theobald (1985), *Political change and underdevelopment. A critical introduction to third world politics*, Duke University Press, Durham.

Reyntjens, F (2013), *Political governance in post-genocide Rwanda*, Cambridge University Press, New York.

Sachs, J et al. (2004), 'Ending Africa's

poverty trap', *Brookings Papers on Economic Activity*, vol. 35, no. 1, pp. 117–240.

Sheridan, MB (2009), 'Clinton building ties with Angola'", *Washington Post*, 10 August.

Snyder, JL (2000), *From voting to violence: democratization and nationalist conflict*, Norton, New York.

Stasavage, D (2005), 'Democracy and education spending in Africa', *American Journal of Political Science*, vol. 49, no. 2, pp. 343–58.

Straus, S & Taylor, C (2012), 'Democratization and electoral violence in sub-Saharan Africa, 1990–2008', in D Bekoe (ed.), *Voting in fear: electoral violence in sub-Saharan Africa*, United States Institute of Peace, Washington, DC, pp. 15–38.

Subramanian, A & Roy, D (2003), 'Who can explain the Mauritian miracle? Meade, Romer, Sachs, or Rodrik?', in D Rodrik (ed.), *Search of prosperity: analytic narratives on economic growth*, Princeton University Press, Princeton, pp. 205–43.

Szeftel, M (1998), 'Misunderstanding African politics: corruption and the governance agenda', *Review of African Political Economy*, vol. 25, no. 76, pp. 221–40.

Themnér, L & Wallensteen, P (2012), 'Armed conflicts, 1946–2011', *Journal of Peace research*, vol. 49, no. 4, pp. 565–575.

van de Walle, N (2014), 'The democratization of clientelism in Africa", in DA Brun & L Diamond (eds), *Clientelism, social policy, and the quality of democracy*, Johns Hopkins University Press, Baltimore, pp. 230–252.

van de Walle, N (2010), 'US policy towards Africa: The Bush legacy and the Obama administration', *African Affairs*, vol. 109, no. 434, pp. 1–21.

Wallensteen, P & Sollenberg, M (2001), 'Armed Conflict, 1989–2000', *Journal of Peace Research*, vol. 38, no. 5, pp. 629–44.

Webster, E & Adler, G (1999), 'Toward a class compromise in South Africa's "double transition": bargained liberalization and the consolidation of democracy', *Politics & Society*, vol. 27, no. 3, pp. 347–85.

Williamson, J (1994), 'In search of a manual for technopols', in J Williamson (ed.), *The political economy of policy reform*, Institute of International Economics, Washington, DC, pp. 11–28.

Woo-Cumings, M (1999), *The developmental state*, Cornell University Press, Ithaca NY.

Woods, N (2008), 'Whose aid? Whose influence? China, emerging donors and the silent revolution in development assistance', *International Affairs*, vol. 84, no. 6, pp. 1205–21.

World Bank (various years), *World Development Indicators*, http://data.worldbank.org/data-catalog/world-development- indicators

World Bank (1989), *From crisis to sustainable growth – sub Saharan Africa: a long-term perspective study*, World Bank, Washington, DC.

Wright, J & Winters, M (2010), 'The politics of effective foreign aid', *Annual Review of Political Science*, vol. 13, pp. 61–80.

About the contributors

Rita Abrahamsen is professor of African politics and international relations at the Graduate School of Public and International Affairs at the University of Ottawa.

David M. Anderson is professor of African history, in the Global History and Culture Centre at the University of Warwick. His publications on the history and politics of eastern Africa include *Histories of the Hanged* (2005), *The Khat Controversy* (2007) and *Politics and Violence in Eastern Africa* (2015).

Philippe Le Billon is professor of political geography at the University of British Columbia, and a Fulbright research chair at the University of California, Berkeley. He previously worked with the Overseas Development Institute and the International Institute for Strategic Studies, both in London.

Emanuele Fantini is a senior researcher at UNESCO-IHE Institute for Water Education and associate researcher at the Programme in Comparative Media Law and Policy at the University of Oxford. His working experience in development cooperation includes both long-term and consultancy positions for the Italian Ministry of Foreign Affairs, multilateral institutions, local authorities and NGOs.

Jonathan Fisher is senior lecturer in African politics in the International Development Department of the University of Birmingham. Between 2013 and 2014 he was an honorary research fellow in the UK Foreign and Common-wealth Office's Africa Directorate.

Zoë Marriage is reader in development studies at SOAS, University of London, where she convenes the MSc Violence, Conflict and Development. Her core areas of research are security and central Africa.

Helena Pérez Niño is a post-doctoral fellow at PLAAS, the Institute for Poverty Land and Agrarian Studies at the University of the Western Cape. She holds a PhD from SOAS, University of London and conducts research on the political economy of conflict and commodity production in Southern Africa.

Marie-Emmanuelle Pommerolle is assistant professor in political science at the University Paris I– Panthéon Sorbonne, a member of the Institut des mondes africains (IMAf), and currently director of the French Institute of Research in Africa (IFRA), based in Nairobi.

Luca Puddu is a research fellow at the Department of Social Sciences and Institutions, University of Cagliari, and a research associate with the Institute for Global Studies in Rome and Bruxelles.

Nicolas van de Walle is the Maxwell Upson professor of comparative politics in the Government Department of Cornell University.

Index

Note: page numbers in **bold** indicate tables or figures and *n* following a page number refers to an endnote with relevant number.

elections, 119, 125, 133*n1*; EU aid, 123–5, 129, 130; financial support despite electoral reservations, 119–20, 132–3; and France, 5, 125, 134*n20*; *illusio* of electoral credibility, 126–8; multilateral donors and electoral reform, 123–5; Onel (*Observatoire national des elections*), 122–3; opposition parties, 127; political leverage, 119–20; and the UN, 133; UNDP aid, 123–4, 131; voter registration, 123, 125, 130–32

Cammack, D., 168–9

Canada, aid and the war on terror, 32

Carothers, T., 168

Chiluba, Frederick, 28

China: and Angola, 141, 147, 163; economic success, 171–2; and Ethiopia, 96, 113; and Uganda, 86; unconditional loans, 163

Chitiyo, Knox, 60

civil society, 169; Cameroon, 120–21, 127, 129–30, 169

Clapham, C., 94, 97

Clinton, Hillary, 163

Cold War, and democracy in Africa, 23

Collier, D., 165

Combined Joint Task Force-Horn of Africa (CJTF-HOA), 37

Commonwealth: and Cameroon, 123, 124; and Rwanda, 59

Compaoré, Blaise, 37

Congdon, John, 103–4

Congo, Democratic Republic of (DRC): M23 militia, 53–4, 55, 56–7, 84; Rwanda's military operations, 17*n11*, 44, 47, 52–7, 60, 61; Second Congo War (1998), 45–6, 52–3; Ugandan invasion, 82

Cook, Robin, 27

Cooley, A., 6

corruption, 164, 171–2, 173; Angola, 152; Uganda, 80

Cuba, and Ethiopia, 94

democracy: definition missing from development discourse, 24–5; disillusion with, 163–4; donors' low expectations, 7; and economic growth, 166–7; and economic liberalization, 25–31; impact of foreign aid, 8–10; and international security, 31–8; limited

coverage in World Bank report, 35–6; perceived as inevitable outcome of modernization, 23; and private sector rent seeking, 172–3; shifting conceptualization, 13, 21–2, 38–9; unaffected by aid suspension, 28–9

democracy fatigue, 161–5

democratization: and aid conditionality, 8, 24, 162–3; ambivalent link with elections, 132; Angola, 140–47, 155; Ethiopia, 105–6; impact of foreign aid, 8; Mozambique, 140–44, 147–8, 155, 157*n6*; Rwanda, 49–51; vs donor interests, 105–6, 114

Denmark: aid and the war on terror, 32; Ugandan aid, 73–4

development, diplomacy and defence (3Ds), 33–4

DFID (Department for International Development): bilateral aid to Rwanda, 45, 47–8, 49, 54, 58; and national security, 33

Di Palma, G., 26

Dollar, D., 8

donors: compromises in interactions with Kagame, 13–14, 62; contradictions and plurality of interests, 98, 103–6, 108–114; culture shock, 164; and internationalized political field, 120–21; motives for funding autocracies, 4–8; need to examine unofficial narratives and views, 10–11; new donors (emerging powers), 3, 6, 98, 163; role of private companies, 92, 99, 103–5, 109–113, 112–14; self-interest, 5; self-interest of local officials, 7, 99, 172

DRC *see* Congo, Democratic Republic of (DRC)

Dreher, A., 3

East Asian Model, 171–3

economic growth: African increase, 161; and authoritarian governance, 165–6; and good governance, 24; no effect on socio-economic living conditions, 30–31; and state-business relationship, 169–71

economic liberalization, and democracy, 25–31

elections: ambivalent link with democracy, 132; anathema to sound

and regional security, 72–3; *see also* DFID (Department for International Development)

United Nations: and Cameroon, 133; Darfur peacekeeping troops, 60; Ethiopia's cotton farming project, 102; lack of credibility in Rwanda, 57–8; report on M23 militia, 84; UNDP and Cameroon electoral reform, 123–4, 131

United States: aid and war on terror, 31–2, 96; continuous aid to Ethiopia, 12, 93; development, diplomacy and defence, 33; development and security policy, 33; initial reluctance to deal with Museveni, 71; Malawi aid suspension, 29; Millennium Challenge Corporation (MCC), 162–3; political aid conditionality, 24; Ugandan aid and economic reconstruction, 74–6; Ugandan military assistance, 72–3, 78–83

UPDF (Ugandan People's Defence Forces), 70–71, 72, 81–2

Uvin, P., 7

war on terror: democracy and security issues, 31–2, 36–7; and Ethiopia, 32, 36, 96; and Kenya, 37–8; and political conditionality, 163; and radicalization, 34; and Rwanda, 32, 36, 37; Trans-Saharan Counter-Terrorism Partnership (TSCTP), 34, 37; and Ugandan military assistance, 79–83

Whitfield, L., 4

World Bank: aid to Ethiopia, 93, 96; aid to Rwanda, 48; *Sub-Saharan Africa: from crisis to sustainable growth*, 23–4, 26–7; Ugandan economic recovery programme, 71–2, 74–6; *World development report: conflict, security and development*, 35–6

Young, C., 7

Zaire, Mobutu's deposition, 82
Zambia, undemocratic practices, 28